E. W. Scripps and
the Business of Newspapers

The History of Communication
Robert W. McChesney and John C. Nerone, editors

A list of books in the series appears at the end of this book.

E. W. SCRIPPS

and the

Business of Newspapers

Gerald J. Baldasty

University of Illinois Press

Urbana and Chicago

© 1999 by the Board of Trustees of the
University of Illinois
Manufactured in the United States of America
1 2 3 4 5 C P 5 4 3 2 1

Library of Congress Cataloging-in-Publication Data
Baldasty, Gerald J.
E. W. Scripps and the business of newspapers /
Gerald J. Baldasty.
p.   cm. — (The history of communication)
Includes bibliographical references and index.
ISBN 0-252-02255-6 (acid-free paper)
ISBN 0-252-06750-9 (pbk. : acid-free paper)
1. Scripps, E. W. (Edward Willis), 1854–1926.
2. Newspaper publishing—United States—
History—19th century. 3. Newspaper publishing—
United States—History—20th century. 4. Journalists—
United States—Biography. 5. Publishers and publishing—
United States—Biography. I. Title. II. Series.
PN4874.S37B35   1999
070.5'092—ddc21
[b]   98-25357
CIP

For Randy Beam

Contents

Acknowledgments

I am indebted to many for their assistance during this project. A grant from the Scripps Howard Foundation provided crucial financial support for research trips. Thanks, too, to William R. Burleigh of Scripps Howard for his support and interest. The University of Washington provided additional support for this work, both through a research grant and a professional leave that allowed me to complete much of the writing.

At Ohio University, home of the E. W. Scripps Correspondence, faculty at the E. W. Scripps School of Journalism did much to advance my research; my thanks to Robert Stewart, Joe Bernt, Marilyn Greenwald, Phyllis Bernt, Pat Washburn, and most of all to Dru Evarts for her great and generous hospitality. The staff at the OU Library manuscripts and archives division was the most public service–oriented group I've encountered in many years of research travels. My thanks to George Bain, Karen Jones, Sheppard Black, and Doug McCabe.

I did much of the writing of this manuscript as a visiting fellow at Indiana University's Institute for Advanced Study. My thanks to James Patterson, director; to fellow visitors Marion Gray and Fred Suppe; and most of all to Ivona Hedin, assistant director. Thanks, too, to the IU Journalism School faculty, particularly to Trevor Brown, Cleve Wilhoit, David Nord, Linda Lawson, and Andy Rojecki.

Several colleagues offered important insights and suggestions at key points in this project. In particular, my thanks to Don Pember, University of Washington; Steve Lacy, Michigan State University; Carol Smith, Fort Lewis College; Carolyn Stewart Dyer, University of Iowa; Richard Kielbowicz,

University of Washington; George Juergens, Indiana University; John Bowes, University of Washington; John Nerone, University of Illinois at Urbana-Champaign; and Barbara Cloud, University of Nevada–Las Vegas. Other colleagues provided helpful support and ideas as well. My thanks to Robert McChesney, University of Wisconsin; James Darsey, Northern Illinois University; the late Robert Burke, University of Washington; Stephen Ponder, University of Oregon; Richard J. Baldasty, Spokane Falls Community College; and Roger Simpson, University of Washington.

Cindy Blanding, Leslie Harding, and Anna McCausland at the University of Washington Interlibrary Borrowing Services often were my lifeline to research sources. Other UW librarians, notably Carla Rickerson and Glenda Pearson, were enormously helpful throughout this project. My thanks, too, to Terry Kato of the UW Microform and Newspaper Collections.

I am also indebted to Jan Ames, Ted Curtis Smythe, James Baughman, the late Mike Jordan, Jacqueline Blix, Howard Voland, Julie Burke, Paula Reynolds, Jill Wiske, and Ed Bassett. Staff members in the School of Communications at the University of Washington provided enormous support; my thanks to Kellus Stone, Pat Dinning, Carol Wagener, and Karen Nagai. Thanks, too, to Karen Hewitt at the University of Illinois Press and to Patrick Grace and Martin Burgess at the Seattle Public Library and Nancy Hines at the University of Washington Classroom Support Services

Finally, I have benefited enormously from the cogent criticism and suggestions of Randal A. Beam. This book is dedicated to him with gratitude for his ideas and never-wavering support.

Chronology

1873   Establishment of Detroit *Evening News,* James Scripps editor.

1878   Establishment of the Cleveland *Penny Press* (eventually the Cleveland *Press*), E. W. Scripps editor.

1880   Establishment of the St. Louis *Chronicle,* E. W. Scripps editor.

1881   Purchase of the Cincinnati *Penny Paper* (later the Cincinnati *Post*) by the Scripps brothers, James, George, and Edward.

1883   E. W. Scripps obtains control of the Cincinnati *Post* and the St. Louis *Chronicle.*

1887–89   E. W. Scripps serves as president of the Scripps newspapers in Detroit, Cleveland, Cincinnati, and St. Louis. Deposed by his brothers James and George in late 1889.

1890   Establishment of the *Kentucky Post* at Covington. Establishment of the Scripps-McRae League (with Milton A. McRae) to run the three newspapers E. W. Scripps controls (St. Louis, Cincinnati, and Covington). E. W. Scripps buys Miramar Ranch near San Diego.

1892   E. W. Scripps finances acquisition of the *San Diegan-Sun* and becomes a minority stockholder.

1895   E. W. Scripps purchases the Los Angeles *Record.* George H. Scripps joins Scripps-McRae League, which gains control of the Cleveland *Press.*

1896   E. W. Scripps purchases the Kansas City *World.*

1897   E. W. Scripps starts Scripps-McRae Press Association (a telegraph news service).

1898 E. W. Scripps purchases the San Francisco *Report* and starts Scripps-Blades News Association (a telegraph news service in western states). Reorganized in 1901 as Scripps News Association.

1899 Scripps starts the Seattle *Star* and establishes the Akron *Press*.

1900 Scripps establishes (and kills) the Chicago *Press* and also kills the San Francisco *Report;* gains control of the *San Diegan-Sun*. George H. Scripps, brother, dies.

1902 Establishment of Newspaper Enterprise Association (a news features syndicate). Scripps acquires the Des Moines *News* and establishes the Spokane *Press*.

1903 Scripps establishes the San Francisco *Daily News* and Tacoma *Times,* acquires the Toledo *News* and Toledo *Bee* (merges them into the Toledo *News Bee*).

1904 Scripps establishes the Sacramento *Star* and acquires the Columbus *Citizen*.

1905 Scripps establishes the Fresno *Tribune*. The St. Louis *Chronicle* merges with the St. Louis *Star Sayings* to become the *Star Chronicle*.

1906 Scripps establishes the Denver *Express*, Evansville *Press*, Pueblo *Sun*, Terre Haute *Post*, Dallas *Dispatch*, Portland *News*, Oklahoma *News*, Memphis *Press,* and Nashville *Times* and also acquires Publishers Press. James E. Scripps, brother, dies.

1907 Merger of Publishers Press Association, Scripps-McRae Press Association, and Scripps News Association into United Press Associations. Acquires the Berkeley *Independent*.

1908 E. W. Scripps turns over business management to son, James Scripps.

E. W. Scripps and
the Business of Newspapers

Introduction

The late nineteenth and early twentieth centuries witnessed the emergence of the modern American newspaper. Political advocacy, so long the mainstay of the American press, gave way to an emphasis on neutrality, "facts" rather than opinion, and highly diversified content, including short stories, sports, recipes, and news about leisure activities. Newspapers became increasingly complex business organizations, and advertisers emerged as their major source of revenue.

The modern newspaper was the result of sweeping changes in American society; urbanization and industrialization in particular created new roles for the press.[1] Several entrepreneurs, including Joseph Pulitzer, William Randolph Hearst, and Edward Willis Scripps, did much to capitalize on these larger social trends. Like their counterparts in other businesses of that era (Rockefeller in oil, Armour in meatpacking, and Duke in tobacco), they revolutionized their industry's organization, operations, and norms.

Pulitzer, Hearst, and Scripps had much in common. They enlarged the reach of daily journalism by courting the great masses. They relied on a reform-minded journalism that exposed corruption and injustice. All three were captains of their industry, running large, capital-intensive corporations. There were differences among them, too, and those are an important part of their imprint on modern journalism.

Pulitzer (1847–1911) pioneered in the development of the modern newspaper, a mass-circulation publication filled with a vast array of content (sports, fashion news, and cartoons as well as more traditional political and business news) presented in a lively and sometimes sensational manner. As George

Juergens writes, pre-Pulitzer newspapers were dowdy and gray, both in appearance and substance. Pulitzer enlivened the American newspaper with illustrations and photographs, multicolumn headlines, entertaining news, and a democratic spirit. His newspapers also reflected a deep commitment to public service and led crusades against corruption, fraud, and the injustices of urban life. Pulitzer "conferred a dignity of sorts on popular journalism, a raison d'être beyond profits and losses, that ultimately influenced all newspapers, and that is still reflected in the lip service the press renders to its role as servant of the people."[2]

Hearst (1863–1951), Pulitzer's chief rival during the 1890s, imitated many of Pulitzer's journalistic innovations. He orchestrated the entertainment aspect of the mass-circulation newspaper. As his New York *Journal* proclaimed in 1896, "The public is even more fond of entertainment than it is of information."[3] Hearst's newspapers were heavily involved in staging news events, whether hiring lawyers for accused criminals, lending support to Cuban rebels, or running soup kitchens. During the 1920s Hearst's big-city tabloid newspapers opened their own murder investigations and challenged the accused to sue if they dared. As William Swanberg writes, "Hearst's constant effort was to get the biggest, the best, the unexpected, the bizarre, in any kind of news coverage, regardless of expense."[4] Hearst also hoped that his expanding newspaper empire would provide the foundation for a political career—even the presidency. He failed in that pursuit because "the electorate had the good sense to turn him down and vindicate the essential soundness of the democratic system."[5]

While Pulitzer and Hearst experimented with news and entertainment content, Scripps (1854–1926) experimented with the news business. Scripps was not ignorant of journalism; he had worked both as a reporter and editor as a young man, and his newspapers carried both news and entertainment content. But his passion, and lasting legacy to his industry, was the development of the modern newspaper as a business. Scripps was the prototype of the modern publisher, concentrating on long-range planning, performance goals, budgets, circulation methods, revenue sources, and a broad range of other business concerns. His career and legacy were shaped by creating a centrally managed and economically efficient chain of newspapers. Everything he did, including embracing working-class issues and concerns, revolved around the goal of creating a newspaper chain. He succeeded and pioneered the model of a modern newspaper organization.

Scripps aspired to more. Unlike Pulitzer and Hearst, he never was happy about the huge presence of advertising in modern American newspapers. Instead, he wanted to reform journalism by wresting it from its close ties to advertising and commercial elites. But such efforts never found industrywide support, and to this day advertisers remain the key patrons of the American press. Scripps succeeded in creating a string of small, cheap, working-class newspapers that were unusually independent in their dealings with advertisers. But, unlike the vast majority of American newspapers, the lack of advertising revenues limited the size and quality of Scripps enterprises. It is ironic that the newspaper chain, often derided now as the archetype of big-business journalism, was an element in Scripps's scheme to resist commercialization.

Scripps's business style differed greatly from those of Pulitzer and Hearst. While they waged their great circulation wars in New York City, Scripps concentrated on the nation's smaller cities, such as Seattle, Dallas, and Denver. He disdained advertising while they embraced it. He published small (four- or eight-page) newspapers, whereas they issued much larger editions. Scripps also tried (somewhat unsuccessfully) to avoid direct (same-city) competition but recognized that Pulitzer and Hearst were his chief rivals.

Scripps was not the only chain-builder in the late nineteenth and early twentieth centuries. Eight other chains were established before 1900, although none had the size or breadth of Scripps's.[6] Pulitzer operated only two newspapers—one in New York and the other in St. Louis. Hearst, too, created a substantial newspaper chain in the early twentieth century, although his expansion began after Scripps and with much different goals. Hearst's chain was as much a political organization to boost Hearst as it was a business entity. Unlike Scripps, Hearst was not a particularly astute business manager; by the 1930s he had racked up such enormous debts that he found himself on the brink of bankruptcy.[7] Battling insolvency, he was forced to kill several newspapers and sell real estate and radio stations as well as a substantial part of his art collection. Swanberg writes, "He had proved himself fiscally the world's worst executive."[8]

Although Pulitzer and Hearst have attracted substantial attention from researchers, Scripps has drawn less interest. His relative obscurity derives from several factors. First, he avoided public attention during his lifetime, preferring to work behind the scenes in business and politics. Second, he never owned well-known, mass-circulation newspapers that would draw attention to him. Third, his substantial business correspondence has been available to researchers only since 1990. The low profile that characterized Scripps's business practices has also characterized research about him.

This book seeks to raise that profile by detailing Scripps's newspaper career, spanning from the early 1870s through his first official retirement in 1908.

During that period, he established or bought more than forty newspapers and created a telegraphic news service (United Press Associations) and an illustrated news features syndicate (the Newspaper Enterprise Association). This book focuses on three aspects of Scripps's business career. First, it details the three business strategies he developed to build his newspaper chain: low cost, market segmentation, and vertical integration. Those strategies were the key for the development of his chain and influenced the quantity, quality, subject, and format of newspaper content. Second, this book describes Scripps's efforts to create newspapers free from advertising and commercial influence. He viewed this process not only as healthy for democracy but also as a smart business move that would keep the press closer to most of its customers. Finally, this book describes the management structure Scripps developed to coordinate and control his far-flung media empire.

The Changing American Newspaper

Scripps's approach to the newspaper business was a response to the far-reaching changes that characterized American journalism during the late nineteenth and early twentieth centuries, particularly to competition, rising costs, organizational complexity, and the rise of advertising.

Competition

Competition among publishers and editors for readers and advertisers was intense in this era. During the roughly forty years straddling the turn of the century the number of daily newspapers in the United States nearly tripled, from 909 in 1880 to 2,461 in 1916.[9] If Scripps's estimates were correct, at least 1,500 newspapers were started and died between 1880 and 1910. Newspaper circulation grew faster than the population itself; the average household consumption of newspapers rose from .36 in 1880 to 1.16 in 1920.[10] Publishers of existing newspapers often worked to prevent the start of new newspapers or sabotage them in their infancy by organizing advertising boycotts, monopolizing national telegraphic news services, or disrupting circulation efforts.

Scripps's market segmentation strategy reflected his sense that the best way to start and operate newspapers was to seek new readers rather than compete with established newspapers directly. He believed that most U.S. newspapers either ignored or were hostile to the working class, thus leaving a sizable and lucrative audience ready for new—Scripps—ventures. He set out to manufacture a product that workers would buy. Scripps newspapers offered relevant news that emphasized labor issues in an easy-to-read format directed toward a less-educated audience. Home delivery efforts targeted working-class neighborhoods. The business decision to target workers also led to extensive regulations on advertising to assure that the Scripps newspapers would not become too closely tied to business interests and forsake their chief readership.

Costs

Newspaper costs increased dramatically during the nineteenth century. Start-up costs, less than $1,000 early in the century, had risen to well above $500,000 by 1900 for many big-city newspapers. Operating costs were also high. *Printer's Ink,* an advertising trade journal, estimated in 1890 that most big-city newspapers had operating budgets exceeding $400,000 annually.[11]

Rising costs were not obstacles for wealthy publishers such as William Randolph Hearst. Scripps, however, had not begun his newspaper career with a huge personal fortune. Only through strict economy could he start newspapers and create a chain. His low-cost strategy was the chief characteristic of his newspaper operations, influencing all aspects of production and news-gathering. Start-up costs for Scripps newspapers ran a third or a fourth of the industry average of that era, allowing Scripps to conserve capital to establish more newspapers. Operating costs were kept low, too, through small staffs, relatively modest salaries, spartan offices, and a pinch-penny mentality.

The low-cost strategy also complemented Scripps's market segmentation strategy. He ran a low-cost operation not only to conserve capital but also to keep his newspapers within the reach of working-class readers. Scripps sold his newspapers for just a penny (both home delivery and street sales) at a time when most of his competitors' newspapers sold for 2 cents (home delivery) and 5 cents on the street.[12] The price made Scripps's newspapers highly affordable for workers but placed even greater emphasis on low cost by providing revenues far below those of an average newspaper of the era. The low-cost strategy also dictated the nature of expansion. Scripps avoided eastern cities, where costs were higher than in the Midwest or West.

Scripps's vertical integration strategy—represented by the United Press Associations and the Newspaper Enterprise Association—derived from concerns over competition and costs. The telegraph news service allowed Scripps to expand wherever he chose, circumventing the Associated Press's efforts to monopolize markets for its members. The NEA distributed illustrations and feature news throughout the chain, avoiding duplication and spreading costs among the ever-growing number of Scripps newspapers. In 1907 Scripps told a business associate, "Your [NEA] assessment is $15 per week, or $780 per annum. The present expenditure on the N.E.A. is about $100,000 per year. Thus for $780 your paper gets $100,000 worth of editorial work."[13]

Organizational Complexity

Newspapers became more complex organizations during the late nineteenth century, placing greater emphasis on managerial coordination and control. In the 1830s most American newspapers were cottage industries, edited and produced by a staff of one or two people. By 1900, however, many metropolitan newspapers had hundreds of employees in separate departments that had different tasks: news-gathering, printing and production, circulation, advertising, and accounting. As in other industries, specialization, departmentalization, increasing capital and operational costs, and intense competition led to the advent of full-time business managers. In the newspaper industry, the publisher emerged as that manager, "a man of business, business over all. He conducts the paper that it shall yield a profit."[14]

Scripps was emblematic of the modern publisher, "a man of business, business over all." His ambitious plans for building a newspaper chain and his three business strategies (market segmentation, low cost, and vertical integration) required extensive coordination and control. Scripps and a few key lieutenants closely supervised each newspaper, controlling costs, enforcing reliance on the telegraph news and news features services, and monitoring all content. Control was centralized, and supervision was intense. Profits, a key to expansion and success, were mandatory. As Scripps said, "It is the duty of newspaper businessmen, as well as all businessmen, to make money."[15] Even his anti-advertising campaign reflected business concerns. He reasoned that too close a tie to social and business elites would destroy his newspapers' ability to be true to their key market.

Advertising

By the late nineteenth century, advertising provided nearly two-thirds of the revenue for most urban newspapers. Advertising played a major role in many aspects of the modern newspaper. First, it took up a lot of space—one-half to two-thirds of each day's edition. Second, advertisers helped shape the entire content of the American newspaper. Their emphasis on reaching consumers led publishers and editors to create content designed for large, upscale reading and consuming audiences. Divisive or potentially boring topics such as politics got short shrift, and reports on sports, fashion, theater, and—as the Pittsburgh *Leader* promised, "whatever you most like to read"—were featured.[16]

Some advertisers wanted extensive control over content and resorted to boycotts to force some publishers to back down from political views. Hearst's New York *Journal* lost substantial revenues when advertisers deserted after it endorsed William Jennings Bryan for president in 1896. But the wealthy Hearst was able to withstand the pressure, and by Christmas of that year the advertisers had returned.[17]

Scripps believed that extensive reliance on advertising was a bad business practice because it ceded autonomy to advertisers. He also believed that reliance on advertising would inevitably make newspapers the representative of elite business interests rather than institutions that served the people at large. So he restricted advertising in an effort to keep his newspapers independent of the rich and powerful and thus better able to reach and represent the working-class readers he sought.

Significance

E. W. Scripps is important because he was a major figure during a period that witnessed the rise of the modern American newspaper. He played a key role in that process, serving as a prototype of the modern publisher and building the first national newspaper chain. Scripps is important, too, because he was the first major publisher to confront one of the enduring issues in American mass media, the power of advertisers. He wanted modern newspapers to depend primarily on readers rather than on elite business interests for revenues, arguing that the latter led to censorship by business and timidity and self-censorship in the press. Scripps failed to reform American journalism, however, because few seemed to share his fear of commercialization of the media.

Scripps's three business strategies (market segmentation, low cost, and vertical integration) merit scrutiny for several reasons. First, they influenced how news was gathered, processed, and distributed. The link between business strategies and content is not a new idea; the competition for readers between Pulitzer and Hearst in New York City in the late 1890s spawned a wave of sensationalism and fabrication. But content is also influenced by strategies that are far less obvious than struggles for street sales.

In the Scripps newspaper chain, market segmentation, low cost, and vertical integration all had an impact on content. Such business strategies also helped create a chain that was highly profitable to its owners, successful in competition, and accessible to readers. As such, they contributed to establishing a model of newspaper ownership that has become dominant in the late twentieth century. Conversely, the chain, in turn, sustained and extended the business strategies. It provided leverage for further growth (a major goal as long as E. W. Scripps was in charge), nurtured vertical integration, and sustained cost control and market segmentation. The chain itself allowed Scripps to achieve efficiencies that most other media organizations did not have.

Finally, market segmentation, low cost, and vertical integration represent the conscious use of marketing in the newspaper industry. As circulation became a zero-sum game in the twentieth century, competition increased the emphasis on marketing and market segmentation strategies. Much attention has been paid to newspaper marketing since the mid-1980s, but the issue dates at least from the turn of the century and deals with how a newspaper can survive in a changing environment.

Conclusions

The late nineteenth and early twentieth centuries witnessed the emergence of the modern American newspaper. E. W. Scripps was a key figure in that process, pioneering a new model of operations—the newspaper chain—that would come to dominate the industry by the late twentieth century. Scripps also sought to limit the power of advertising in the press, arguing that the resultant commercialization undermined the press's ability to serve the public and democracy. Three strategies—market segmentation, low cost, and vertical integration—all contributed to the business success of his newspapers and influenced the nature of news and information.

The Struggle for Control

I remember your early disapproval of me, your doubt—almost a
conviction, first that I was unfit for any part of the printing business, second that I could never be a writer, later an editor, and
lastly . . . that I had any business qualities whatsoever.
—E. W. Scripps to James E. Scripps, March 18, 1892

IN 1905, WHEN THE managers of the San Francisco *Daily News* proposed
enlarging that newspaper contrary to E. W. Scripps's wishes, he reminded them
that he was the "controlling stockholder": "There is no good kicking. There
is no good evading. There is no good of arguing. . . . I am not going to mince
words in writing or talking. The reasons why I always take 51 per cent of the
stock of a newspaper should be evident."[1] On another occasion he sent an order
to Milton McRae, his long-time partner: "Read carefully. This is important.
This is not an argument. This is not a complaint. This is not a subject for discussion."[2] Another time, Scripps berated his Seattle editor for failing to obey
orders: "I will excuse no more for failing to obey an order and keep an agreement about money matters. You must play this game fair and square, living
up to the rules we have agreed upon or leave the table."[3]

Obey orders, follow rules, no arguments. In the early twentieth century
E. W. Scripps was the dominant voice in his newspaper empire. He was the
majority stockholder and chief executive, setting policy and identifying goals.
He demanded ready compliance from employees and fired those who balked.[4]
Scripps's chain reflected his personality, vision, and business strategies. He was
in control.

Gaining control, however, had not been easy. Scripps spent nearly twenty
years in pursuit of position and power. Only in his forties did he acquire the
power and resources to create a newspaper empire unimpeded by others. By
today's standards, such power by that age might seem a sign of great success,
but to Scripps, never humble about his abilities, the wait had been far too long.

Those apprenticeship years did much to shape Scripps's views about journalism, business, and, most of all, control.

The Early Years

Born on a farm in Illinois in 1854, Edward Willis Scripps was the youngest of thirteen children born to James Mogg Scripps in three marriages. Young E. W. Scripps was bright but bristled at following rules, so school was often a trial for him (and for his teachers). His mother found him difficult and demonstrated little interest or affection in him. Only his half-sister Ellen, eighteen years older, doted on him, serving as a surrogate mother and teaching him to love books and ideas. She was his alter ego throughout life, one of the very few people who understood him and whom he trusted completely.

As a youth, Scripps displayed the entrepreneurial spirit that would serve him so well in building a newspaper empire. He hired boys—at low wages—to help with the plowing, speeding the work by turning the project into a contest. The lads gladly competed to see who could do the work fastest, leaving E. W. Scripps to supervise and read a book. On another occasion, he created a small but profitable business cutting wood; Scripps hired others to do the heavy work while he solicited more orders.[5]

When he was eighteen, Scripps left the farm for Detroit, where his half-brother James was editor of the *Tribune*. James, nineteen years older than Scripps, had been a distant and gruff figure in Scripps's childhood but emerged as a key figure during his adult years, a teacher, disciplinarian, and focus for rebellion. Their battles spanned most of their adult lives, beginning in 1872 when Scripps first arrived in Detroit and ending only in 1906 with James's death.

James's editorship of the Detroit *Tribune* ended in early 1873 when fire destroyed its offices. With insurance money from his ownership of the newspaper's job printing plant, James started his own paper, the *Evening News* on August 23, 1873. The newspaper reflected a new style of journalism that had begun to take root in the 1870s. It was independent in politics, cheap (selling for just 2 cents compared to 5 cents for its competitors), half the size of other newspapers, and—unlike virtually all papers of that era—aimed at the working class.[6] Scripps later recounted that the little *Evening News* challenged the elites who had long escaped scrutiny:

> Rich rascals, rich men who were affected by petty meannesses, so called respectable men in political offices who were doing wrong things, clergymen who had faults that unfitted them for church service or even decent society, professional

men—doctors, lawyers, and even judges on the bench—who had depended upon the cloak of their respectability, or position, to cover a misdeed, and many other citizens, soon found that, as far as the reporters of the Evening News were concerned, they were living in glass houses and that they had no means of protecting themselves from public exposure.[7]

The *Evening News* was an enterprise financed and run primarily by three Scripps siblings: James, George, and Ellen. James provided the original capital and the working-class journalistic formula. George brought substantial capital to the venture soon after its start, and Ellen wrote extensively for the new publication. When the newspaper was incorporated, James took thirty shares, George sixteen, and Ellen two. Michigan law required five stockholders for forming a closed corporation, so E. W. Scripps and John S. Sweeney, a cousin, each received one share. That single share of stock provided the basis for E. W. Scripps's newspaper empire, serving as collateral as well as legal leverage in later years.

Scripps's success at the Detroit *Evening News* came more from his own persistence than from the benefit of family connections. James refused his brother's request to be a reporter, mocking the younger man's grammar and spelling. Scripps became a circulation solicitor instead and again demonstrated his entrepreneurial skill. His task was to create and service a city delivery route; instead, he organized twenty routes and supervised younger boys who made the deliveries. Before long, his routes accounted for half of the newspaper's circulation.[8] He then developed country circulation, first as a solicitor and then hiring canvassers. He proved adept at judging the character and responsibility of potential employees.

Despite these successes—and the income from managing various newspaper routes—Scripps still wanted to be a reporter. James still resisted. Scripps insisted, working first for free in the newsroom, learning to write by watching others, and becoming valuable by performing tasks no one else wanted. Older reporters learned that they could sleep in because young Scripps would perform the early-morning work of rewriting news from other newspapers. Even James recognized Scripps's talent, and before long he was assistant city editor and later city editor.

Scripps was restless, however, even as city editor. In 1878, when his brother George asked him to go to Europe, he welcomed the break. The trip was important for several reasons. First, it strengthened his ties to George, fifteen years his senior, a lonely bachelor crippled in the Civil War. George usually deferred to James in running the family business, but he was a major stockholder and would figure prominently in disputes between Scripps and James in the years ahead. Second, Scripps later recounted that on that trip he resolved never again to be "anybody's hired man."[9]

When he returned home in mid-1878 he urged James to start a newspaper in Cleveland. Both James and George liked the idea, although James opposed Scripps's plan to serve as founding editor. Scripps's arguments, coupled with George's support, finally triumphed, however. Cousin John Sweeney was the first business manager. James and George, financing the venture, each took 30 percent of the new company's stock, leaving 20 percent each to Scripps and Sweeney. Scripps's collateral for the stock was his single share of the Detroit *Evening News* stock.[10]

Scripps had much to learn as he started the Cleveland *Press*. He had acquired a basic sense of working-class journalism from the Detroit newspaper, but he had little sense of the newspaper business. James and George provided just $10,000 capital. The paper, begun in November 1878, lost money at first, produced a small profit after six months, but then was soon losing money again. When the original capital was gone, James and George provided another $2,500 but ordered a 25 percent cut in expenses. Scripps protested vehemently, arguing that cost-cutting would destroy the *Press*, but James and George won the fight. They held a majority of the stock. Scripps was forced to practice "the most extreme economies," doing a cash-only business, demanding immediate payment for advertisements and sales, and monitoring finances daily to keep track of all spending. He worked fifteen to seventeen hours a day.[11]

The *Press* eventually became a success despite the cost-cutting. Scripps learned a key lesson: "There, in that case, was demonstrated to me, more clearly than in any other case that I have met with, that men make money and that money does not make money. It is the man who makes the newspaper and not the man's capital. *Everything else being equal, the more money that is spent on founding a paper, the less apt it is to be successful; and, even being successful, the less will be its success.*"[12]

Still, Scripps was impatient. After just a year in Cleveland he was eager to move on. The "humdrum," day-to-day operation of newspapers bored him. He wanted to start other newspapers, but his brothers balked. They fought over expansion: Scripps was always in a hurry, his brothers content to manage a few properties. Scripps resented their caution. At twenty-six he wrote, "I wish my unconfident brothers could see far enough into me to know my capabilities. If they would but give me their countenance and means, I could . . . push their interests throughout the length and breadth of the country and make them millionaires."[13] In late 1880 Scripps told his sister Annie that he was looking for a new newspaper venture but warned her not to mention it to James, who "doesn't want me to be in such a hurry."[14]

In 1880 Scripps convinced his brothers to finance the establishment of a new newspaper, the *Chronicle*, in St. Louis, with him at its helm. Within five months, however, he was ready to flee, "impatient to get away from this horrible mud hole city."[15] A month later he told George, "I am not pleased with this slow pokey life of waiting for the paper to pay."[16] He was always looking for new projects and considered starting newspapers in Chicago and Pittsburgh.[17] Scripps was ambitious and badgered James for power and control in the family business. In 1880 they fought over Scripps's demand to be president and general manager of the *Chronicle*. Scripps told Annie:

> James E. and I are enjoying one of our semi-monthly squabbles. I carried my point in regard to being elected president and obtaining a general supervision of the concern. . . . he did not think I would dare presume to such a step when I knew he opposed it. However, I did. . . . and now he is trying to sit down on me and make me feel small. He has only succeeded thus far in causing me to stop writing him and to lay my plans for a separation as soon as possible. I am tired of his domineering selfishness and egotism and I am quite strong enough now to walk alone.[18]

Scripps wasn't "quite strong enough" at that point, but he recognized that a break with James would come at some point. "The affair may blow over as others have but it will recur again and again until sooner or later the rupture absolute will come." He told Annie that he was engaged in a contest for supremacy with James. "It is very hard work for a young man to join issue with his superiors in age and at first command the respect of his associates. It is harder still for him, whatever his qualifications may be, to become the leader of his elders."[19]

His arguments with James were something of a game for Scripps. "A little manly independence is necessary in dealing with our big brother," he informed Annie. "He [James] looks upon the rebellion of his baby brother as monstrous. So do I. That makes it all the more enjoyable."[20] On another occasion he characterized his disputes with James as a game. "It pleases the old man to play the part of a conservative hold back and for myself it would be too disgustingly tame if I did not have some one to raise a row with."[21] Scripps did not always describe these battle in such a benign fashion, but the fact that he often prevailed in family disputes may well have contributed to his view.

Scripps succeeded in gaining responsibility and power within the family business through his own agitation, James's lack of interest in running a growing number of newspapers, and support from George and Ellen. In 1883 Scripps parlayed his minority ownership in the St. Louis *Chronicle* and in the Cincinnati *Post* (10 percent in each paper) into a majority by buying out other minority shareholders and by inducing James to sell him additional shares.[22] With these two newspapers under his control, Scripps began to compete earnestly with James. Setting a goal of forty thousand circulation for the *Post* in 1885, Scripps noted, "I will then have overtaken my big brother and have nothing else to do but strongly forge ahead of him."[23] Scripps's distaste for detail persisted. As the *Post* and *Chronicle* grew in the mid- and late 1880s he turned much of the day-to-day management over to Milton McRae, who had worked as an advertising solicitor first at the Detroit *Evening News* and then at the *Post*.[24]

During the 1870s and 1880s Scripps's key goal was to become a successful newspaper businessman. He told Annie that the Cleveland *Press* "was never started for the purpose of accomplishing a great good." Rather, it was a business proposition. He later recounted that his only key goal in taking control of the Cincinnati *Post* was "to establish the paper on a self-supporting basis . . . and cause it to make enough money to yield me an income of between five and six thousand a year."[25] His concerns about advertising would not become prominent until the late 1890s.

Controlling the Cincinnati and St. Louis newspapers was not enough for Scripps; he wanted to run all four of the Scripps family papers. By 1887, at age thirty-three, he succeeded. By then he had demonstrated his business acumen, turning the once-dismal Cincinnati *Post* into a spirited, popular, and profitable enterprise. James, in poor health, was eager to take a break from business to seek comfort and cure at European health spas. Scripps had finally gotten what he long had wanted—presidency of the family business.

Even though he was only a minority stockholder in two of the newspapers Scripps set out to be a forceful executive. In a whirlwind presidency, he strove to create an efficient, centralized newspaper company. He modernized newspaper plants, started a news bureau and advertising office in New York City, and organized shared news coverage. But his presidency was stormy. Some newspaper managers resisted his centralization plans, and cousin John Sweeney continued to jockey for power and favor of the majority stockholders, James and George. Scripps was generally successful in controlling Sweeney, but the battle was time-consuming and nerve-wracking.

As costs rose because of plant modernization and heavy spending on joint-news projects, and dividends dropped, James and George deposed Scripps as president, leaving him with control of just the Cincinnati and St. Louis operations. Furthermore, James called in some of his loans to his younger brother;

only a loan from sister Ellen prevented the loss of Scripps's stock in the Cleveland and Detroit newspapers. Scripps was humiliated and bitter. Although the two brothers were forced to deal with each other in the coming years due to intertwining ownership of the papers, social ties were sundered. The antipathy between the two increased after George's death in 1900; James vainly battled the will that left most of George's property to Scripps.

Between 1872 and 1889, however, James had taught his younger brother much about the business; Scripps would later credit him with inventing the Scripps brand of working-class, low-cost newspapers.[26] His sudden dismissal provided one more lesson: the need for "one man power." Scripps realized that he would never be able to forge a strong, efficient company as a minority stockholder subject to the advice or meddling of others. Only "one man power" was effective: "There being a number of proprietors and no one having a control—this danger of anarchy which always accompanies democracy should be constantly guarded against and no better way of doing this can be found than by a constant effort toward one man power and responsibility."[27]

In the 1890s Scripps retreated from the newspaper business to devote time and energy to the development of Miramar, his new ranch outside San Diego. The challenges there were many: finding water, building roads, planting trees, and building a home for his expanding family.[28] His newspaper properties still drew his attention, although he left most of the work to his new partner, Milton McRae, with simple instructions: "To make money—large money out of our concern has now become your duty—beyond which there is no greater duty."[29]

During the early and mid-1890s, the Scripps-McRae League experienced limited but significant expansion. McRae started the *Kentucky Post* at Covington as an offshoot of the Cincinnati *Post* in 1890. By 1893 George Scripps had become somewhat alienated from James and joined his younger brother and McRae, bringing control of the Cleveland *Press* with him. These two highly profitable Ohio newspapers formed the nucleus of the Scripps newspaper empire. Their profits supported Scripps's Miramar development and generated much of the capital needed for future expansion. In 1896 McRae purchased the Kansas City *World*. Scripps himself dabbled in newspapers on the West Coast; in 1892 he financed the purchase of the *San Diegan-Sun* by Paul Blades and E. C. Hickman, and in 1895 he bought the Los Angeles *Record*, putting Blades in charge of it.

Reliance on McRae worked well in the early and mid-1890s while profits were high and Scripps wanted to avoid business to concentrate on the development of Miramar. By the late 1890s, however, he had completed much of his ranch work and was gradually reinvolving himself in the management of his newspapers. He was instrumental in the establishment of the Scripps-McRae Press Association, the chain's midwestern-based telegraph news association, in 1897 and in a similar telegraph news operation in the West (the Scripps-Blades News Association). Impatient and imperious, Scripps began to second-guess McRae, charging that he had allowed the midwestern operations to become too dependent on advertising revenues. Scripps ordered that his newspapers refuse lucrative patent medicine advertising—over McRae's objections—and then perversely blamed McRae for declining revenues. In 1899 he announced that he was "returning to active work," his "recent long retirements from active oversight and management had ended."[30]

Control

Back at the helm, Scripps remembered his advocacy of "one man power." He functioned as the chief executive officer, engaging in virtually all aspects of his chain's operations—from starting newspapers to killing them. He defined the company's objectives (expansion), strategies for achieving those objectives (market segmentation, low cost, and vertical integration), procedures or rules for general operation, and methods for measuring performance.

As the "chief stockholder" of his newspaper company, Scripps demanded compliance with his objectives, strategies, and rules. He could not monitor every newspaper or employee, particularly when expansion increased in the early twentieth century, so he created a central office to execute his strategies and supervise compliance. Tasks were divided by function, with one manager directing finances, another legal issues, and, after 1902, a third supervising news. Scripps saw the central office as an extension of himself: "That office is my office. When it speaks or writes, it is my voice or writing."[31] On another occasion he told western editors and business managers that he would not tolerate criticism of the central office. "When you criticize the cost of the Central or Atwood office, you are simply claiming that I am not worthy of my position of headship, and that I am not so well fitted to run my business as you are."[32]

Each of the central office managers was ostensibly equal, and each served in what Scripps called his "cabinet." In practice, however, Lemuel T. Atwood was the first among equals. Atwood had begun his career with Scripps as a reporter on the Cincinnati *Post* and eventually rose to become its editor. In the late 1890s he became Scripps's chief enforcer. He held Scripps's power of attorney, was the chain's treasurer, and was clearly Scripps's agent. Scripps told McRae that "Atwood's real position was this: he knew what I wanted done. I knew that he comprehended my instructions."[33] Although Atwood surveyed all aspects of operations, he and his staff of clerks and auditors focused primarily on financial matters central to Scripps's low-cost strategy. Scripps predicted that Atwood and his staff would keep "everlasting after the boys for irregularities and waste."[34] He told Atwood, "I desire you in your position of responsibility in financial matters to adopt a policy of being perfectly rigid and exacting in the matter of enforcing my economical rules in the cases of all the properties."[35] Atwood carried out Scripps's orders zealously; many of the chain's editors and business managers found him to be a relentless stickler for details. He also served as editorial secretary of the chain until 1902, although there is little evidence that he paid substantive attention to journalistic issues.

The supervision of the news product—and thus of the market segmentation and vertical integration strategies—was enhanced in 1902 with the appointment of Robert F. Paine as editor-in-chief of the chain. Paine had begun his writing career at the Cleveland *Press,* and his frank but cheerful personality had long appealed to Scripps. Paine was one of a very few people who came close to being friends with Scripps. He served as editor of the Cleveland paper in the 1890s and was the founding manager of the midwestern telegraph news service in the late 1890s. He left the Cleveland editorship in 1902 to start the Newspaper Enterprise Association and take on chainwide editorial supervision. As editor-in-chief of the Scripps newspapers, he alone routinely read and critiqued their content, offering advice on how to make them both interesting and loyal to working-class readers.

Atwood and Paine were ideal choices for Scripps's central office. They reflected the chief characteristics of his own personality: Atwood the authoritarian preference for rules and orders and the overwhelming concern about expense and Paine the devotion to the working class and the belief that journalism should agitate the privileged. Together, they assured that each newspaper in the concern followed Scripps's vision of journalism and business.

Other members of the cabinet were Jacob C. Harper and McRae. Harper joined the central office in 1899 as the chain's legal counsel. Scripps recognized that an interstate business, subject to a wide variety of state statutes, needed a lawyer.[36] Harper's managerial responsibilities expanded as he became the regional manager of some of the Scripps newspapers established in 1905 and 1906. McRae remained an active member of the Scripps management team after the 1890s, although Atwood had taken over many of the duties he had performed in the 1890s. He served as general manager of midwestern (Scripps-McRae League) newspapers until 1905, arranged the acquisition of newspapers in Toledo and Columbus, and also procured newsprint for the entire chain.

Scripps frequently badgered and berated him in cabinet meetings, although the men retained close ties for years.

Scripps defined broad policies and specific rules to speed expansion and implement his strategies of market segmentation, low cost, and vertical integration. He and his central office monitored each newspaper to gauge performance and check compliance with policies and rules, providing incentives for compliance or punishment for violations. Through all of this, he tolerated no dissent. He noted that he did not care to argue with employees over policy or rules. "I think it is more economical, in time and money, to give a discharge instead."[37]

Conclusions

By 1899, in his mid-forties, Scripps was back to full-time newspaper work. During the next decade he would oversee the extensive expansion of his chain, including the establishment or purchase of twenty-one newspapers and the creation of a news features service (the Newspaper Enterprise Association) and a national telegraph news service (the United Press Associations).[38] The guiding principles and practices during that decade of expansion all derived from his long apprenticeship with his brother James. E. W. Scripps's newspapers would be small, cheap, politically independent, and working class. E. W. Scripps's newspaper company would also reflect the lessons he had learned from his many battles with James: "One man power" would be a hallmark of the chain. The company was a highly centralized operation under the direct control of its chief stockholder—E. W. Scripps.

Expansion

I will be constantly tempted to make new newspaper ventures.
—E. W. Scripps to J. C. Harper and Milton A. McRae, October 16,
1900

IN LATE APRIL 1905 E. W. Scripps met with the manager of his northwestern newspapers, E. F. Chase, to plot expansion of the growing Scripps newspaper chain. They created a list of nineteen cities, primarily in the western United States, where "our concern ought to have . . . papers" and agreed to start operations immediately in Fresno, San Jose, Missoula, Vancouver, Denver, Ogden, Salt Lake City, and Reno.[1]

Although Scripps did not start newspapers in most of these cities, the meeting with Chase illustrates his zeal for planning new ventures. Throughout his long career, he was always eager—even impatient—to buy or start another newspaper. In 1880, just four months after the debut of the St. Louis *Chronicle,* he told his sister Annie that he was looking for a press for his next project. "I am anxious to keep the ball rolling."[2] A few years later he told her, "I fear I will not long rest content till I get another iron in the fire and begin negotiating for some other paper."[3]

Expansion had been the source of constant friction between Scripps and his older brothers James and George. Scripps wanted to expand rapidly, his brothers did not. He was in a hurry, they weren't. Moreover, they wanted Scripps to buckle down and actually manage a newspaper rather than scurry off to new ventures.

Operating on his own after 1889, Scripps was free to establish new newspapers, leaving much of the day-to-day management to others. In the early 1890s he was preoccupied primarily with development of his California ranch, Miramar, and expansion was a relatively minor consideration. After he returned to active management of his newspaper companies in the late 1890s, however, he again displayed great zest for expansion—starting or buying twenty-one newspapers between 1899 and his retirement in 1908. He also created an infrastructure for news; both the United Press Associations and the Newspaper Enterprise Association facilitated expansion.

In 1899 the nucleus of the Scripps newspaper company was the Scripps-McRae League: the Cleveland *Press, Kentucky Post* (in Covington), Akron *Press,* Kansas City *World,* and St. Louis *Chronicle.* A small West Coast group had started with the purchase of the *San Diegan-Sun* in 1892, and Scripps bought the Los Angeles *Record* in 1895 and the San Francisco *Report* in 1898. By 1908 he had added newspapers in Washington, Oregon, California, Colorado, Indiana, Tennessee, Ohio, Texas, Illinois, Oklahoma, and Iowa. Expansion was purposeful as well as extensive and rapid. Three criteria guided the choice of markets:

—Could a newspaper in this city strengthen the chain's news-gathering abilities (particularly the telegraph news services)?
—Could a newspaper in this city aid other nearby Scripps newspapers in getting regional news?
—Was there a market for a Scripps newspaper in this city? Could it be started cheaply? Specifically, would it be the city's first penny newspaper aimed at the working class?

These criteria reflected the three business strategies Scripps used in building his chain. The telegraph news service was part of vertical integration; new newspapers would be both clients and contributors to the telegraph news service, defraying costs while providing news for other Scripps properties. The emphasis on starting working-class ventures cheaply reflected both the market segmentation and low-cost strategies.

Aiding News-Gathering Abilities

Early nineteenth-century newspapers were highly partisan journals dedicated more to debate than to presenting facts. By midcentury, however, editors had learned that readers had an almost insatiable appetite for fast-breaking news; serving those interests could be highly lucrative. In the late nineteenth century many Americans were interested not only in local events but also in the latest national and world news. Editors competed to get the news first and bragged about their scoops.[4] Many readers bought newspaper extras for the details of a major boxing match or an important battle in some distant locale when such reports arrived outside regular publication times.

The medium for fast-breaking, non-local news was the telegraph, and by the late nineteenth century telegraphic news had become an essential part of any credible and popular newspaper.[5] Major events that attracted intense public interest, such as the assassination of President William McKinley in 1901, underscored the importance of telegraphic news. In 1898 the Pittsburgh *Leader* claimed that its telegraphic services made "it what it is today, a model American newspaper."[6] Beginning in the late 1840s, various organizations supplied telegraphic news, and by the early 1890s, two rival companies, the Associated Press and the first United Press, supplied routine dispatches and special telegrams to client newspapers.[7] The Scripps newspapers were clients of the United Press, which was directed by Walter P. Philips.

Scripps and Telegraphic News Services

Scripps's major involvement in telegraphic news services began in 1889, when he and his lieutenants established an auxiliary telegraph news service to supplement dispatches from the United Press. When the United Press collapsed in 1896–97, Scripps was left with only the small auxiliary report. He refused to join the Associated Press because its franchise system would have impeded expansion of his newspaper chain and because the AP insisted that Scripps kill his auxiliary report.[8] Scripps expanded his auxiliary report, creating the Scripps-McRae Press Association (SMPA) to serve his midwestern papers. In 1898 he started a western service, the Scripps-Blades Press Association—renamed the Scripps News Association (SNA) in 1901—to serve his three California newspapers. The two regional services exchanged news with an eastern company, the Publishers' Press Association (PPA), that Scripps did not control until 1906. In 1907 he merged the three services into a single entity: the United Press Associations.[9]

Two major challenges faced the Scripps telegraphic news companies during the late 1890s. The first was economic. Providing news via telegraph was expensive; the SMPA's initial operating costs in the Midwest were $10,000 a month.[10] The second challenge was journalistic. A successful telegraphic news service needed reliable agents to report and transmit the news. The Associated Press could depend upon its member newspapers—many of them metropolitan dailies—as sources of news for its report. The upstart Scripps companies, however, had to scramble to provide that news. Many of the early Scripps telegraph clients were small newspapers that lacked extensive newsgathering abilities.[11]

Expansion was a logical response to the challenges facing the Scripps telegraph companies. Additional clients would provide revenue to defray costs and improve news-gathering and telegraphic links.[12] Both the SMPA and the SNA grew rapidly. The SMPA had 55 clients in 1897, 75 in 1898, 104 in 1902, 123 in 1904, and 154 by 1906. The SNA grew from 15 clients in 1902 to 32 in 1904 and 60 in 1906.[13] In 1906 the associations served 214 clients; only 15 percent were Scripps newspapers. Establishing *Scripps* newspapers was an ideal method of expanding the telegraph news client base because they were required to subscribe to the Scripps telegraphic news services. There was no danger they might defect for a cheaper or better report. Scripps also required his editors to cover the news of their city and vicinity for the telegraphic news service, a control that did not exist with non-Scripps papers.

Scripps's options in Chicago—"the great newspaper center of the west"—in 1900 illustrate how starting a new operation could help the telegraphic news service. He knew that the Scripps-McRae Press Association needed a Chicago presence, but Chicago's leading newspapers were affiliated with the Associated Press, leaving the *Democrat* as the SMPA's sole client there.[14] The *Democrat* often failed to provide Chicago news to the SMPA, apparently leaked SMPA scoops to the AP, and was close to bankruptcy.[15] Unwilling to depend on the *Democrat* any longer, the SMPA's general manager, Robert F. Paine, outlined two options. The first entailed creating a Chicago news bureau financed by the SMPA; the second entailed starting a Scripps daily newspaper staffed with those same SMPA employees. Both plans would improve SMPA news-gathering, but the newspaper had a distinct advantage: It held the promise of local revenue to offset some SMPA costs.[16] Scripps concurred, and the Chicago *Press* was born. "The Chicago Press was started and has so far been maintained because it was a necessity. . . . the S.M.P.A. is compelled to have a newspaper in Chicago," he wrote.[17]

The needs of the Scripps telegraphic news companies in turn created the impetus for starting newspapers. Scripps told Paine that he had established the western Scripps News Association to serve his California newspapers and then had "started more western papers in order to get the S.N.A. clients."[18] "I have recognized that the S.N.A. needed more clients in order that as an association it would grow stronger and be able to give its old as well as its newer clients a better report," he told his western editors. "Entirely at my own risk of capital, I caused to be founded a number of other newspapers, and the management of the S.N.A. has been extremely active and successful in obtaining other clients, who by contributing to the general cost, enabled the S.N.A. report to be continually and largely improved."[19]

San Francisco was the major news center on the Pacific Coast, and the failure of the *Report* in 1900 eroded the SNA's news-gathering abilities.[20] In 1903 Scripps started another newspaper in San Francisco, primarily to help the

SNA. Even before publication began he claimed that the SNA had "increased in value prospectively because of its association or connection with the proposed San Francisco enterprise."[21] The "main reason for the Daily News' existence was to supply news to the Scripps News Association," he told Paine. "Scripps News started the paper with their own money and credit. . . . If the Daily News didn't print a line of local [news], they were [still] bound to bring it to the office for S.N.A."[22]

Scripps started a newspaper in Denver in 1905 to serve as a bridge between the SNA in the West and the SMPA farther east: "I had two telegraph news associations, separated by a large geographical expanse, over which I had to haul backwards and forwards news matter, at a great expense, there being no intermediate clients between the two districts. I wished to erect in Denver, the half way point, a 'telegraphic pole' to carry my wire and to help support the same."[23]

Similarly, the needs of the telegraphic news services prompted the establishment of the Dallas *Dispatch*. A. O. Andersson, the southwestern agent of the Scripps-McRae Press Association, argued that the SMPA needed to open a Texas bureau to improve its overall coverage, better serve Texas clients, compete with the Associated Press, and attract more clients in the fast-growing Texas afternoon newspaper market.[24] Dallas was the obvious location for such a bureau because it was the center of the state's population as well as the divisional headquarters of Western Union, the nation's leading telegraph company. Eighty percent of all telegrams to and from any Texas point were handled at Dallas. "No other point in the state would be as desirable a location for an SMPA agency, as the dispatches all would go through Dallas any how on arrival, and again on being redistributed."[25] Andersson reported that improving SMPA service in Texas "necessarily involves the collection of a certain amount of Texas news at Dallas," a job that would be greatly improved through a newspaper based in the community. "If the Scripps McRae interests control a paper in Dallas, the press association will be materially benefited."[26]

It was critical that the Dallas venture be reliable, so the Scripps organization moved quickly to preempt the start of a penny paper planned by the Cloverleaf chain—drawing sharp protests from Cloverleaf's management.[27] Cloverleaf was closely associated with the Scripps newspapers, and all Cloverleaf publications were clients of the Scripps telegraphic news services. But Scripps and his associates doubted that a Cloverleaf paper in Dallas would help the SMPA in news-gathering. Jacob C. Harper, the Scripps chain's chief attorney, told Scripps that Cloverleaf newspapers in St. Paul, Minneapolis, and Omaha had "almost wholly neglected press association interests," thus shifting the burden for covering news in their regions to Scripps newspapers.[28]

Just as the needs of the telegraphic news services dictated where some newspapers should be started, they also helped prolong the life of others. In 1908 the Portland *Daily News* was still unprofitable after nearly two years in operation.[29] Scripps and his associates considered killing it but eventually decided not to do so. As he said, "The Portland paper would have been abandoned on account of its misfortunes except for this reason: it was a necessary link in the Pacific Coast news chain."[30] Paine saw "no excuse" for the Portland *News* "save that it is a lease wire client for the United Press Associations."[31] Scripps had also delayed closing the Nashville *Times* in 1907 despite its losses because it served as a key southern center for the telegraphic news services. He and his associates finally decided that the *Times* would never do well, however, and reluctantly suspended publication.[32]

Plans for expansion farther east materialized only after the purchase of the Publishers Press Association in 1906. That same year and also in 1907 Scripps contemplated establishing newspapers in Philadelphia and New York, while Harper suggested buying or starting newspapers in New Jersey.[33] The Philadelphia *News Post* did not begin publication until 1912, however, and the *Telegram* in New York City was not acquired until 1927.

Aiding Other Scripps Newspapers

A major premise of the Scripps telegraph news business was that each Scripps newspaper had the responsibility of relaying the news from its vicinity to all Scripps newspapers and other clients. When the battleship U.S.S. *Bennington* exploded in San Diego harbor in 1905, for example, the *San Diegan-Sun* was responsible for covering the catastrophe and assuring that other Scripps newspapers received the information promptly.[34]

The notion of mutual assistance influenced the geographic patterns of expansion. Scripps often established newspapers so they could share regional news. The result was a set of fairly concentrated newspaper groups in Ohio, California, and the Pacific Northwest and uncompleted groups in Colorado, Oklahoma, Indiana, and Texas. By 1908 the Ohio group included newspapers in Cincinnati (and Covington, Kentucky), Cleveland, Columbus, Akron, and Toledo. The California group included San Diego, Los Angeles, San Francisco, Fresno, and Sacramento. The northwestern group included Seattle, Spokane, Tacoma, and Portland. Newspapers in Denver and Pueblo were the first in Colorado, with proposed expansion in Colorado Springs.[35] Oklahoma City was the center of a proposed Oklahoma group, with anticipated additions at Guthrie just north of Oklahoma City and Shawnee east of it.[36] The two Indiana newspapers were in Terre Haute and Evansville. In 1908 Dallas represented the first stage of a Texas group, and a newspaper was started in Houston in 1911.[37]

Scripps classified his holdings in major news centers such as Seattle, Dallas, or San Francisco as "pillar" newspapers, whereas those in smaller cities were "buttress" papers established to support the pillars. As he said, "The position I took was there are two classes of newspapers in my league; that one class that forms the pillars of the edifice and that class that forms the buttresses."[38] The Sacramento *Star* covered the California state capital, providing important news to the three pillar newspapers in San Diego, Los Angeles, and San Francisco. Both the Fresno and Sacramento operations provided news of the inland valleys of California to the newspapers on the Coast. "Sacramento and Fresno were considered by me as supports rather than pillars in my California edifice," Scripps said.[39] In a similar fashion, the Tacoma and Spokane properties supported the pillars in Seattle and Portland. Even though the Spokane *Press* was losing money, Scripps sustained it because it provided his coastal papers with news of eastern Washington. "Sometimes I have felt willing to wipe the Spokane paper out of existence and take the whole plant and go somewhere else with it; but against this idea I have the feeling that the interests of the Seattle *Star* and Tacoma *Times* require that the third big City of the State should have a sister newspaper in it."[40] "Like you," E. F. Chase told Scripps, "I do not want to see the Press stop, because we need Spokane in our work up this way."[41] Scripps replied, "I think personally I am prompted to hold on to the Press because we need the Spokane field in our business of the Washington league."[42]

Portland, the last newspaper added to the northwestern group, was seen as a necessary complement to the others. E. H. Wells, founder of the Seattle and Tacoma newspapers, noted the value of having a Portland property: "We will have to get that city sooner or later to complete the chain. It is in close neighborhood to our Seattle and Tacoma enterprises, and in every way a desirable point to cover."[43] Scripps also contemplated starting other newspapers in the "small cities" of Washington state—Wenatchee, Walla Walla, Yakima, Bellingham, and Aberdeen—because they would help his larger papers in that state.[44]

Other proposed expansion—none of it carried out—was seen in the same light. Scripps anticipated starting newspapers in Eureka, San Jose, and Stockton to strengthen the California group and in Dayton to buttress the Ohio group. He envisioned the Terre Haute and Evansville newspapers, both established in 1906, as the start of a broader Indiana group; the next step, he said, would be a newspaper in Indianapolis, and Milton McRae described the Memphis and Nashville papers as "the nucleus for the Tennessee group."[45]

The Influence on Content

Expansion based on the needs of the telegraphic news service and on pillar and buttress considerations influenced the type of news that appeared in the Scripps papers. Extensive reliance on newspapers within the chain meant that news from cities where Scripps newspapers published appeared more frequently in Scripps newspapers than in those that relied on a different telegraphic news service. News from cities with Scripps newspapers constituted almost half of the telegraphic news in the Scripps properties in Portland, Sacramento, and San Diego, whereas it averaged only 17 percent of the telegraphic news of their rivals in those markets, all of whom subscribed to other news services (fig. 1; table 1, appendix 1). An analysis of the two Portland afternoon newspapers in 1907 illustrates the impact that had on news. The front page of the October 4, 1907, issue of Scripps's Portland *Daily News,* for example, carried four articles from Scripps cities: two from Seattle (both about crimes), one from Kansas City (about religion), and one from San Francisco (about a court case there). Its afternoon rival, the *Evening Telegram,* had none of these articles.

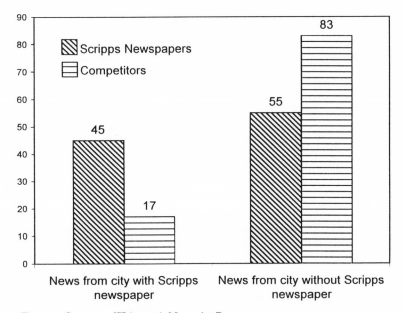

Figure 1. Sources of Telegraph News, by Percentage

Market Analysis

The third element in the expansion evaluation process involved market analysis. Scripps and his associates gathered and analyzed two kinds of information about each city: general characteristics (population, business volume, transportation facilities, and the size of the working class) and the nature of newspapers already serving that market (price, political affiliation, news style, and affinity for labor).

General City Characteristics

Dallas, as Andersson reported in 1906, could easily support a Scripps newspaper. It had ninety thousand inhabitants, was the center of a territory with 2.5 million people, and transportation routes were good: "Eight systems of railways converge at Dallas, over 15 lines radiating in as many directions. Eighty-four passenger trains are handled daily in the Dallas depots. Twenty-five passenger trains depart between 1 P.M. and 8 P.M." Consequently, supplies such as newsprint could be delivered without difficulty, and the afternoon train schedule would facilitate distribution to nearby towns. The city was a congenial place for families (the ideal customers). Dallas, which had a substantial working-class population, was "the leading manufacturing city in Texas." Business was diversified, growing, and prosperous, providing the foundation for extensive advertising from a wide variety of businesses. "Dallas has six months of summer," Andersson observed, "but none of the summer siesta spirit which I noticed in Mobile, Birmingham, Jacksonville and other Southern cities. . . . the newspaper advertising columns carry a good line of local patronage in the [summer] season."[46]

Other market studies analyzed similar city characteristics. In 1906, when C. H. Fentress, business manager of the Cleveland *Press,* examined the suitability of Oklahoma City, he reported on population, living conditions (schools, churches, city improvements, and utilities), advertising base (the number of, prosperity of retail stores), and transportation routes.[47] J. P. Hamilton reported on Denver's population, business activity, and working-class base when he proposed starting a newspaper there.[48] When Scripps was considering starting a paper in Tacoma, Washington, J. C. Harper wrote to a lawyer in that city to gauge local business prospects. "You ask if Tacoma is growing," Emmett Parker replied. "Building has been progressing for two or three years past such as we have not seen since the boom times."[49]

Most Scripps newspapers were started in small and medium-sized cities, where, McRae contended, such ventures were cheaper, easier, and more likely of success than in big cities. Scripps agreed. "I note what you say as to the advisability of our confining our efforts to the small cities. Practically, the small cities means the system of planting little acorns to grow into big oaks."[50] Too, Scripps newspapers could grow with the population. When E. H. Wells was editing the Tacoma *Times*, Scripps told him that his circulation should grow by two thousand for every ten thousand new residents.[51]

Another aspect of expansion concerned the sizes of various cities. Scripps attributed some of his early success, particularly in Cleveland, to the *Press*'s ability to exploit that city's population growth. In 1880, just two years after the *Press* began publication, the city had a population of 160,146; by 1890 it had grown to 261,353 and to 381,768 by 1900.[52]

Chicago had a population of 1.7 million when he started the *Press* there in 1900, and San Diego had only 17,000 inhabitants when he bought the *San Diegan-Sun* in 1892. By 1906, however, Scripps had concluded that the critical mass necessary for one of his cheap independent newspapers was a population near forty thousand. The success of the Sacramento *Star* proved that a Scripps newspaper could do well in a town that size, he said. Fresno, with a population of just twenty thousand, would be too small.[53]

Existing Newspapers in Specific Markets

The single most important consideration in expansion was whether a market existed in a city for a Scripps newspaper. The ideal market was one in which the existing newspapers were partisan, relatively expensive (about 5 cents per copy), cozy with local corporate interests, and hostile or at least indifferent to labor. In those cities, Scripps could reach an untapped market with independent, pro-labor, penny papers.

The bulk of a twelve-page market analysis report on Evansville, Indiana, in 1904 concentrated on the city's two most prominent newspapers: the morning *Courier* and the afternoon *Journal News*. H. Y. Saint, a long-time Scripps employee, reported that both were relatively expensive, selling for 5 cents a copy on the streets. Both were politically oriented (one Democratic, the other Republican), and neither espoused working-class interests. A small, weekly, labor union newspaper was the only major outlet for labor issues. Saint reported that neither the *Courier* nor the *Journal News*'s management expected new competitors because they controlled the Associated Press's news service in Evansville. The advertising manager of the *Courier* had told Saint that "he didn't think a new newspaper enterprise would pay, because they could not get the A.P. dispatches." In sum, Saint thought the Evansville market was a good one for Scripps. Merchants were encouraging, and prospects were good:

> There is a good field in Evansville from the circulating standpoint. There is an opening for a newspaper. I do not think the existing papers are covering the field . . . for advertisers told me that they were compelled to do their own advertising by circulars. . . . The local papers are political in tone, are not honest and their owners are not overly popular. A paper could be conducted more cheaply in Evansville than in most any city that I know of. Fuel is cheap, labor is cheap and rents are low.[54]

Andersson reported from Dallas in 1906 that there were no labor union newspapers in that city and that both major newspapers (the morning *News* and the evening *Times Herald*) ignored labor interests. Both were tied to the political status quo, the *News* being "the recognized organ of the corporations in Texas." It and the *Times Herald* were also relatively expensive; both sold for 5 cents on the streets. The newspapers were boring. The *News* "rarely prints any sort of an item which would give the slightest offense anywhere. . . . its local stories are dull and dreary. It would be against the News' policy to print a live story in a breezy manner. The whole paper is inordinately respectable and heavy." Andersson concluded that "there is a wide field in Dallas untouched by the existing papers. A very large element of the community seems to be unrepresented in the local press at this time, and it will be our aim to further their interests and to satisfy their demands for a clean, live, honest, snappy paper at low cost."[55]

Other market studies paid similar attention to established newspapers. J. P. Hamilton reported that the two afternoon newspapers in Denver (the *Post* and the *Times*) sold for 5 cents a copy and that both were also unsympathetic to labor interests. "It can be seen that the masses get what the classes care to give them, and only that." Labor was particularly hostile to the *Post* because of its stance in the previous gubernatorial election, when it "sold out to Peabody, Union Labor's bitterest enemy, and defeated Adams, a true friend of the workingman."[56] McRae likewise said that the older established newspapers in Nashville were high-priced (one sold for 5 cents, the other 2 cents) and represented corporate, not labor, interests there. "It is considered that there is a good field in Nashville for a 1 cent independent newspaper."[57] From Oklahoma City, Fentress reported that the three daily newspapers there (the *Daily Oklahoman*, *Oklahoma Post*, and *Times Journal*) all sold for 5 cents a copy and were partisan. Fentress concluded that "there is a good opportunity to work up a good street sale upon a one cent basis, and I am sure that the right management can show a handsome circulation with a year's time."[58]

The desire to establish newspapers in cities without well-established 1 cent papers directed expansion away from large eastern cities, where they were more common.[59] In 1906 and 1907 Scripps contemplated entering two eastern markets (Philadelphia and New York City) with an unusual product: an advertising-free newspaper.[60] Eventually, in 1911, he started one, the *Day Book* in Chicago, which published until 1917.

Market studies were also instrumental in derailing preliminary plans to start newspapers elsewhere. In Salt Lake City, for example, location would have helped the telegraph news services.[61] Closer analysis revealed, however, that the market segment Scripps wanted to reach was already being served. R. G. Conant reported that Salt Lake City already had a penny newspaper run along Scripps lines and begun by a former Scripps employee: "Its make up is almost identical to our own papers and it makes great grand stand plays about attacking the city light and street railway franchise extensions and such other matters—in fact, it fills the very field that our own papers do in every city."[62] Market analysis of San Jose showed that the two existing afternoon newspapers there would be formidable competition and that the city had neither the population or advertising base to support three. Scripps attempted to buy the *News* but failed. The market report recommended that "San Jose should be passed for the present. . . . the time is not ripe for us to go into that city."[63] Somewhat similar conditions existed both in Toledo and Columbus, but the Scripps organization was successful in purchasing newspapers in both cities. Milton McRae engineered the purchase of the Toledo *Times,* Toledo *News,* and Toledo *Bee* in 1903 and the Columbus *Citizen* in 1904.

With hindsight, Scripps and McRae agreed in 1905 that a city where one newspaper had "an extraordinary lead over all competitors" was not a good site for a Scripps newspaper. They learned this lesson from their experiences in Chicago, St. Louis, and Kansas City, where their newspapers had fared poorly against a well-entrenched and popular competitor.[64]

Limits to Expansion

Two key factors slowed expansion during Scripps's years as chief executive: limited capital and lack of personnel.

Capital—Scripps's method of doing business limited his access to capital. In an effort to protect his financial independence and avoid untimely calls on loans, he tried to avoid borrowing money from banks. He relied instead on profits from his wealthier newspapers (notably the Cleveland *Press* and the Cincinnati *Post*), although both suffered in the late 1890s from the common postwar circulation and advertising decline. The uncertainty brought about by the bitter, drawn-out (1900–1903) family battle over George Scripps's estate limited financial discretion and thus impeded expansion.[65]

The financial picture changed in 1903 as profits rose and the family litigation ended favorably for Scripps. In 1903 he first realized the extent to which employees could finance expansion. Experimenting with a new way of raising capital, he solicited Scripps employees for the capital for the Tacoma *Times,* and the project quickly was oversubscribed. Within a year, he established the Newspaper Savings and Investment Society to funnel employee contributions. Employee funds were part of the capital used in starting newspapers in Dallas, Terre Haute, Memphis, Nashville, and Oklahoma City.[66]

Substantial sums were expended between 1903 and 1906, when thirteen newspapers were started and three purchased. The cost of these—plus additional money spent to start the NEA, buy the PPA, and purchase additional ranch property near Miramar—exhausted Scripps's supply of ready capital. At the end of 1906 he said that rapid expansion had made money scarce; further expansion would have to wait.[67]

Personnel—Even when money was not tight the shortage of well-trained Scripps employees limited expansion. In 1905 and 1906 R. F. Paine—by then editorial superintendent of the entire chain—said that finding enough qualified men to start Scripps newspapers was a huge challenge. Each newspaper was expected to train employees in the Scripps style of journalism, preparing them for jobs elsewhere in the chain. The expansion of 1903–6 quickly depleted the supply of trained employees, and in 1908 J. C. Harper said that any expansion in Texas had to be delayed—not from a lack of money but from a lack of men to run the newspapers. "It is felt that until we have properly manned the papers which are already in existence that we ought not to take on others."[68]

Conclusions

"Expansion is one of the shibboleths," Max Balthasar said when he was general manager of the Scripps News Association.[69] He was being too modest; expansion was a shibboleth of the entire Scripps organization. Scripps had fallen short of his goal of blanketing the country with fifty to a hundred cheap, small, working-class newspapers, but he was far more successful than any of his contemporaries in starting and buying them.[70] Not every new venture was successful, however. The most dismal failure of this era was the San Francisco

Report, which Scripps bought in 1898 and killed in 1900.[71] He also killed the Nashville *Times* in 1907 and the Kansas City *World* in 1908. The Pueblo *Sun* and the Fresno *Tribune* never performed well and were killed in 1910 and 1912, respectively.

Despite these failures most newspapers Scripps established were profitable. By 1908 he had a thriving group along with a national telegraph news service to support further expansion. His elder sons, James and John, did not demonstrate his zeal, however, and it was not until his son Robert and Roy Howard were running the organization during the 1920s that expansion became common again.

Scripps succeeded in expanding his newspaper empire because he built carefully and strategically. Vertical integration meant that he built a strong foundation for the chain in the telegraph news services. Stymied by the Associated Press's monopolistic practices, he could expand because of his ready source of non-local news. In turn, he started newspapers in news centers such as Dallas or San Francisco that supported the telegraph services and helped other nearby Scripps operations. His strategies of market segmentation and keeping costs low also directed expansion, directing Scripps to markets where his particular style of journalism had a good chance of success. Not only did these three strategies dictate how Scripps expanded his business, but they also influenced the construction of news. The symbiosis between telegraph services and the Scripps newspapers in particular provided a distinct geographic bias to non-local news.

Controlling Costs

I don't like to spend money except under the most favorable conditions.
—E. W. Scripps to E. H. Wells, January 1, 1903

Do not be afraid to be called a skin flint or a miser. You can acquire no more valuable reputation.
—E. W. Scripps to Hyacinth Ford, November 7, 1906

THE FIRST ISSUE OF Scripps's Seattle *Star* on February 25, 1899, was small (just four pages) and printed on the cheapest, thinnest newsprint available. Its debut had been scheduled for the day before, but its old, worn press would not run. News content was also sparse—the product of just three inexperienced reporters working at minimal salaries—and type was in such short supply that the newspaper was produced in two stages. Many newsboys refused to sell the *Star*. They did not want to hike to its office in a run-down building in a low-rent district outside Seattle's central business district. Those who did show up were surprised to find that, contrary to common practice, they had to pay for their newspapers in advance, and the *Star* did not allow them to return unsold ones.[1]

All of this—used presses, cheap offices and newsprint, small staffs at low wages, and a cash-only business—reflected the penny-pinching methods of the *Star*'s chief stockholder, E. W. Scripps. When he agreed to start the newspaper, he had admonished the staff to "shave expenses . . . down to the bone. The cheapest white paper is the best. Proof reading is only a frill. . . . All show is damn foolishness. . . . pinch every penny."[2] In Seattle, editor E. H. Wells and business manager E. F. Chase tried to do just that. As Wells said, "There is no chance to save a penny that is neglected." Hours were long and salaries small. Chase wore threadbare clothes, and Wells borrowed money from Scripps to support his family. Chase reported, "It gets tiresome, living almost without spending any dough at all."[3]

Such penny-pinching was an integral part of the business strategies (market segmentation, low cost, and vertical integration) Scripps used to build a national newspaper chain. His newspapers were cheap; they sold for just a penny during an era when many of their rivals still sold for 2 to 5 cents. That pricing decision was purposeful. Scripps wanted to ensure that his publications were within the reach of his target audience, the working class. The pricing decision also limited revenue compared to other newspapers of the era and thus dictated stringent controls over expenditures. Vertical integration by means of a news features service (the NEA) and telegraph news service (the United Press Associations and its various forerunners) reduced news-gathering and production costs.

Scripps's low-cost strategy was essential to the creation of his chain. It preserved capital, limited operating costs, reduced dependence on advertisers, and kept his newspapers accessible to the working class. At the same time, it became such a central focus that it threatened to undermine his newspapers. It severely limited their ability to cover local news—increasingly a staple of American journalism. Small staffs hampered local-news coverage and dictated dependence on mass-produced, relatively low-cost features, and reliance on cheap but worn presses and old type often resulted in newspapers that were hard to read.

Learning to Economize

Penny-pinching did not come naturally to Scripps; it was a lesson he had been taught—sometimes forcibly—by his elder brothers James and George. Scripps later said that his tenure at the Detroit *Evening News* shaped his attitude toward finances. "The one great characteristic my brother [James] impressed upon the News. . . . was economy. Money was saved and was to be saved at every possible point. Business was to be conducted on a cash basis only—that is to say, no capital was to be borrowed and no bonds issued. Thrift and always thrift."[4]

In his autobiography, Scripps recalled that James reduced newsprint costs by allowing the *Evening News* to have unusually narrow page margins. The staff was small, hours long. Scripps's sister, Ellen, produced a large amount of copy cheaply by rewriting news from a variety of newspapers.[5] No waste was tolerated; "from top to bottom, in every department, large and small, the most minute attention was given to economy."[6] "Why even the paper that we reporters had to write our copy on was always used twice," he remembered, "after we had written our articles and sent them to the printer, on clean paper, the 'devil' of the composing room used to gather up all of the written pages and then return them to us, the writers, so that we could use the other side for fresh copy."[7]

His elder brothers continued to enforce economies on Scripps during these "apprenticeship" years, both in Cleveland and St. Louis. When he began preparations for the St. Louis *Chronicle* in 1880, Scripps told the prospective editor, Stanley Waterloo, that salaries would be substantially below market—"at the lowest possible figures. On the matter of salaries, both of my brothers were fixed beyond all argument." Waterloo was to "look for profits rather from the increase in value of stock than from salaries."[8]

From the 1890s on, Scripps became much more concerned about finances and economizing. Extensive expansion taxed his limited capital and placed greater emphasis on cost-cutting, and he began to watch expenditures closely, telling one employee that "every dollar is a drop of my blood." Success came through economy, Scripps claimed. "The ability to control expenses is about the only ability on which purely business success can depend."[9]

Scripps defended his penny-pinching ways by claiming that "it is not the money that makes a newspaper, it is the men. More newspapers have been ruined by the editors having too large an appropriation than have failed as a result of the editor having too little." A poor editor with large amounts of money could hide his failure "for an indefinite period." In contrast, "if the editor is a poor editor and has a small fund you find him out quickly."[10] Efforts to control costs figured prominently in three areas: start-up costs, news-gathering and production, and distribution.

Start-Up Costs

The first step in controlling costs was to limit the amount of money used in starting a new newspaper. It was a lesson dinned into Scripps by his brothers when he started the Cleveland *Press* in 1878 and the St. Louis *Chronicle* in 1880; on his own, he continued that policy. He attempted to limit spending on equipment (such as presses, Linotypes, and office furniture) and operating expenses (such as salaries and newsprint) until a new newspaper broke even. The modest debut of the Seattle *Star* in 1899 exemplifies the cost controls he imposed.

Scripps wanted to limit start-up costs for several reasons. First, most new newspapers failed, regardless of their level of capitalization, and Scripps wanted to limit expenditures until he was fairly certain of success. Second, limiting start-up costs prevented a drain on his limited capital, thus allowing expansion elsewhere. Better to start five cheap newspapers at $20,000 each than two deluxe ones at $50,000, he reasoned. Third, Scripps was convinced that limiting the initial expenditure in a newspaper shaped its future. Elaborate offices or expensive presses would spawn lavishness and thus waste precious money.[11]

Beginning with the *Star*, he insisted that founding editors and business managers of new newspapers submit a detailed prospectus, outlining estimates of all start-up costs. Scripps then treated these prospectuses as quasi-contractual agreements between himself and local management. In 1903, for example, E. H. Wells, prospective editor of the Tacoma *Times,* submitted a proposal that included estimates for acquiring and installing all machinery and related supplies necessary to start publication: a press, a Linotype, motors for both, type, a casting box for cuts, a keg of ink, a ton of metal, a ton of newsprint, tools for installation, a proof roller, saw and table, typewriters, office furniture, wiring and lights, stationery, rollers, office signs, and carpentry work. Wells estimated that the *Times* would break even after ten months, but during that period money would be needed to meet operating costs.[12] Proposals for starting newspapers in Sacramento, Oakland, Salt Lake City, Nashville, Reno, and Denver all followed the same format. Scripps insisted that these proposals be quite specific; he rejected the first draft of the Denver prospectus as too general.[13]

The prospectus was to be followed closely. Wells was required to keep daily accounts to compare actual expenses to prospectus estimates. Scripps wrote, "You can tell every day whether you are getting above or below any appropriations you have allowed for yourself."[14] When W. H. Porterfield wanted to depart from the prospectus for the Sacramento *Star* by adding a second Linotype before the newspaper had broken even, Scripps refused. "I have no idea of ever giving my consent to your enlarging your plant of machinery until after you have proven your ability to profitably conduct your business with your present plant."[15]

The single largest expenditure for a new newspaper was a press. To delay spending money on a printing press, some Scripps newspapers relied on flatbed presses at commercial printing firms until circulation reached several hundred. After that, they relied on used presses bought relatively cheaply from other Scripps newspapers.[16] The Tacoma *Times* started with a press from the defunct Scripps Chicago *Press* and other machinery from the Seattle *Star.* The Sacramento *Star* started with presses previously used by the St. Louis *Chronicle* and the Los Angeles *Record.* The Portland and Terre Haute operations began with machinery that McRae purchased from a newspaper plant in Oshkosh, Wisconsin. The Seattle *Star* bought used presses from the Cleveland *Press* in 1901 and from the Cincinnati *Post* in 1902.[17]

Reliance on used machinery met Scripps's requirement of controlling costs but did not guarantee high quality. Many Scripps editors complained that they had inferior presses and inadequate machinery. In 1901 Chase reported on "the poor apology for a machine that we have."[18] "I can see no unpleasant aspect to the situation except that we cannot print a decent looking sheet," Wells told Scripps. He recounted trying to publish photographs of a "sensational wedding in this town between an ex-judge of eighty-four and a blusher of thirty-six from Montana. I tried to print their pictures and got a couple of ghastly shadows into the paper."[19]

But such complaints did not generate much sympathy. Scripps argued that "typographical appearance and polished literary style" were the "equal enemies of journalism." Both were "intended for show" and ran contrary to cost controls. On another occasion he told Jacob C. Harper, the chain's chief attorney, that "typographical form in a newspaper has about the same relation to the real spirit and character of the newspaper as a man's coat has to the man's character. . . . Grant would have been no better a general had he always worn a dress suit, nor would he have been less competent as a general had his uniform been gray instead of blue."[20]

Overall, Scripps was successful in controlling start-up costs for most of his operations. He established newspapers for $10,000 to $35,000 at a time when other medium-sized dailies cost two or three times that amount. The Cleveland *Press* was established for $15,000, the *Kentucky Post* for slightly under $10,000, the Tacoma *Times* for $16,666, the Evansville *Press* for $21,000, the Dallas *Dispatch* for $35,000, and the Sacramento *Star* for $20,000.[21]

News-Gathering and Production

Extensive cost controls also meant that the Scripps newspapers ran on a proverbial shoestring. Efforts to control expenses in news-gathering and production included cheap offices, controlled size, cheap newsprint, staffing, salary levels, reliance on inexpensive content, budgeting, and general rules and exhortations.

Cheap Offices—Scripps was eager to limit any expense that did not generate revenue, so the chief characteristic of his newspapers' offices was their cheapness. In 1906 E. H. Bagby, manager of the Los Angeles *Record* told the new editor of the Memphis *Press,* "Insignificant and inconspicuous offices have invariably marked or been the emblem for the creation of each of the western properties."[22]

Scripps newspaper offices usually were in low-rent areas outside of the central business district. Old warehouses were commonly used. In Spokane, the *Press* was located in that city's tenderloin; the San Francisco *Daily News*'s office was in an industrial area south of Market Street, a mile or two from San Francisco's central business district in 1903; and the Portland newspaper's first office was on the east side of the Willamette River, several miles from downtown. Scripps doubted that these relatively out-of-the-way locations would hurt business. "Only a very small part of a newspaper business. . . . depends upon that casual sort of custom which only comes because it is convenient," he said. He told one manager to be particularly wary of real estate people when hunting for office space. "Never tell them you are looking for an office for a newspaper. They have their own ideas about where a newspaper should be. Instead tell them you are going to start a laundry or a blacksmith shop. The prices quoted will be one half to one quarter what you would otherwise pay."[23]

Once newspapers were well established, Scripps would buy land and erect an office building—primarily to avoid spiraling rental costs. But cost controls still applied. When he planned to construct an office for the Sacramento *Star*, he told its manager, "Really, all you need in the way of a building are good enough brick walls, a roof and a firm floor with the roof supported by iron or timber up-rights." Scripps developed a generic, warehouse-style building that guided all building projects.[24]

Modest offices were important beyond the actual cost savings derived from low rent. Scripps argued that the style of an office set the tone for a newspaper's entire operation: "Just as a man and his wife and family will live up to the style of the house they occupy rather than live down to the income that the family enjoys, so the newspaper management and a staff of newspaper employees live up to, think up to, and work up to the style and custom of a newspaper that would ordinarily occupy such an office, rather than conduct themselves according to the income and financial ability of a newspaper."[25] When E. L. Rector and A. R. Hopkins, the founding editor and business manager of the Pueblo *Sun*, agreed to pay $50 a month for an office, Scripps worried that "this proportionately high rent" would harm the new venture. "If business can be done in the new office of the Sun on exactly the same scale that it would have been done in the $25 per month office, no great injury can result, but I feel it is necessary to sound a note of warning on the subject."[26]

Plush offices were also thought to be bad for well-established newspapers. By 1906 the Los Angeles *Record* had produced substantial profits for Scripps, yet he worried that its new building would "result in an unnecessary increase in expenses and a reduction of the net profits." As he told Lemuel T. Atwood, the chain's treasurer, "Think of it, they have forty-two phones in that office." Scripps later told E. H. Bagby, the *Record*'s manager, that he regretted the new office. "We only live to learn," he said. "I have learned that the only way to prevent new and commodious business quarters from being a detriment is to absolutely prevent the building and furnishing of the new offices in any other way than as the cheapest possible covering for the plant."[27]

Controlled Size—From modest offices, Scripps employees produced small newspapers. Most were four-page sheets in an era when rivals published eight to twelve pages daily. Page size differed as well. Pages on Scripps's newspapers ran about two-thirds the size of those of rival publications; most had seven columns rather than eight. The four-page format was an article of faith. Scripps proudly proclaimed that he had started all of his newspapers as four-page publications. They were more popular and thus more salable than big papers. "All things being equal, the smaller the sheet of a newspaper, the more interesting, the more popular and the more salable it is," he proclaimed.[28]

Four-page newspapers were economical, too, requiring less newsprint or composition work than larger operations. As Richard Kaplan notes, James Scripps had introduced the notion of small newspapers as a method of reducing costs for newsprint—and thus facilitating the low price that made the Detroit *Evening News* so accessible to the working class.[29] Scripps continued his elder brother's formula, even after the prices of newsprint declined during the 1890s. "I have never been able to double the size of a paper without more than doubling its cost," he maintained.[30] He insisted that profits for larger newspapers were reduced by additional newsprint, increased circulation and transportation expenses, typesetting for articles and advertising, additional machinery (for typesetting and presswork), and a "full staff of pressmen, stereotypers, printers, editors, mailing room, men, etc."[31]

Scripps allowed his newspapers to expand to eight pages (and, in the case of some of the older midwestern properties, to ten pages and more) if profits remained high. The Cincinnati *Post* and Cleveland *Press* continued to generate substantial profits even after being enlarged, but that was not always true for newspapers such as the Seattle *Star* and Los Angeles *Record*.

Cheap Newsprint—Saving money on newsprint was another way to control costs. "Every penny that we save on white paper is a penny added to our net profits," Scripps said.[32] In addition to printing small, four-page newspapers and using a poorer-quality newsprint, Scripps also instructed managers to use the thinnest newsprint their presses would accept and use narrow margins.[33]

Scripps newspapers bought newsprint jointly to obtain bulk discounts. In 1905 Milton McRae estimated that these purchases saved the chain nearly $45,000 a year. Because newsprint was sold by weight, managers had instructions to weigh every roll upon delivery—to monitor contract compliance. Offices kept inventories low to avoid tying up cash and because cheap newsprint often broke on the presses after it had aged.[34]

Staffing—Staffs at most Scripps newspapers were small too, thus limiting salary expense. Except at the older midwestern operations in Cleveland, Cincinnati, and St. Louis, the staffs of Scripps's publications usually were a third of those of rival newspapers. In 1908 Wells compared the size of editorial staffs at northwestern Scripps newspapers with those of afternoon rivals. The Spokane *Press* had three reporters compared to ten for its afternoon rival the *Chronicle;* the Tacoma *Times* had three, whereas its rival had twelve; the Portland *Daily News* had three compared to nine at the afternoon *Telegram;* and the Seattle *Times* had twelve reporters to just four on Scripps's Seattle *Star.*[35]

The editorial staffs of most Scripps newspapers established early in the twentieth century amounted to three or, at most, four people. Five persons composed the entire editorial, circulation, and advertising staff of the Denver *Express.* J. P. Hamilton, the business manager, told Scripps: "We take turns in sweeping out the office, going after the mail, and carrying the forms from our office to the printing establishment. During my spare time, I solicit subscribers, keep the books and chase advertising. Must walk at least fifteen miles a day. Am getting the kind of exercise I have needed for so many years."[36] Production staffs were small, too. In 1904 Wells reported that "the smallest number of men allowed by the unions are employed in the mechanical departments of the [Tacoma] Times. . . . There is not an extra man around the place."[37]

Salary Levels—Not only were staffs small but salaries for the news staff were also low—all in an effort to limit expenses. (Printers, who were unionized, earned relatively higher wages.) Instead of market-based salaries, editors and business managers usually held a minority of the stock in their newspapers. As Scripps had explained to Waterloo in 1880, "I expect to get my pay for the first year's or two year's work from the increase in the value of my stock."[38]

Salaries for editors and business managers were particularly low until a newspaper broke even. Chase and Wells started at $15 each at the Seattle *Star.* Chase reminded Scripps that they were working at low salaries to get the newspaper through its early days. "The bargain was that the salaries should remain unchanged until the Star broke even. Just as soon as the Star is making the proper . . . profit . . . we shall surely think that the salaries of the Editor and Business Manager of the Star should be considerably more than $25 a week each."[39] George Putnam earned $12 a week as editor and business manager of the Spokane *Press* in 1902 and 1903, when $25 or $30 was a common salary for that job at other newspapers.[40]

The object was to induce people to work as cheaply as possible. In the early 1890s Scripps and his lieutenants assessed the productivity of salaried reporters on the Cincinnati *Post* by computing the average cost of a column of news that each reporter generated. Some worked cheaply—generating a column for as little as $1.21; the more expensive reporters were warned to work faster and produce more (and thus to bring their per-column average down). "Inefficient" reporters would be transferred from salary to payment by volume generated ("space" pay).[41]

Experienced reporters often left to work for higher wages elsewhere. In 1881 R. W. Harris told Scripps he had left the St. Louis *Chronicle* "solely from necessity" because his salary "was not sufficient to meet my expenses and live decently." Waterloo told Scripps that he could not afford to match Harris's new salary at the St. Louis *Republican.* "We must expect to lose our good men regularly." In 1900 H. B. Clark told Scripps that the best reporters at the Seattle *Star* were hired away by the other Seattle newspapers at higher salaries, leaving the editor there with cub reporters. Once those cubs were trained, they, too, were lured away by salary offers 25 to 100 percent higher than the *Star* paid. "It makes things hard for the Star in one way," Wells noted. "We are forever breaking in new men and our office has become the recruiting ground for both the Times and the PI."[42]

Other Scripps newspapers faced similar problems in hiring or retaining employees. H. B. Canfield, editor of the Los Angeles *Record,* reported in 1902 that both the Los Angeles *Examiner* and the *Evening Express* raided his staff. Paine observed that Scripps salaries were seldom competitive; few capable of being editors would willingly take a $15 or $20 weekly salary when even inexperienced reporters on other newspapers were getting that much or more. Thomas Dillon, editor of the Portland *Daily News,* quit after eighteen months because his salary was so low. In 1908 B. F. Gurley, editor of the Denver *Express,* lost "every man in his editorial staff except one consumptive. The two best men he had left to accept more lucrative positions."[43]

Paine found it difficult to hire employees for the Scripps-McRae Press Association (the Midwest telegraph news service). "It is proving a terribly difficult job to get men, young, bright men, who don't want $35 per week as a starter. . . . On the coast here any young scrub can command at least $20 per week and the sole argument I have been able to use has been the greatness of our concern and the opportunities with it, and the fellows can't usually see it."[44] Porterfield reported that salaries and business expenses were very low at the *San Diegan-Sun.* Such economy had consequences. "There isn't a single up-to-date man on the whole property. . . . Both the reporters are lazier than time, the carriers are insolent and independent, the foreman is a crank who hasn't been out of San Diego for a generation, and so it is right down the line."[45]

None of this appeared to trouble Scripps. He told the editor of the Los Angeles *Record* that the newspaper was "really the gainer by this condition" by making jobs there an ideal path for ambitious and energetic young men who wanted to get into journalism. Scripps argued that young, relatively inexperienced reporters were ideal employees because they worked for less and their writing was "more natural and more easily understood. . . . Ninety nine per cent of all the good work that has been done on my newspaper has been done by men who produced their best work when they were getting the least pay."[46] Scripps told one editor that "untrained newspapermen, fresh from the ranks of the laymen, crude as their work would be, were necessarily more sympathetic . . . to the great mass of common people." Journalistic training and experience lead a reporter "away from the masses. . . . For myself, if I were editing a newspaper today, I would rather have my whole staff of untrained 'cubs' than have it made up of men recognized as proved and experienced journalists."[47]

Scripps newspapers generally did not raise employees' salaries when an outside offer was made. In 1899 McRae told the Cleveland *Press*'s business manager to do nothing when an advertising solicitor had a chance to earn more money at another newspaper. "I think it would be well to let Mr. Beswick leave the Press at once unless he is willing to accept our judgment as to his value. . . . Even if you retain such a man as Beswick, when he demands an increase peremptorily it is bad business policy." On another occasion McRae said, "The man who wants to quit because he is not getting enough salary has a perfect right to quit and nineteen times out of twenty, we don't want to prevail upon such a man to stay in the concern."[48] Charles Mosher, editor of the Cincinnati *Post* in 1900, did not raise a copy editor's salary to keep him from going to the rival *Times-Star* because "I believe it would have spoiled him and made him really less valuable to the paper."[49]

Not only were salaries low but benefits were also few, as was true at most U.S. newspapers. Although Scripps transferred employees from one newspaper to another, moving expenses were seldom allowed. There were no pensions. Vacations were not a basic right for every employee but rather seen as rewards for hard work. In 1906 Paine explained that "there is no such thing as an employee being 'entitled' to a vacation. . . . The granting of a vacation is simply an investment by the company in the improvement of its good men, and it is a necessary and profitable investment when properly made." Paine also stressed that employees should earn their pay; past performance did not excuse current illness or decline. In such situations, he advised, "He is a good fellow and we all like him. You feel that you don't need him. Give him, at once, two weeks notice."[50]

With low salaries and virtually no benefits, Scripps's newspapers had some difficulty in attracting and retaining good employees. Some were willing to put up with low wages as reporters because they hoped to advance in the expanding chain to editor or even regional manager of a group of Scripps newspapers, positions that included stock ownership and dividend income (chapter 4). Others, such as Robert F. Paine, could have earned more elsewhere but were ferociously loyal. Not all endured in the hope of promotion or out of loyalty, however. In 1905 Scripps discovered that some of the Seattle *Star*'s staff were engaged in graft and fired them for taking bribes to kill news unfavorable to local speculators. He was shaken, but Paine told him that inadequate salaries invited such behavior.[51]

Reliance on Inexpensive Content—Scripps's efforts to control costs extended to news, too. From the late 1880s on, he attempted to reduce the costs of news production by generating common content for all Scripps newspapers to avoid duplication and spread costs. It was decidedly cheaper, Scripps maintained, for his newspapers to generate content as a single "concern" than as a set of independent units.[52]

The pioneer in creating such cheap, common content was Ellen Browning Scripps. During the late 1870s she had written short articles of general interest news ("Random Notes," "Matters and Things," or "Personal Paragraphs") for both the Detroit *Evening News* and the Cleveland *Press*. E. W. Scripps, then a fledgling editor in Cleveland, liked the articles because they filled space and were both interesting and free.[53]

The effort to generate cheap, shared news increased greatly in the late 1880s, when E. W. Scripps was managing the four Scripps League newspapers—the Detroit *Evening News*, Cleveland *Press*, Cincinnati *Post*, and St. Louis *Chronicle*. In 1887 he ruled that "each paper must be bound to send to any or all the other papers such news and cuts as are called for."[54] He instituted regular meetings of editors to stimulate joint activity and began a common short-story service.[55] He also deployed reporters to New York and Washington, D.C., to provide articles that all four newspapers would publish.

The search for cheap news continued after Scripps was removed from the League presidency by his brothers in 1889. In 1890 the Cleveland *Press* and the Cincinnati *Post* shared a state capital correspondent in Columbus, Ohio, and in 1891 they shared an artist who divided his time between the two cities. Despite the break between Scripps and his brother James, the four original Scripps newspapers shared coverage of the presidential nominating conventions and campaigns in 1892, 1896, and 1900. In the mid-1890s the newspapers under E. W. Scripps's control (the Cleveland *Press,* Cincinnati *Post,* and St. Louis *Chronicle*) shared the costs of covering a popular prizefight and two notorious murder trials. They also routinely exchanged articles and engravings for illustrations.[56]

By 1900 these activities were formalized into the Scripps Editorial Alliance (SEA) under Atwood's direction in Cincinnati. In 1900 he invited approximately twenty-five prominent politicians (including Theodore Roosevelt, Albert Beveridge, C. J. Depew, Marc Hanna, John Hay, Henry Cabot Lodge, William McKinley, Thomas C. Platt, Eugene V. Debs, Thomas Reed, and William Jennings Bryan) to write short articles (for free) about the issues in that year's presidential election. After the election, Atwood attempted to organize a steady supply of short stories and news features.[57]

In 1902 Scripps expanded his efforts by creating the Newspaper Enterprise Association (which superseded the SEA), which provided cartoons, features, editorials, and a wide range of other editorial material. Scripps said he started the NEA to create a high-quality illustrated news service while spreading costs across all of his newspapers, which the NEA did successfully, even with changes in production brought about by Linotypes and other mechanization.[58] Between 1891 and 1893, for example, the *Post* paid an average of $6.38 for each column of non-advertising content it generated.[59] It paid an average of $9.37 per column for pictures and art and $7.34 per column for news features—all of which would be major parts of the NEA service. Local news, which the NEA would not produce, averaged $4.38 a column.[60] The *Post* shouldered these costs by itself. By contrast, the June 1907 production of the NEA cost an average of $12.26 per column.[61] No one newspaper bore that cost, however. With twenty-four Scripps newspapers then in operation, the average cost of this material was about 51 cents per column, about one-twelfth of the average cost of a column for the *Post* in the early 1890s.[62]

Scripps ran the NEA not only with an idea of generating cheap newspaper content but also of facilitating expansion. The rate charged for the NEA was based on gross revenues. Scripps's richest and largest newspapers (in Cleveland and Cincinnati) paid nearly half of NEA expenses, whereas newer (and poorer) operations paid very little.[63] In its first six months of operation (in 1906 and 1907), the Pueblo *Sun* paid just 9 cents per column for NEA material; a rate increase raised its average cost for 22.5 cents per column.[64] In 1905 the Seattle *Star* paid $10 a week for the NEA and used an average of about thirty-eight columns of NEA material weekly at an average cost of 26.3 cents per column.[65] Scripps claimed that he could start a new newspaper anywhere in the country with just one reporter and one editor, provided he also had the

NEA. "All of my baby papers by reason of their extreme poverty and during their extreme youth depended almost absolutely for substance editorially on the N.E.A."[66]

Scripps ordered his editors to use NEA material and suggested it account for at least 25 to 35 percent of each issue.[67] In 1906 Paine, the NEA general manager, said that the NEA accounted for more than half of the content of the Evansville *Press* and "fully three fourths" of the Terre Haute *Post*.[68] A content analysis of four Scripps newspapers established between 1903 and 1906 indicates that NEA material constituted an average of 62 percent of nonadvertising content (fig. 2; table 2, appendix 1). For the newer properties, the cost was roughly equivalent to the salary they would have paid a seasoned reporter—$12 to $15 a week.[69]

Wells reported that the NEA had been particularly useful when he started the Tacoma *Times:* "If it had not been for this material, I would have been hard pressed to get out a paper with the small, raw force that I have. As it is, the Times has a decent appearance, which is helped out measurably by fine press work."[70] In Seattle, it made the *Star* competitive even though it had a small staff. Wells said that without the NEA, "We would have to largely increase our editorial expenses, something that would be extremely difficult to do. Our contemporary The Times, employs a very large force of competent men, including thirteen of the best reporters that can be found, and spends money

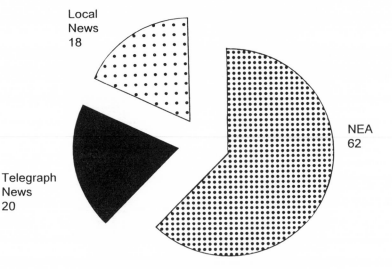

Figure 2. Sources of News in New Scripps Newspapers, by Percentage

like water to get news near and far. Against this effort we can put half as many reporters and the N.E.A. And we can win out with the N.E.A."[71] A content analysis of well-established Scripps newspapers in 1907 shows that the NEA averaged 48 percent of all content, even after the early issues (fig. 3; table 3, appendix 1).

The NEA not only reduced the staff size needed to produce a Scripps newspaper but also cut production costs. Its special mission encompassed illustrations: photographs, cartoons, and other drawings. Given production processes, these illustrations were much cheaper for individual newspapers to use than local news articles. Local copy had to be written, edited, and then typeset, requiring the labor of three persons (reporter, editor, and typesetter). Extensive reliance on local news would also require two (or more) typesetting machines. In contrast, NEA illustrations arrived in mats by mail. Metal castings (cuts), necessary for the printing process, were made cheaply locally from the mats.[72] The result was editorial content that was cheaper to produce than local news articles—both in terms of labor and machinery. The editor of the Spokane *Press* said, "You know, I'm running a one [type-setting] machine office and if I have cuts and cartoons enough, need only one shift. The N.E.A. saves the day."[73] Paine told the manager of the *San Diegan-Sun* that using the NEA could cut composition costs and thus produce newspaper content "at ridiculously low cost." NEA news articles came in proof form and so still required type-setting. They did not require reporting or writing, however, and frequently were not edited locally.[74]

Scripps envisioned that the NEA would someday become the nucleus of a

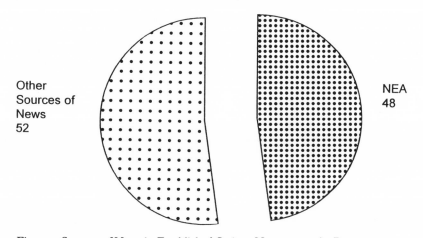

Other
Sources of
News
52

NEA
48

Figure 3. Sources of News in Established Scripps Newspapers, by Percentage

national newspaper. "The ultimate end and ideal of the plan is to make up and edit in one office all the matter fit for a national paper that can be published anywhere in the country under any name, without even the support and co-operation of a local staff."[75]

The mandatory use of NEA material, coupled with small newspaper staffs, meant that the Scripps newspapers often had far less local news than competitors. That was not true for the older Scripps newspapers such as the Cleveland *Press,* Cincinnati *Post,* and St. Louis *Chronicle,* but it was very much the case for small, NEA-heavy publications established as the chain grew. Scripps newspapers in San Diego, Sacramento, and Portland had far less local news than their competitors—about 22 percent compared to 50 percent for their rivals (fig. 4). The fact that they were half the size of their competitors meant that the competitors ran at least four times more local news (table 4, appendix 1).

The relative lack of local news did not trouble Scripps. Although he contended that he was always willing to spend money for news, he did not care very much about local stories. He contended that the Pueblo *Sun* was "the best and most salable of all our infant papers from the start" because "the editor, having no money to spend on local news . . . [was] compelled to depend on N.E.A."[76] Some of his managers, however, were particularly concerned that

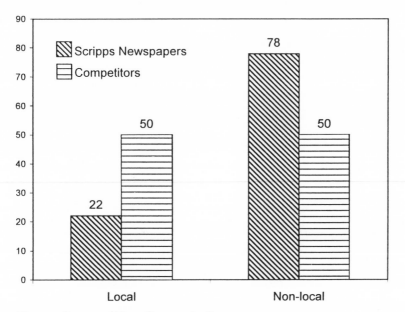

Figure 4. Sources of News Content, by Percentage

the poverty of local news would erode circulation. Harper, superintendent of newspapers in Dallas, Oklahoma City, Evansville, and Terre Haute, maintained that local news was the prime reason that the Cleveland *Press* and the Cincinnati *Post* had done so well during the 1880s. Porterfield, regional manager of most of the California Scripps newspapers in 1906 and 1907, observed that some San Francisco *Daily News* readers had complained about a lack of local news. The editor there, he said, could work hard but could not "furnish local news for his readers with two or three reporters." Porterfield also decried the lack of local news in the Berkeley *Independent* and the Fresno *Tribune*. The *Independent* suffered from a glut of NEA material and "too little local stuff. . . . It has been comparatively easy to get new subscribers but very hard to hold them." One issue of the *Tribune* was "the worst local newspaper ever gotten out" because of a lack of local news. "There was just one local story, outside of the sporting page, in the entire paper, while the Herald [the *Tribune*'s competitor] had four good ones and a lot of little ones." In Seattle, Wells echoed Porterfield's complaints, saying that Scripps newspapers in Spokane, Seattle, Tacoma, and Portland were deficient in local news because of tiny staffs.[77]

Budgeting—In an effort to control costs, Scripps also required his newspapers to operate on a monthly budget or "deadline." In July 1900, for example, the Seattle *Star* had a deadline of $81 a day, raised to $85 a day a few months later. Scripps probably was delighted when Clark told him that the *Star* was keeping to that deadline even though it was nearly impossible to do so. "We are known as 'pinchers' but people that pay their bills. And we have no debts." On another occasion, Clark told Scripps that "we are living, all of us, closer to the wind than we ever did before."[78]

Budgeting had been introduced during the late 1880s. Each business manager presented an estimated budget for approval before the start of a month, outlining all anticipated expenditures and revenues. At the end of the month, budgets were reviewed and deviations from the estimates (whether above or below) noted. Newspapers could acquire limited "surpluses," although overspending was strongly discouraged. Budgets were also drawn up for six-month and one-year periods.[79]

The budgets were intended to force local managers to limit spending. As Scripps observed, "It makes no difference how much a business grows, the tendency to spend money on odds and ends grows, and the only possibility of getting a profit at all is to absolutely prohibit such expenditure."[80] He also used budgets to avoid debt and anticipate unusual expenditures (some months had five weekly paydays and some years had fifty-three). "It is your business," he told the business manager of the new Denver *Express,* "and it is absolutely necessary for you to so manage your affairs that you will never be short for a penny."[81]

General Rules and Exhortations—Beyond these specific categories of expenditures, Scripps and his lieutenants monitored all expenses closely. Scripps contended that his newspaper companies should not pay for "luxuries": ice in the summer, pencils, lunches or dinners for those who worked extra hours, soap, toilet paper, or paper towels. Atwood instructed one editor that each reporter "is to pay for his own carfare, buy his own lead pencils and . . . pay for all of those little personal expenses contingent on the discharge of his duties."[82] McRae told the business manager of the Cleveland *Press* to buy used twine for wrapping bundles of newspapers for out-of-town shipment; the Cincinnati *Post* had been doing so for years. "Money saved is money made and this is one way to do it."[83]

Beginning in 1900, a company accountant began to scrutinize each of the midwestern newspapers' expenditures. He charged that the Cleveland *Press* had purchased too many brooms over an eight-month period, that the St. Louis *Chronicle* had improperly spent $1 on streetcar fare for two employees, and that the Cincinnati *Post* had improperly paid $3.45 for meals for men working on an extra edition.[84] The business manager of the *Press* protested:

> It seems to me that we can hardly dispense with the item for lead pencils. We are now buying the cheapest pencil we can, the cost being 65 cts per gross. . . . The auditor says that $3.17 of postage item was unnecessary. I do not know how he figures exactly how much postage we should have used. . . . I think it will be a mistake to cut off our Toilet Supply service. Towels and soap are always necessary, and while the men might get such service at the hotel or saloon wash rooms, it would undoubtedly come out of our time, and, it is absolutely necessary in my opinion to have some such service for the ladies.[85]

Some rules did not generate savings. McRae told Scripps that the ban on buying toilet paper meant that staff members used old newspapers. "Newspaper clogs up the pipes, which are not large, causing overflow and damage, naturally plumbing bills will follow."[86] McRae reported paying several plumbing bills for the same problem.

Every penny counted. As Paine told one new editor, "The money question, my boy, is always a hard one for the real newspaper maker."[87] When Hyacinth Ford became business manager of the San Francisco *Daily News* in 1906, Scripps told him that "the first thing that you . . . have to learn, is how to save money": "Never buy anything today that you can put off until tomorrow or next year. Never add any expense for anything until you shall have felt the supreme necessity of such an expenditure for at least three months. . . . Do not put on any frills. Do not be afraid to be called a skin flint or a miser. You can acquire no more valuable reputation."[88]

The constant focus on finances drove some Scripps editors to dubious deals, particularly over public printing contracts. In the late nineteenth and early twentieth centuries, U.S. cities usually called for sealed bids from local newspapers for the printing of local ordinances and announcements. The newspaper submitting the lowest bid became that city's "official printer." Scripps believed the public to be uninterested in such official advertising and discouraged editors and business managers from competing for the contracts. Other publishers, however, had no such doubts and wanted to obtain the printing contracts at as high a rate as possible, so they offered kickbacks to competitors (including Scripps newspapers) who would collude in the bidding process. Scripps editors had no interest in the bidding, but the lure of easy revenue induced them to pretend to compete. In Seattle and San Diego they agreed to such deals before Scripps angrily ordered them to desist (and, in the San Diego case, to return the money already paid).

Distribution

Scripps attempted to keep distribution costs low by concentrating on city rather than country circulation, limiting overhead, seeking slow and stable circulation growth, and closely monitoring circulation rates.

City Circulation—Scripps preferred city circulation over country or rural circulation because it was cheaper. He estimated that country circulation cost three times as much as city circulation with little profit. Urban populations were denser than rural ones, so news-gathering was relatively focused and distribution much cheaper than in distant suburbs or rural areas.[89]

Scripps's preference grew out of his experiences in Cleveland, Cincinnati, and St. Louis. In Cleveland, he had concentrated first on building just local circulation and was quite successful.[90] He then tried to build country circulation by covering two other nearby communities but said he found that "the compound cost of getting this news reported and other extra expenses, went way beyond the receipts from circulation."[91] Even when country circulation did not lose money it never was as profitable as city circulation. In Cleveland, the *Press* had an average circulation revenue rate of $4.22 per thousand newspapers sold between January 1896 and May 1898; its average country rate during that same period was $4.01.[92] Another report concluded that the *Press* had higher circulation revenues rates than the Cincinnati *Post* during March 1897 because it depended less on country circulation. The *Press* had a circulation revenue rate of $4.31 per thousand newspapers sold, whereas the *Post*'s rate was only $4.04.[93]

During the period of great expansion of the chain, Scripps told editors to concentrate on city circulation only. In 1907 he told managers of the newer eastern newspapers—Evansville, Terre Haute, Nashville, Memphis, Dallas, and Oklahoma City—that "the circulation of the papers is to be strictly local, that is to say within the city limits of the city of publication."[94]

In practice, the newer publications in the West relied more on city circulation than did the older eastern newspapers. In 1903 the Spokane, Seattle, San Diego, and Los Angeles ventures derived 77.4 percent of their circulation revenues from city circulation (and just 22.6 percent from country circulation). Scripps told Atwood that no more than a hundred copies of the Los Angeles *Record* were sold twenty miles from the city center.[95] By contrast, the older eastern newspapers had substantially larger country circulations. In Cincinnati, 58.7 percent of circulation revenues came from country circulation in 1902; in Cleveland, 41.3 percent; and in St. Louis, 56.2 percent.[96]

Circulation Overhead—Scripps believed that most circulation departments constituted unnecessary expenses and consequently kept them small and limited in function. Circulation managers were to create routes for home delivery, oversee carriers on those routes, and recruit and deal with newsboys if street sales were allowed. At new newspapers, business managers filled this position; only well-established newspapers had full-time circulation managers. To avoid office expense no records were kept of subscribers; only the carriers knew who their customers were.[97]

Slow and Stable Circulation Growth—The lack of a large circulation force did not mean that Scripps did not value circulation. He had begun his career doing circulation work for his brothers at the Detroit *Evening News* and said that a growing circulation was the only real measure of a newspaper's quality. The business manager of the San Francisco *Daily News* was instructed to work on three things: "getting circulation, getting more circulation and getting the most circulation you possibly can in the least possible time."[98]

Economy guided circulation work. For new newspapers, that meant a slow-growth policy, with little money spent on anything other than news-gathering and production. Scripps said that new newspapers should not rely extensively on sales representatives (solicitors) to create demand. Rather, content itself should be sufficient to create demand. Scripps told the editor of the Spokane *Press,* "A fool manager depends upon solicitors. A wise manager concentrates all his thoughts upon the one effort, to produce every day some one thing, or some several things, in the editorial or news columns which the public must have."[99] On another occasion he said, "I count every dollar put into the hands of a circulation solicitor to be a dollar thrown away."[100]

Solicitors promoted the Tacoma *Times* for a few days before its debut edition in late 1903, but once started it relied solely on carriers and word of mouth for circulation growth. It had only three small delivery routes at first, coordinated by the business manager. "Other routes will have to wait," the editor said. "Of course we could go ahead faster by spending some money in the circulation . . . but none of us want rapid progress at greater expense. The gist of my instructions from E. W., as you know, were to go slow and sure on the least possible expenditure."[101]

Once a newspaper was well established, however, Scripps believed that money spent on circulation was a good investment if circulation was growing of its own accord. In that situation, solicitors were not so much sales representatives but circulation clerks who merely helped people subscribe.[102] Even then, Scripps preferred solicitors who were low-key in their sales pitches: "Everything else being equal, I really prefer a poor solicitor to a good one. I mean I would prefer the kind of a man who has no special power of persuasion or 'jollying' an individual into putting down his name. The kind of solicitors we want is simple, plain industrious fellows who will present the idea of taking the paper to a possible subscriber in such a way as will only procure those subscribers who do not need much persuasion. This kind of subscriber is more apt to stick."[103]

Circulation Rates—Scripps and his lieutenants closely monitored circulation receipts for each newspaper. In part, that was to gauge the relative popularity of each, but it was also to gauge costs. Each business manager figured a circulation rate per hundred, referring to the gross circulation receipts received for every hundred newspaper sold. Newsboys bought the newspapers at a half a cent each, so the maximum circulation rate was 50 cents per hundred papers. That rate was difficult to reach, however, because it included all newspapers printed, even if they were not sold.

Consequently, Scripps attempted to limit the production of newspapers that produced no revenue. Business managers had orders not to run more newspapers than could be easily sold, and newsstands were bypassed because they insisted on returns.[104] Free newspapers—to employees, advertisers, or others— were considered an extravagance. As Harper told the staff at Denver, "I consider that every copy of a newspaper that is given away is a positive injury to the business."[105] Even Scripps paid for his subscriptions.[106] His newspapers also broke with the tradition of supplying local advertisers with each issue that carried their ads. They were expected to buy a copy themselves; only non-local advertisers received free copies.[107] "There shall be no free papers given," Scripps told editors from a half-dozen new publications in 1907. "No officer or employee or patron of the company shall receive a free copy. Employees of the papers are entitled to get papers only for their actual use in the office. . . . for inspection, for checking ads, or for reference and correction."[108]

Conclusions

When Hyacinth Ford became the business manager of the San Francisco *Daily News* in late 1906, E. W. Scripps told him, "The first thing that you, as a young business manager have to learn, is how to save money. . . . Cut and squeeze everything in the way of expenses in your office."[109] Such economizing was a hallmark of Scripps's career as an editor and publisher. As he told one associate in 1903, "I don't like to spend money except under the most favorable conditions."[110]

This emphasis on economizing reflected Scripps's low-cost strategy, which in turn reflected the realities he faced: Capital and revenues were limited relative to those of many of his competitors. Scripps had not begun his career with wealth, and he feared that reliance on other financiers would strip him of independence. Expanding the chain nationwide necessitated great care in the use of his own money. Second, Scripps limited revenues by restricting advertising and selling newspapers for just a penny. Scripps's publications were forced to operate on a proverbial shoestring if they were to remain true to his goal of being independent working-class newspapers. Without that strategy he would not have been able to create a chain. Nor would he have been able to create newspapers relatively impervious to advertising pressure.

There were trade-offs, however. The low-cost strategy broadly affected operations. Staffs were small, salaries low, offices nearly bare, and machinery old. Every expense—including pencils and toilet paper—was monitored closely. Scripps relied on prospectuses to limit start-up costs and budgets to restrict operating costs. Editors were assessed on ability to keep costs low rather than news acumen. The value of a reporter was sometimes figured in the cost per column of copy generated rather than in the quality of writing and reporting.

Such economizing naturally influenced content. To save money on composition and newsprint, Scripps newspapers were small. Many ran just four small (tabloid) pages in an era of eight- and ten-page large (blanket) sheets, which meant carrying less news than competitors—or that whatever they presented would be extensively condensed. Low salaries meant that Scripps publications often lost experienced reporters to rivals; a revolving-door concept perhaps best describes Scripps's labor relations. Old presses sometimes produced hard-to-read newspapers, local news received short shrift because staffs were small, and vertical integration (the Newspaper Enterprise Association) facilitated the supply of much cheaper non-local content. News features, photographs, illustrations, human-interest editorials, and cartoons were common because their cost to each newspaper was quite low.

Management

If management is not everything, it is certainly much more than three-fourths of the whole proposition.
—E. W. Scripps to J. C. Harper, March 29, 1905

IN LATE 1903, as E. H. Wells was starting the Tacoma *Times,* E. W. Scripps exhorted him to keep a daily record of "every dollar of expense incurred."[1] Every expense was to be noted, "Even the items of taxes, rents, insurance, etc., although paid only yearly, should be reduced to a daily item and put on the books, so that it will not be said, when these bills are paid, that they were 'extra-ordinary,' etc. The items of taxes and insurance are just as much of an expense, running every day, as the item of labor, or white paper."[2] That daily record would provide a full and up-to-date report on how the new publication was faring.

Two years later, shortly before H. N. Rickey became editor-in-chief of midwestern Scripps newspapers, Scripps advised him on how to succeed in his new position. The key to success was to be prepared for all contingencies. "In our business there is no such thing as an extraordinary expense and an unexpected emergency. Everything that is costly, embarrassing and troublesome that can occur which must cause our chief men to strain every nerve and energy to meet and overcome, is to be expected." Hard work alone would not mean success. "Your success depends upon your power to think right."[3] The advice reflected his efforts to assure the systematic operation of the rapidly growing chain. Close attention to costs at each newspaper and long-range planning, as he urged, were part of the system Scripps created to manage a business with hundreds of employees across the country.

Managerial control took several forms.[4] First, Scripps defined broad policies and specific rules designed to implement market segmentation, low cost, and vertical integration. Second, he and his managers monitored each newspaper (as well as the telegraph news services, Newspaper Enterprise Association, and national advertising bureau) to gauge performance and check compliance with policies and rules. Third, they offered incentives for compliance with rules and policies.

Scripps and his central office (chapter 1) were the center of the chain's business administration. As the chain grew, another layer of administrators emerged, and regional managers (e.g., a California editor, a southwestern editor) aided the central office in its oversight and provided further direction to newpapers under their control.

This highly centralized management style, characterized by extensive rules and close surveillance, left little autonomy to editors and business managers at individual publications. Control was most extensive on financial matters; individual newspapers had virtually no autonomy there. Control was less extensive over news, which, unlike finances, could not be scripted and budgeted a month or more in advance. The rule that Scripps newspapers use NEA material extensively, however, brought a third or more of the space in each under direct control of central management. Although the newspapers were independent of outside influences such as advertisers, big business, and politicians, editors had little independence inside the chain. Scripps and a handful of senior managers were the de facto editors of much of the content of the chain's newspapers. Local editors' autonomy applied to local news and to decisions about how to present content generated by the chain's central news-producing agencies.

Rules

Rules were a natural consequence of the efforts to make business more systematic in the late nineteenth century.[5] They were an important element of managerial control and identified the way in which work was to be done, providing standards and guidance while reducing autonomy among the rank and file. Scripps devised hundreds of rules to guide the growing corps of editors and business managers, many of whom had little experience in business or in journalism and virtually all of whom were distant from Cincinnati or Miramar. Such rules were necessary, he said, because "the conduct of a modern newspaper, like that of any other business, requires a certain number of rules and regulations."[6] Many of these rules are detailed elsewhere in this book; they are mentioned here to focus on their managerial function.

Scripps's rules derived from his three strategies of business. To implement vertical integration, he required each newspaper to become a client of his telegraph news services and a member of the Newspaper Enterprise Association.

As for market segmentation, Scripps wanted newspapers that provided news in a way that would appeal to working-class readers. To that end, he created the 40-60 rule: 40 percent of expenditures went to the news-editorial department and 60 percent went to the business department for advertising and circulation solicitors, production, and distribution. Scripps argued that most newspapers spent far less than that amount on news production, even though "news on paper" was the essence of the industry. "The idea of the 40-60 rule was that newspapers depend for their existence and prosperity upon not only the intelligent, but the liberal, use of money by the Editor *spent on getting news.*"[7] He limited advertising space, both to protect news space and decrease the power of advertisers who might lure his publications away from their working-class orientation.

The low-cost strategy produced a large number of rules. One dictated a cash-only business at each newspaper to prevent debt. Another held that Scripps (or Atwood) had to approve all salaries and all raises. Another rule, designed to control spending, dictated that each newspaper could not spend more than 85 percent of its receipts each month (thus producing a 15 percent profit). Scripps said, "In this connection, I would say that any man who is unable to so business manage a newspaper as to keep its expenses within the required sum, and at the same time to cause an increase in circulation and volume of business, is not fit to be business manager." Editors were forbidden to divulge circulations because Scripps believed that unprofitable circulation-padding invariably resulted. No newspapers and no advertising were to be given away; advertisers had just thirty days to pay their bills or they would be cut off. Editors and business managers were required to create and adhere to budgets for all expenditures.[8]

Rigorous controls over all expenditures were mandatory. In an effort to obtain a realistic assessment of spending, Scripps required each editor and business manager to make routine expenditures that occurred infrequently, such as taxes (which came due every twelve months) or the replacement of printing presses and other machines (which occurred about every five years—or sixty months). Consequently, each newspaper was required to make monthly payments to the central office of one-twelfth of taxes and one-sixtieth of estimated plant replacement costs.[9] As Scripps explained the rationale for the plant fund, "We cannot count as net cash divisible profits all the money that a newspaper makes in any one year. If we should, for instance, actually divide all of the cash profits made by a newspaper each year, it would only be a question of time when the newspaper company would have to assess its stockholders, or borrow money, or run in debt for a new plant."[10]

Scripps wanted to end what he saw as a cycle of three or four years of large profits followed by a year of heavy expenditures due to plant replacement—a cycle that gave an inflated assessment earnings and encouraged spending. Setting money aside monthly in a plant fund would provide a more accurate view of business conditions while also preparing for the future. "Wear and tear is going on under our eyes all the time, and as business advances, new and better equipment must be had, *not unexpectedly, but as a matter of course,"* he said.[11]

Other funds were established to anticipate possible demands for money. Beginning in 1905, each newspaper had orders to contribute monthly to a libel fund, reflecting Scripps's contention that legal expenses were as much unexpected expenses of running a newspaper as bills for newsprint. When the Seattle *Star's* business manager claimed that he did not need a libel fund, L. T. Atwood told him that such a fund was part of wise planning. "I consider that it is very desirable on the part of every newspaper, to have a fund of this kind laid by. Otherwise, when the libel judgment comes, it is generally really a crushing blow to the finances of the company."[12] Also in 1905, the central office fund set the libel fund monthly assessments for midwestern newspapers: the Cleveland *Press,* $300; the Cincinnati *Post,* $200; the Toledo *News-Bee,* $175; the Columbus *Citizen,* $100; the St. Louis *Chronicle,* $100; the *Kentucky Post* at Covington, $50; and the SMPA, $250. That same year the chain began a self-insurance fund against fire damage, in part for planning purposes and also to reduce premiums paid to insurance agents. Atwood announced a $100,000 goal for the fund.[13]

Following these rules was a requirement in the Scripps chain. Would-be editors and business managers mentioned many in their prospectuses for new newspapers. In 1906, when Jay A. Gove and R. G. Conant wanted to start a Scripps newspaper in Nashville, they promised that it would conform to the rules:

It will cultivate a numerous clientele of small advertisers, and will discourage too extensive use of space by a few large advertisers. . . . As to circulation, effort will be confined to the City of Nashville, Tenn., and its environs and a large and influential circulation there secured before any effort is made to reach outlying territory. . . . No statements of circulation shall be published or given the public or advertisers. The paper shall refrain from all attacks on the editor or publisher or corporations conducting or controlling other newspapers on account of a feeling of rivalry or competition. . . . Neither of us, nor anyone else connected with the project, shall have any authority to contract any debts of any kind . . . without the consent of yourself or a majority of the stockholders. All purchases shall be paid for in cash as soon as business customs shall permit, and salaries shall be paid in cash on pay days.[14]

The same promises were made by the prospective editors or business managers of the Spokane *Press,* San Francisco *Daily News,* Tacoma *Times,* Seattle *Star,* Sacramento *Star,* Dallas *Dispatch,* Oklahoma City *News,* Pueblo *Sun,* and Denver *Express.*[15]

Scripps demanded obedience to his rules. He told W. W. Thornton, general manager of the Scripps-McRae League in 1905, "I wish to remind you that I expect there will be no dispensation granted for any rule that is in existence while you are in office." On another occasion he told E. H. Wells to stop making excuses for failing to follow orders: "You must play this game fair and square, living up to the rules we have agreed upon or leave the table."[16]

Surveillance

Scripps and his upper managers created an extensive system of surveillance to measure the degree to which individual newspapers followed the chain's rules. Surveillance had several aspects: monthly statements, visits by managers, summonses to Scripps's ranch, and a close monitoring of content. Information gathered was frequently disseminated widely throughout the chain via the extensive use of carbon copies.

Monthly Statements

Each Scripps editor had orders to send a fairly detailed statement on his newspaper to Scripps and Atwood each month. Editors of new publications were required to provide weekly statements.[17] Scripps said the statements were the best indicator of how each newspaper was performing. They were "made for the purpose of conveying to the minds of all parties concerned as nearly as possible, the exact and actual condition of our business."[18] As he noted, he did not have time to read each newspaper regularly, so monthly statements were a good way for him and Atwood to check on expenditures, receipts, and circulation growth. "I am carefully watching your statements," he told the business manager of the Seattle *Star* in 1901.[19]

The statements were particularly useful in monitoring rules derivative of the low-cost strategy. They provided detailed information on receipts (how much from circulation and advertising); total inches of advertising published; average per-inch advertising rates; expenditures (what had been spent on editorial department, telegraph, composition, business office, janitor, supplies, transportation and mail, composition, presswork and stereotyping, newsprint, ink, fuel, light, power, insurance, taxes, rent, repairs, interest, and payroll); and average circulation. Each newspaper also reported earnings per hundred copies (counting spoilage and unsold papers). Scripps said that the rate per hundred was a key indicator of successful management: "A great many spoiled papers show lax business management and supervision of the press room."[20]

Both Scripps and Atwood used the statements to monitor expenditures. After reviewing the January 1903 statement for the Spokane *Press*, he told Atwood that the manager was wasting money by trying to build circulation too quickly. "The newspaper publisher who starts out to build up a circulation by canvassing for subscribers generally bankrupts himself before he discovers a fundamental truth concerning our business—which is that a successful newspaper must depend entirely upon its quality for its custom, and not at all upon slick solicitors." Atwood instructed the Spokane manager to reduce expenses.[21] In 1904 he also criticized the business manager of the Seattle *Star* for not controlling costs in 1903. "This is a very important matter so far as the Star is concerned and I ask that you give immediate attention to it and let me hear from you in regard to the matter."[22] In 1907 Scripps told the San Francisco *Daily News*'s managers that their statements showed too much spending on miscellaneous items. He ordered them to control expenses by creating a "deadline" (budget) for each department and sticking to it: "It makes no difference how much a business grows, the tendency to spend money on odds and ends grows, and the only possibility of getting a profit at all is to absolutely prohibit such expenditure."[23]

Scripps, Atwood, and central office auditors used the monthly statements as the basis for detailed analyses of each newspaper. Atwood, for example, compared the Los Angeles *Record*'s statements for 1899 and the first six months of 1900 to those from the first eleven months of 1901. Profits had declined, and Atwood asked the business manager to explain. The monthly statements were the basis for Atwood's reports on annual profits.[24] In late 1904 Scripps told the San Francisco *News* editor and business manager that the statements from August 1903 through September 1904 demonstrated that the newspaper was increasing spending on circulation promotion while decreasing spending on news. "This certainly indicates an unhealthy condition," he warned. "There is no good getting new subscribers unless you are going to make a paper that will hold them."[25]

The statements were also used as the basis for comparisons across the chain. Scripps compared the new newspapers to the Cleveland *Press* during its early days. In 1901 he observed that the Seattle *Star* was comparable in most regards to the early *Press*. He also sent copies of the Cleveland statements to the *Star*'s business manager, telling him to study them closely. In 1906, when the Los Angeles *Record* was eleven years old, Scripps compared its statements to those of the *Press*'s for 1889—when it likewise was eleven. That comparison confirmed that the *Record* was doing well.[26] By comparing newspapers of similar age or size he could find variations that might reveal problems or successes. At his order, the business managers of the Los Angeles *Record* and the Seattle *Star* exchanged monthly statements beginning in 1901. He wanted them to learn from each other and also hoped to create rivalry that would spur growth.[27]

Standardized statements also facilitated comparison.[28] When editors failed to fill out their statements accurately, Scripps reprimanded them. In 1905 he told Wells that the incomplete statements from the Tacoma *Times* had prevented him from comparing that newspaper with others in the chain "in order to discover the exact condition of every paper during every month."[29] Scripps and Atwood insisted that statements be precise; when one manager referred to an expense of "about" $4,500, Scripps took him to task: "It is the word 'about' which makes it impossible for me to make any calculations. The sooner you learn that it is necessary to fix a definite amount, which shall not under any circumstances be exceeded, and the sooner you show this by your statement, the better it will be for your business." Messy or incomplete statements also attracted Scripps's ire. He berated Paul Blades, manager of the Los Angeles *Record* in 1900, for "unintelligible" statements. "For God's sake, send me a statement which tells me the real statement," Scripps ordered.[30]

Statements were expected at Atwood's office in Cincinnati and his Miramar ranch by the third or fourth day of the next month. Both he and Scripps sent scolding letters to employees who failed to file reports on time.[31] In 1902 Scripps complained to E. H. Bagby that the October statement for the Los Angeles *Record* was late. "This is the 15th of November and no Record statement or report of Record circulation at hand. . . . There is a period of time, between the 4th and 10th of every month, that I am naturally giving my thought to the different businesses and comparing their statements. Any monthly statement from any paper that does not come in before that time not only causes me irritation but an actual loss to the delinquent paper in that practically a month of my attention is lost to that paper."[32]

Atwood and his auditors supplemented the statements with other information they had solicited from individual newspapers and with analysis of specific newspapers. In 1903, for example, the central office staff measured the amount of advertising in the Los Angeles *Record* and the Seattle *Star* and compared it to each newspaper's statement for June. The *Star*'s statement was correct, whereas the *Record* contained a good deal more advertising than it had reported. Thus, its rate per inch was substantially lower than reported (34.7 cents instead of 43.7 cents).[33]

Visits to Newspapers

Another method of managerial surveillance came through occasional site visits. Scripps attempted to visit each newspaper annually through 1905. After that, his visits declined while those of his cabinet—particularly Paine and Harper—increased.[34] The visits provided an opportunity for observing local conditions, giving advice, and encouraging workers. The editor of the Seattle *Star* described the visit of E. W. Scripps and his brother George in 1899: "Mr. Scripps and party arrived Friday evening and will remain here until Tuesday. George H. and E. W. both like the town. They told Chase [the business manager] and myself that they were well pleased with the conduct of the Star and would continue to stand by the firm even after ten thousand [dollars] had been spent. At the same time they told us that if we could pull through on the ten it would be of the greatest personal benefit, more than we imagined."[35]

Central office auditors also visited each newspaper to inspect ledgers, supervise book-keeping, and report back to Atwood in Cincinnati. In 1900 Charles J. Stein began an extended visit to the newspapers in San Diego, Los Angeles, and San Francisco. As Scripps told Atwood, "It is desirable for Mr. Stein to keep constant watch of the affairs of the western papers so as to assist you." Stein's task was to bring greater order to local accounting practices and supervise each newspaper's business office.[36] Scripps told the manager of the Los Angeles *Record* that Stein would "not assume control unduly" but that he would "nevertheless have the right to supersede local and general management during his presence in the offices." H. B. Clark, head of the western telegraph news service, told Stein that Scripps wanted him to keep a close eye on business practices in the West, "sailing around from place to place, pounding and criticizing and encouraging each and all members of the business departments of the several papers."[37] When Stein visited the Seattle *Star* in 1903, he had to help the cashier there untangle the accounts. He told Atwood that "Copeland, the Cashier, was completely at sea and was very much relieved when, after several days of hard work, the whole of the different funds, i.e., Building, Reserve, Paper and Commercial account, were straightened out and placed upon the books." Stein also reported on the *Star*'s circulation ("moving upward"), expenditures on a new building (over budget), and advertising revenues. "With the exception of the overdraft [on the new building] and the mix up in the cash account, I found everything in good order." When he visited the San Francisco *Daily News* in 1906 he reported that too much money was being spent on acquiring new circulation.[38]

In late 1906 another central office auditor, H. W. Coombs, was sent to the

West Coast to continue Stein's work. Atwood told each western editor and business manager that "I shall expect prompt attention to be given to any recommendations or changes he may inaugurate in the matter of accounting or finances, as though the order emanated from me." Charles F. Mosher, another central office auditor, visited Scripps publications in the Midwest.[39]

Visits to Miramar

Scripps also relied on visits to Miramar as a means of supervising his newspaper chain. His cabinet met there, and editors from throughout the chain trekked to California to hear his advice.[40] Both Chase and Wells from the Seattle *Star,* for example, visited Scripps in 1905 to hear his views.[41] Scripps said that any employee was welcome at Miramar but warned that "we have so much respect for our guests that we never bore them by entertaining."[42]

Due to proximity, California editors and business managers were invited most frequently for talks, advice, or criticism. In 1905 Scripps, angered by W. H. Porterfield's actions at the Sacramento *Star,* ordered, "Come to Miramar on the first train and please send no more telegraphs about not worrying."[43] In 1906 he told the business manager of the *San Diegan-Sun* that a short meeting at Miramar would help the newspaper greatly. "You certainly are doing wrong in not coming out here and catching a few minutes with me if no longer. I don't think it's necessary to have a long talk. I know what ought to be done, and I know what can be done, and I know that I can tell you in five minutes what to do, that will greatly facilitate your work."[44] In 1908, when the Los Angeles *Record*'s profits and circulation were stagnant, Scripps summoned its editor and business manager to Miramar. "But I don't want you gentlemen to come to me as employees having to face a disgruntled or disappointed employer. Both of you have far more personal interests in the fortunes and misfortunes of the Los Angeles Record than I have."[45]

Monitoring Content

Statements and visits (particularly by auditors) focused primarily on the financial performance of each newspaper and on compliance with the low-cost strategy. Supervision of actual content was the responsibility of Robert F. Paine, the chain's editorial superintendent, who made sure that editors implemented the market segmentation and vertical integration strategies by using NEA material and creating interesting newspapers for working-class readers. Scripps, however, sometimes did read the newspapers himself.[46]

It was Paine, however, who read most of the Scripps newspapers, paying attention to general content, page makeup (including headline size and place-

ment of photographs and illustrations), and NEA usage. In 1905 he told the
editor of the Tacoma *Times*, "I am reading your paper daily." He advised editors on what kind of news was most interesting to readers, criticized some
newspapers for too much attention to dull topics (such as politics), and discussed where to use illustrations and cartoons to best advantage and how to
condense general news. He cajoled editors to make extensive use of NEA
material and at one point in 1906 instructed the Kansas City *World*'s editor
to provide reasons for every NEA article he did not run.[47]

In 1902 Paine conducted a detailed analysis of a single issue (August 22) of
the Los Angeles *Record*, praising it for the extensive use of the NEA (352 inches
in an eight-page publication) and for finding local angles on NEA articles.[48]
In 1903 he analyzed a twelve-day run of the Seattle *Star* and told Scripps that
it was downplaying news by carrying too many advertisements.[49] In 1905 Paine
tallied the space in the *Record* and found that only seventeen and a quarter
columns out of sixty-four were devoted to news. The heavy volume of advertising, he informed the editor, had turned the *Record* into "another of those
horrible bill posters" rather than a good newspaper.[50] Also in 1905, Paine ordered the business manager of the Sacramento *Star* to stop running advertisements in prominent places on the front page, which belonged to news.[51]

Paine often sent his analyses directly to editors, although he sometimes sent
them to Scripps instead. Scripps, in turn, referred to Paine's analyses and cri-
tiques in writing to editors and business managers. In 1905 he sent Paine's cri-
tique of the *San Diegan-Sun* to Porterfield, noting, "Under my instructions, Mr.
Paine has been making a careful study of all the coast papers for two weeks and
has written to me at some length concerning the various newspapers." Paine
had concluded that the *Sun* was not using enough NEA material and devoted
too much attention to local disputes over water. He also reported that Friday
editions of the Los Angeles *Record* had too many advertisements, and Scripps
told the editor and business manager to increase news content on Fridays.[52]

Round-Robin Letters

Carbon copies of letters disseminated orders and ideas widely through the
chain. Scripps's secretaries routinely made multiple copies of his letters and
sent a copy not only to the chief addressee but also to others who should know
Scripps's opinions or decisions on any particular topic. Atwood was supposed
to receive copies of all correspondence to and from Scripps and filed them so
the central office would have a complete set of Scripps's rulings and directions.
Other members of the cabinet (Paine, Harper, and McRae) routinely received
carbon copies of letters relevant to their particular duties, and when they wrote

to each other they usually sent carbons to other cabinet members and Scripps.[53] The copies served as a source of information and at times led to intervention. In 1905 Scripps wrote to Porterfield, "I note by copies of letters from N.E.A. that your editor is about to throw down the short story plan and to revert to the old absurdity of continued stories. I trust you will be able to induce him to abandon this project.[54]

Compliance

Scripps demanded loyalty. Employees were expected to follow his rules and heed his advice without hesitation. Editors or business managers who failed to do so were fired. George Putnam was fired, for example, when he insisted on expanding the Spokane *Press* to eight pages contrary to Scripps's small-paper predilections. Yet Scripps did not seem to rely on the threat of dismissal to motivate employees. Rather, he created a series of incentives that rewarded loyalty and performance while binding employees tightly to the chain: a policy of promoting within, profit-sharing (via employee stock-ownership), and management salaries based on performance.

Promotion

Lower-level employees (such as reporters, advertising solicitors, or circulation workers) could be prime candidates for jobs as editors or business managers at new Scripps newspapers. "It should be our practice," he urged, "always to select our editors from the young men employed on our papers." For the young employees, the policy held the attraction of promotion, greater responsibility, and potentially substantial income. For Scripps, the policy assured that new editors or business managers were already schooled in the Scripps style of low-cost, working-class journalism. As he said, "I have never yet been successful in going outside of my own concern to get managing men."[55]

H. N. Rickey began as a reporter on the Cleveland *Press*, rising through the ranks to be its editor and then editor-in-chief of Scripps-McRae newspapers. E. L. Rector, a business department employee at the San Francisco *Daily News*, became the first business manager of the new Pueblo *Sun* in 1906.[56] The Denver *Express*'s first editor was Boyd Gurley, who had worked at Scripps newspapers in Los Angeles and San Francisco as a reporter and city editor.[57] Many of Scripps's personal secretaries were also promoted. H. B. Clark became a founding manager of the Seattle *Star*, business manager of the *Daily News*, manager of the Scripps News Association, and eventually the president of United Press. J. P. Hamilton became the first business manager of the *Express*, and George Putnam established the Spokane *Press*.[58]

Successful editors and business managers of individual newspapers could hope to run additional operations. After Porterfield took over the *San Diegan-Sun*, Scripps held out the possibility of further advancement. "I know of at least two good jobs where you could earn more money than you are earning on the Sun, but I am not going to promote you until you have shown that you can do something smart, all alone, by yourself."[59] Successful in San Diego, Porterfield went on to establish newspapers in Sacramento and Fresno, and by 1907 he was manager of most of Scripps's California operations.

Profit-Sharing and Stock

Scripps allowed many employees to share in company profits by buying stock in his newspapers and telegraph news services. He stressed that his belief in profit-sharing did not come from socialist or philanthropic impulses but from an "object to increase my profits."[60] Workers who received dividends from company stock would work harder than salaried employees. "No one believes more than I do in the system of commissions and premiums or bonuses. My experience has taught me that I can get better results from a man if he is paid a part of the profits of his work."[61]

Employees were enthusiastic about holding stock in the Scripps chain. Wells, founding editor of the Seattle *Star*, said, "I take a keen interest in the success of the Star as you can well imagine. It pays to hold stock, don't you think! The hired man business is a good thing for those who like it, but I don't." "I want all of this Star stock I can get," said E. F. Chase, the founding business manager of the *Star*. Scripps encouraged employees to value stock-ownership. As he told Wells, "Your Star stock will carry you comfortably in the immediate future and secure you a really fine competence for the future."[62]

Dividends could augment salaries substantially. During a fourteen-month period in 1907 and 1908, the editor and business manager of the Tacoma *Times* received an average of $46.88 a month from *Times* dividends when their monthly salaries were $80.[63] During 1907, when W. D. Wasson was earning $100 a month as editor of the San Francisco *Daily News*, he also earned an average of $43.54 more in monthly dividends.[64] Clark received $13,923.88 in dividends over a fourteen-month period in 1907 and 1908, an average of $732.83 a month. Paine likewise received $6,626.88 in dividends during this period while. Atwood and Harper each earned about $3,100.[65] At the same time, Porterfield, as California regional manager, received $4,021.16 in dividends, and E. F. Chase, the Northwest regional manager, received $3,667.68.[66]

Employee stock-ownership created incentives to follow Scripps's rules, particularly to adopt his low-cost strategy. First, it reinforced Scripps's directive to limit capital investment. In starting new newspapers, he promised editors and business managers that they could buy stock in the new venture after it was making money.[67] That provided an incentive to keep start-up costs low because the price of each share would be determined by the amount needed to start the newspaper. In 1903 Wells promised to start the Tacoma *Times* for $10,000 and was to get 25 percent of its stock for $2,500. When he had spent $13,500, Atwood told him he needed to increase his investment by $875 to reflect 25 percent of the overrun. Porterfield ran into the same situation at the Sacramento *Star*.[68] After the newspaper was established, stockholder-employees would share the financial burden of any further capital expenditures such as buying land or erecting a building. When the Seattle *Star* acquired a new press plant in 1905 it added $5,000 in capitalization. Scripps, with 51 percent of the stock, paid $2,550, and the three employee-stockholders paid the remainder.[69]

Employee stock-ownership also helped keep operating costs low by severely reducing personnel costs. Both Scripps and his employees saw it as a trade-off for salaries that were well below industry norms. "Even if the salary is small at the start," he told Wells, "you would feel that you would still be greatly the gainer, because by your work you improved the value of your stock and its earning capacity. . . . Think only of the paper and the paper will take care of Wells."[70]

In 1905, when W. P. Strandborg had been editor of the Seattle *Star* for almost two years, he asked Scripps for stock in it. He had gotten by on a low salary, he said, "with the understanding that I was to acquire, if successful as editor of the Star, some interest in the stock of the paper; such inducement, indeed, was held out to me when I first came to Seattle."[71] In 1906 LeRoy Sanders asked for a 15 percent interest in the Tacoma *Times:*

> I have been managing editor of the Times during the past eighteen months and have been working at a very low salary with a view of securing a stock interest in the paper. I understand that the Times is soon to be incorporated and I am therefore becoming anxious about the matter. . . . During most of the time that I have been here my salary has been $14 and $15. Recently, I have been drawing $20. I have plugged along for that salary only because I expected to become a part owner some day. . . . Above all else I want a stock interest in the Times.[72]

Scripps kept close control over stock allocation and usually kept a simple majority (51 percent) for himself. "I only desire a sufficient amount of stock to secure to myself personal control of each corporation."[73] He preferred to allocate stock to those actively working on a newspaper and decided which employees could buy stock after closely observing their performance, acting "cold bloodedly . . . to give the stock where it will do the paper good, and not to serve friends, proteges or relatives."[74] Editors and business managers usually received the largest blocks, and other employees received smaller amounts. When the Seattle *Star* was incorporated in 1900, Scripps kept 51 percent of the stock and allocated 17 percent each to editor Wells and business manager E. F. Chase. Clark received 15 percent.[75] When the *San Diegan-Sun* was reorganized in 1905, Scripps took 51 percent of its stock, allocated 48.6 percent to Porterfield, and gave the remainder to three other employees at the newspaper.[76] Employees who left Scripps's employ were required to sell their stock back to him or to someone he designated. He reserved the right to set the stock's value.

Management Salaries

Managers who successfully followed Scripps's orders to earn 15 percent profits could earn a salary equal to 5 percent of gross revenues as long as that sum did not lessen the 15 percent profit. Scripps thought that incentives increased employees' efforts. "My experience has taught me that many a man will do ten percent more work with a five percent bonus," he said.[77] The 5 percent management rule applied to editors and business managers of individual newspapers as well as to regional managers. They could earn the 5 percent management fee if all the newspapers under their control showed a 15 percent profit.

Conclusions

Scripps built his chain through a three-part strategy of market segmentation, vertical integration, and low cost. Those strategies were not self-fulfilling, but required skillful management. As he noted, "If management is not everything, it is certainly much more than three-fourths of the whole proposition."[78] He and his central office were the heart of the entire chain—a centralized administrative structure—and relied on three chief methods. They defined rules or policies that derived from market segmentation, low cost, and vertical integration. They also created incentives for employees to obey those rules and policies and established surveillance systems to check on compliance. All of that reduced the autonomy of individual editors, but Scripps believed that rules were essential to create a unified chain. He told one editor that each newspaper was an integral part of the "whole institution" and that the "greater good of the greater number is the rule that must control."[79]

Avoiding Competition

The past success of the News has been due very largely to the
fact that no one knew that it was successful.
—E. W. Scripps to W. D. Wasson, May 19, 1906

CLOAK-AND-DAGGER SECRECY surrounded the establishment of E. W.
Scripps's newspaper in Portland, Oregon, in 1906. Scripps called the project
"Columbia," keeping the real name of the city a secret from almost all of his
associates. Only three employees were involved in the planning for "Columbia": E. H. Wells, editor of the Seattle *Star;* E. F. Chase, the *Star's* business
manager; and Lemuel T. Atwood, the chain's treasurer and head of the central office. Atwood had orders to hide correspondence on the matter even from
his closest aides, and Wells diverted attention from Portland by shipping the
press and Linotype to another city for storage. The Newspaper Enterprise
Association was told to send news features material for the new newspaper
directly to Wells in Seattle. Both the editor and business manager for "Columbia"—Thomas J. Dillon and Melvin Voorhees—did not learn of their
destination until minutes before they left Seattle for Portland in late August.
They pledged, at Wells's direction, that they would not tell friends or relatives
of their new location.[1]

The Portland newspaper began publication as a 1 cent neighborhood sheet—
the *Eastside News*—rather than as a citywide publication. Its only method of
distribution was home delivery by carriers. It had no street sales, and circulation was small. Its ownership was hidden; all references to the Scripps telegraph
news service or the Newspaper Enterprise Association were deleted from articles supplied by those services. The newspaper carried virtually no advertising during its first month in operation, and when it did start to carry advertisements they were for small businesses in the neighborhood near its office.

Such secrecy reflected Scripps's desire to escape the attention of established

Portland dailies. He wanted his newspaper to serve an untapped segment of the Portland market, and secrecy, he reasoned, bought time to get started without extensive competition. "There is nothing that I so much desire as to have all of the old line of newspapers consider us . . . something pretty nearly beneath their contempt," Scripps told one of his editors.[2]

The desire to avoid competition was an outgrowth of two of Scripps's basic business strategies: low cost and market segmentation. Competition could undermine the low-cost strategy by draining capital, time, and attention. Established newspapers might also vie with Scripps in targeting working-class readers (either through price reductions or changes in content) once they realized that such a sizable segment existed. That would threaten both the low-cost and market segmentation strategies.

Newspaper competition took place in two stages, and Scripps went to great lengths to avoid them both. First, established publishers often attempted to prevent new competitors from gaining a foothold in their markets. Second, once newspapers were established they vied for readers and (except in Scripps's case) advertisers. In both stages the range of competitive behaviors was broad. Newspapers could try to tie up readers through the use of premiums offered for long-term subscriptions, advertisers (through the use of discounts in return for exclusive advertising contracts), or distribution systems. Costly price warfare—both in subscriptions and advertising rates—could bleed poorer newspapers or scare off newcomers.[3]

Learning the Value of Obscurity

In 1878, when E. W. Scripps established the Cleveland *Press,* he demonstrated none of the secrecy that marked the birth of his Portland newspaper. Just the opposite. The young Scripps proudly proclaimed his identity as editor, brashly promoted the newspaper, and excoriated his rival publishers.[4] On November 15, 1878—in its twelfth issue—the *Press* claimed that "a larger number of the PENNY PRESS are now sold in Cleveland than any other paper." On that same day, the *Press* bragged about scooping its older rivals, noting that it was "the only paper in this city that received the news of the recovery of A. T. Stewart's body yesterday." When the *Press* was six months old, Scripps claimed his "thoroughly live and independent newspaper" had revolutionized Cleveland journalism.[5]

Scripps's brashness in Cleveland—particularly the attacks on one of his rivals there—came close to destroying the *Press.* In his early days as its editor, Scripps was particularly outspoken in condemning Edwin Cowles, proprietor and editor of the Cleveland *Leader.* In 1879, when the *Press* was involved in a lawsuit brought by a local industrialist, the sheriff had seized the newspaper plant pending proof that Scripps could post a $100,000 bond. With operations idled on a workday, two inspectors came to appraise the *Press*'s plant, one of whom was Cowles. Cowles relished the shutdown. He refused to check purchase invoices and declared that he wanted to inspect the entire plant. Scripps realized that Cowles intended to drag the appraisal on for hours, preventing publication of that day's newspaper. With luck, he found a wealthy Clevelander to post the bond and was able to cut the appraisal short.[6]

That incident only fanned Scripps's dislike of Cowles, and their war of words continued. In April 1881, in one of its tirades about Cowles, the *Press* referred to "the old man who lost the roof of his mouth by youthful indiscretion, and who now edits the Leader."[7] The imputation of venereal disease led to a criminal libel suit from Cowles, and, although Scripps eventually was acquitted, the suit could have ruined the newspaper and sent him to jail.[8] From such experiences with Cowles, Scripps came to believe that attacks on other publishers were unwise. In 1907 he discussed these cases with the editor of his Denver newspaper and said, "There is no similarity about my present policy of the still hunt and long distance plans, and that *reckless, thoughtless, passionate and ungoverned conduct* of the Press in its early days."[9]

Scripps also learned that the high profile his newspapers maintained in Cincinnati and St. Louis only goaded competitors to work harder, lower prices, and, at times, attempt to disrupt his distribution systems. Scripps's long-running battle against Joseph Pulitzer's *Post-Dispatch* in St. Louis also taught him the virtue of being the only working-class advocate in a city. Pulitzer's progressive journalism led to a natural, nasty, and very expensive battle between the two publishers for the same readers—a fight Scripps eventually lost.

From these experiences in the 1870s and 1880s, Scripps formulated a plan for avoiding competition. He operated in a highly secretive manner, hoping that existing publishers would not take alarm. He also attempted to monopolize the working-class newspaper market, offering to share markets with more conservative competitors while driving other working-class publications out of business.

Seeking Obscurity: The Still Hunt

Scripps characterized his stealthlike entrance into newspaper markets as a still hunt. "The philosophy of our 'still hunt' campaign is that we want to avoid, as far as possible, attracting public attention in mass."[10] He expected that competition would arise eventually but saw the still hunt as a way to delay it until he had his newspaper operating and could turn his attention to the rivalry.[11]

His still hunts were defensive and emphasized secrecy, avoidance of circulation and advertising wars, and a ban on newspaper attacks.

Secrecy

Scripps labored hard to hide his ownership of newspapers. As Linda Lawson has demonstrated, secrecy about newspaper ownership was not entirely unusual in 1900.[12] Some owners tried to hide their affiliations to camouflage inherent conflicts of interest. Standard Oil, railroads, and other commercial interests recognized that public knowledge of their ownership of newspapers would seriously undermine the effectiveness of propaganda-as-news. Scripps appears to have tried to hide his ownership primarily for business reasons. He believed that most publishers would see him as a formidable opponent and so would go to great lengths to prevent his entry into their market. He also reasoned that the public would be more attracted to a struggling young editor who seemed to be running one little newspaper than to a publication that was part of a larger company. Although Scripps's secrecy was based on both concerns, his correspondence with his editors and managers seems to stress the former rationale. He worried that other publishers might engage in costly battles to stop his new little newspapers.

Most made no mention of Scripps at all, listing only the names of their editors and business managers. E. H. Wells relied on such secrecy in founding three Scripps newspapers: the Seattle *Star*, the Tacoma *Times*, and the Portland *Daily News*. In 1904, shortly after the debut of the Tacoma newspaper, Wells told one associate that "Mr. Scripps' name is not mentioned in connection with this enterprise by his own wish. Nobody is known in connection except myself. . . . In Seattle, the same policy was followed. E. H. Wells & Co., there did business, with nobody else known, until later incorporation." Even after incorporation, Scripps's name did not appear on company documents; his stock was held by a trustee—Atwood. When Chase went to Seattle in 1899 to help establish the *Star*, he told none of his former colleagues at the *San Diegan-Sun* or members of his family where he was going.[13] When W. H. Porterfield took over as manager of the *San Diegan-Sun* in 1901, Scripps congratulated him for his salutatory because "it removed the impression of my ownership. For economical reasons, this is better for the Sun."[14] In 1906 the Denver *Express* began listing its editor and business manager in an effort to counteract rumors that Scripps was running it.[15] When Chase visited Salt Lake City in 1905 to survey that market for a new newspaper, Scripps told him to be secretive. "Don't talk about Scripps and perhaps you had better not register in your own name, as newspaper men very likely know of you and of your connection with me, and might surmise things."[16]

Scripps's link to his newspapers was often hidden from even employees so they could not inform competitors. He used a pseudonym, for example, for his subscription to the Seattle *Star*, which was sent to a "Mr. Woods." Scripps also used plain brown envelopes in writing to the *Star*, and secretaries there who typed managers' letters to him were never told where those letters went. The salutation was left blank, and the editor or business manager later filled in "Dear Mr. Scripps" and addressed the envelope.[17] Wells told Scripps that most employees did not know of Scripps's tie to the newspaper. Letters from him were kept in locked desk drawers, and only top managers were to see them.[18] In 1906, seven years after the newspaper's debut, Scripps told his long-time business partner Milton McRae, "To this day I doubt if ten percent of the employees of the Seattle Star know that I have a stock interest in the paper, and I do not believe half of them know of my existence. I have dealt so far as I could in the same way with all the other papers."[19] In 1905 McRae had told Scripps that many Los Angeles *Record* employees had no idea that Scripps owned the San Francisco *Daily News*.[20]

H. B. Clark, one of the founding partners of the San Francisco *Daily News* in 1903, had strict orders to keep that project quiet. Lemuel T. Atwood was necessarily involved in all new projects, and Clark apologized for being rather vague about some details when asking for advice: "The old man [Scripps] was rather insistent that too much should not be generally known. . . . I ask that you say nothing of this outside of E. W. as whatever is done must be done quietly. That is one of the things he himself specified."[21]

Scripps developed a complicated set of ciphers to hide his authorship of letters to key associates in the event that lesser employees or even outsiders would see the correspondence. As part of that system, he frequently sent letters under the signature of his personal secretary. When using telegrams, he sometimes split the message between two telegrams, each with alternating words. The message itself made sense only when someone had both telegrams.[22]

How well Scripps succeeded in hiding his affiliation with his new publications is unclear. Their format and politics—and the use of the Scripps telegraph news services and Newspaper Enterprise Association—all were conducive to educated guesses about ownership. Few people contacted him directly about the newspapers, however, and he took that as a signal that the secrecy was successful.[23]

Avoiding Circulation Wars

Circulation is a prime indicator of a newspaper's worth, showing popularity with readers and providing the basis for advertising rates. Publishers and editors naturally fight rivals that might siphon away circulation. Wars for circulation can include reductions in the cost of a newspaper, platoons of solicitors seeking subscribers in a door-to-door canvass of the city, premiums for new readers, and contests for all. Scripps attempted to avoid circulation wars by seeking new readers, keeping circulation figures secret, and using unobtrusive distribution methods.

New Readers—Scripps did not want to alarm other publishers, so he started newspapers in markets that had room for circulation growth and told editors and business managers to find new readers. When Clark was starting the San Francisco *Daily News,* he told Scripps that it would not bother the two existing afternoon newspapers. "We will neither disturb the Post or Bulletin."[24]

> I find that there are approximately 25000 Bulletins and 5000 Post delivered in San Francisco. There are 420000 people here and evening papers should have 70,000 circulation. That makes 40000 circulation here to be had by somebody without replacing either a Bulletin or a Post. . . . I don't believe out of 3400 carrier circulation we have replaced 150 Bulletins and Posts. . . . I can get this 40,000 people who are not reading evening newspapers. It will not replace any paper now read. At least not for along time. It will of course make new readers for evening papers.[25]

Jacob C. Harper, the chain's attorney and supervisor of Scripps's Evansville *Press* in 1906, also told its editor to seek new readers: "Do not conduct your circulation work on the idea of taking away subscribers from the Journal-News. There are enough people in Evansville who do not take that paper and who will want to take both papers, to give the Press a magnificent circulation. Let your aim be to fill the field, rather than to crowd the other paper out." In 1906 he told the editor and business manager of the St. Louis *Chronicle,* "The theory ought to be, I submit, not to take subscribers away from the Post-Dispatch, but to get subscribers who are not now taking either paper."[26]

Circulation Secrecy—Scripps editors and business managers also had strict orders never to reveal circulation because doing so would invite "disastrous competition." Scripps particularly worried that circulation figures would prompt established newspapers, which usually sold at 2 to 5 cents, to lower their prices to challenge his publications for the cheap, penny market.[27]

Scripps told the business manager of the Los Angeles *Record* to keep circulation a secret from everyone, including employees. When Chase disclosed that information to a few prospective advertisers in 1902, Scripps berated him, saying, "It was my intention that . . . the circulation figures should be a profound secret, even amongst our employees." Chase was forbidden ever to disclose circulation again. A year later the prospectus of the Tacoma *Times* included a provision guaranteeing "absolute secrecy" on circulation, and in 1906 the prospectus of the Denver *Express* promised that circulation would be kept secret from everyone, including employees, "so far as possible." "The important thing is to increase your circulation without letting the other people know of your increase," Harper told the new business manager at the Evansville *Press* in 1906.[28]

It was not an easy secret to keep. Advertisers routinely relied upon circulation figures to gauge a newspaper's marketing value, and refusing to cite them ran contrary to common industry practice. At times, editors or business managers would ask for a variance from the rule, but Scripps was adamant. Disclosing circulation to advertisers was tantamount to telling rival publishers, who would quickly strike back. When Ward C. Mayborn, business manager of the Evansville *Press,* wanted to disclose that publication's circulation to a few advertisers in 1906, Harper warned, "Do you not see that if you report what your circulation is for purpose of securing advertising that this fact will get to The Journal News and they will be able to estimate the progress that you are making." Harper told Mayborn that the *Press* could reach a circulation of ten thousand if the *Journal News* stayed at 2 cents. Disclosing circulation was an invitation to price warfare.[29]

Circulation Methods—Scripps put into practice a series of steps to make sure that other publishers did not know the full extent of his circulation figures. His newspapers did not start with citywide sales, but concentrated on areas where established newspapers had few readers. Scripps newspapers in San Francisco, Portland, Pueblo, and Nashville first circulated only in working-class neighborhoods.[30] Another way to keep circulation a secret was to forego street sales. Most Scripps newspapers that began after 1898 allowed only home delivery by carriers; street sales by newsboys allowed rivals to see sales and thus estimate circulation.

The San Francisco *Daily News,* established in 1903, had no street sales except at the ferry terminal. Newsboys wanted to sell it, but the managers refused, fearing price warfare with the afternoon *Bulletin.* Scripps claimed that no one in San Francisco—either readers or other publishers—had any idea of the newspaper's success. "Our contemporaries think that the owner of the News is an old fool who is parting with his money. They, in their folly, think they know the only way to make a newspaper business success, and as we are not pursuing that way, they are not worrying themselves about our ever becoming successful, and hence, dangerous competitors," he said. "The case would be entirely different even if a half a dozen newsboys were hawking paper on the street and crying it."[31]

In 1905 Scripps said that he was convinced that street sales of the *Daily News* would provoke other newspapers to reduce their price. Its circulation was more than twenty-four thousand—without street sales—when earthquake and fire hit the city in April 1906.[32] After the earthquake, however, the *Daily News* resorted to street sales because regular readers were widely dispersed and living in tents, although Scripps warned the manager to reinstate carrier delivery as soon as possible.

> Our main present reason for objection to a street sale is our desire to always be as obscure as possible, and this largely for the reason that we do not wish to drive our contemporaries to reducing their price, nor for some time to come at least, demonstrate to others than our one cent small paper field is so good that they will desire to enter it. . . . The chief danger I apprehended from the street sale was that the sale might be very large and conspicuous, and that the older papers would be impressed by it and act accordingly.[33]

Street sales continued, however, and within six months the *Daily News*'s chief afternoon rival, the *Bulletin,* had dropped its price to a penny.[34]

Managers of the Evansville *Press* and the Terre Haute *Post* allowed street sales when they began in 1906 and immediately faced newsboy boycotts organized by rival newspapers. Harper advised giving up street sales entirely; withdrawing would be seen as a major defeat and would lull rivals into complacency. In Terre Haute the *Post* did withdraw from street sales and concentrated only on home delivery by carriers. One of Scripps's lieutenants visited Terre Haute and urged a continuation of the low-key approach: "In this way, they may hope to keep the Tribune fixed in its mistaken opinion and be free to work their carrier circulation without any suspicion on the part of the Tribune of what they are really accomplishing." A month later the *Post* was selling fewer than forty daily newspapers on the street and nearly 770 through carriers.[35]

Prospectuses for new newspapers sometimes emphasized reliance on home delivery. In 1906 the prospectus for the Pueblo *Sun* stipulated sole reliance on carriers during the newspaper's first year, and the *Sun* generally followed that policy statement. After two weeks' operation it had 506 subscribers through daily home delivery by carriers and street sales of fifty. The Scripps newspaper in Denver, started with the same pledge, had no street sales at all. After seven months, the *Express* had a daily circulation of nearly 1,940—1,900 of which were home delivery by carrier and forty by mail.[36]

Avoiding Advertising Wars

Advertising was central to the survival and success of most newspapers early in the twentieth century, and publishers naturally fought anyone threatening their major source of revenue. Newcomers posed a real threat. The mere presence of a new publication could depress advertising rates as businesses exploited the situation by seeking discounts in exchange for patronage. Publishers were complicit and offered discounts for long-term exclusive contracts in an effort to monopolize advertising and bankrupt newcomers.

Scripps's business managers had strict orders not to woo away advertisers and start battles with other publishers. When the San Francisco *Daily News* increased its advertising volume in 1906—after nearly three years of running very few advertisements—Scripps was quick to criticize it because he did not want advertisers to flock to his newspapers. That might prompt other publishers to produce small newspapers or lower their prices. R. F. Paine, the chain's editorial superintendent, echoed Scripps's criticism and warned that the *Daily News*'s two afternoon competitors would strike back. "All this going after business is notice to the Bulletin and Post, and other competitors, that you have entered upon a policy that will seriously effect their business, and what reprisals your rivals may attempt I do not know."[37] Scripps advised the editor of the Tacoma *Times* in 1905 not to put much energy into pursuing advertising because "the first effect would be that your contemporary (who considers himself your competitor), with larger space and larger resources, would outdo you."[38]

To avoid such retaliation, most new Scripps newspapers did not welcome advertisers. Those in Fresno, Dallas, Oklahoma City, San Francisco, and Denver refused all advertising at first, and Scripps told the manager of the Denver *Express* not to run any until circulation had reached two thousand. The prospectus for a Salt Lake City newspaper—which was never established—also called for a ban on advertising until circulation reached two thousand.[39] The Oklahoma City *News*, which began publication on October 1, 1906, did not carry its first advertisement until November 8. Even after that, ads were not plentiful. During the rest of November 1906 the *News* published forty-three advertisements in eighteen issues—3 percent of the newspaper's total space. Six businesses accounted for all advertisements: a coal company, a bank, a railroad company, restaurant, gas company, and a furniture store. The ads were small. Forty (93 percent) were ten inches or less, and twenty-one (48 percent) were five inches or less. Only three exceeded ten column inches.[40]

Some Scripps newspapers, however, accepted advertising as soon as they began but did little to encourage it. The Pueblo *Sun*'s editor reported that he made no effort to attract advertisers although he ran ads in his first issue on September 1, 1906. During the first week of publication, the *Sun* printed fifty-nine advertisements. Fifty-five (93 percent) were five inches or smaller, and only four exceeded five column inches. They represented twelve businesses—a bank, wallpaper store, insurance agent, printer, restaurant, Turkish bath, saddle shop, jeweler, gas company, and three boardinghouses—and took up just .5 percent of the *Sun*'s total space. "We have thus far paid little attention to advertising," the editor told Scripps at the end of the first month.[41] The Seattle *Star* carried 959 inches of advertising during its first full month of operation, about 7 percent of its total space.[42]

The dominance of small advertisements in Scripps's Oklahoma City and Pueblo newspapers reflects a conscious decision to avoid large accounts. The prospectuses of the Tacoma, Nashville, Dallas, and Oklahoma City operations all stipulated that each would "cultivate a numerous clientele of small advertisers and will discourage too extensive use of its space by a few large advertisers."[43] No full-page advertisements were allowed in any Scripps newspaper during this period. Most refused anything larger than forty column inches (two full columns), and the Denver *Express*'s prospectus set the limit at twenty. In late 1907—a year after its start—the Dallas *Dispatch* had contracts with forty-one advertisers. Twenty-nine of those contracts called for one- or two-inch advertisements daily, four for three-inch advertisements daily, and two for six-inch advertisements weekly. Only six called for advertisements larger than six inches.[44]

Because department stores usually demanded relatively large advertisements, the size limit was intended primarily to exclude them. Scripps believed that department stores made poor customers, but he also wanted to avoid upsetting established newspapers by doing business with their largest and most lucrative advertisers. Just as his newspapers had orders to seek new readers, they were also to seek new advertisers rather than dislodge those already patronizing established publications. In Terre Haute, the *Post* avoided advertising at first, but when it started accepting ads it ignored department stores and sought out small merchants who had not been advertising at all.[45]

Attacks on Newspapers

Still hunts also included a ban on wars of words with other editors. Scripps editors had strict orders not to bait other editors and not to respond if attacked. Young editors were told that there were two reasons for avoiding such attacks. First, they were not effective in a competitive sense. Readers either sympathized with the newspaper attacked or learned to disdain all journalists. "According to my experience," Scripps said, "it is ten times harder and more costly to gain an inch of advantage over your adversary by attempting to pull him down a half an inch while you make a half an inch upward progress, than it is to make a full inch gain over him by cultivating territory he has not yet, and perhaps cannot, preempt."[46] Second, such attacks only attracted attention to—and competition for—Scripps's newspapers. When W. D. Wasson, editor of the San Francisco *Daily News,* attacked William Randolph Hearst's *Examiner* in 1906, Scripps was quick to berate him. "The Examiner is not our competitor. We do not want anyone to think of us as a newspaper in the same category with the Examiner." He told Wasson that it would be ideal if other newspapers ignored the little *Daily News,* but they would not do so if the *Daily News* attacked them.[47]

It was a difficult rule to enforce, and Scripps battled with editors over it. In Spokane the editors of the struggling *Press* seemed unable to avoid attacks on William Cowles, publisher of the morning *Spokesman-Review* and afternoon *Chronicle.*[48] In Los Angeles, the editors of the *Record* frequently attacked Harrison Otis, publisher of the *Times.*[49] Beginning in late 1903, however, with the prospectus of the Tacoma *Times,* new editors promised to avoid attacks on other editors: "This paper shall refrain from all attacks on the editor or publisher or corporations conducting or controlling other newspapers on account of a feeling of rivalry or competition." Similar pledges were included in the prospectuses for Scripps newspapers in Dallas, Oklahoma City, Nashville, and Denver.[50] In 1907, at a conference with the business managers and editors of the "young eastern papers" (Terre Haute, Evansville, Dallas, Oklahoma City, Pueblo, Denver, Nashville, and Memphis), Scripps reiterated that "if you do not like my rule, and think it is inconsistent with your dignity, let us part company right now."[51]

Controlling the Working-Class Market

A still hunt ideally bought Scripps time in starting newspapers, which he believed should be well established among working-class readers before retaliation from other publishers surfaced. But the still hunt had limits. Once well established, his newspapers would not be able to hide their success, and other publishers might try to invade the lucrative working-class market. Scripps was particularly eager to avoid a battle over working-class readers and so attempted to share markets with more upscale conservative newspapers while preventing the establishment of other working-class newspapers.

Dividing the Market

Scripps's methods of expansion led him away from cities where newspapers were already successfully reaching working-class readers. After they established newspapers, Scripps and his lieutenants sought to educate older publishers to his market segmentation ideas and convince them that there was ample room (and profit) for them and for Scripps. That was no easy task. Most publishers and editors were unwilling to cede an entire market segment, particularly a large one such as working-class readers, to another publisher.

In 1903 Scripps instructed the business manager of his Seattle *Star* to propose a secret arrangement with Alden Blethen, publisher of the afternoon Seattle *Times,* the *Star*'s chief competitor. Scripps offered to keep the penny *Star* at four pages forever if the *Times* (at eight pages and larger) would keep its price at 2 cents. Scripps also proposed that he and Blethen unite to block other afternoon newspapers in Seattle, particularly by preventing a new venture from getting a telegraph news service. He predicted that such an alliance would prove lucrative to both and bar competition.[52] Scripps argued that the presence of the Seattle *Times* on the upper end of the market and the *Star* on the lower end precluded others from entering the field. "Nothing but asinine egotism, or greed can prevent such an understanding between the publishers as will secure, for a long term of years, the present satisfactory condition," he said.

Seattle editors were told to prove their good will toward Blethen by refusing to compete in the bidding for the contract to print the city's legal notices. Blethen wanted the contract, and he approached both the *Star* and the morning *Post-Intelligencer* in an effort to keep them from underbidding him. Scripps instructed E. F. Chase to tell Blethen, "Hereafter, the Times need never to take the Star into consideration as a competitor." The desire for long-term cooperation was also to be made clear: "Tell Blethen you will be glad to have him reciprocate in a general business way to any extent he feels inclined." No formal agreement ever came about, however.[53]

In 1904 Scripps visited Cowles and told him that his little penny newspaper, the Spokane *Press,* posed no real competition to Cowles's publications because it sought an entirely different audience: "The lines that I laid down were that he should go on, just as he has been, being the representative and organ of the Republican party, employees' association, etc., and that he should strive in every possible way to get all the business in sight for his papers, while my boys should devote themselves to the democratic, workingmen constituency, and to that constituency which did not like Cowles and Cowles's paper, and that our boys should do all they could to get every dollar's worth of business they could for their paper."[54] Both afternoon newspapers would make money—and prevent other competition—if they divided the market and concentrated on serving their own segments.[55]

Harper instructed the business manager of the Evansville *Press* in 1906 to be congenial toward the older, well-established afternoon newspaper, the *Journal-News*, which sold for 2 cents. "Let the note be everywhere and to every one, that Evansville is too big and prosperous a city for one afternoon newspaper, that it will support two newspapers, and that you mean to do nothing that will diminish the prosperity of the other paper; you want it also to succeed." The business manager was to make an appointment with the owner of the *Journal-News* "and assure him that there is no intention on the part of the Press to try to interfere with the Journal's field; that you felt there was a field for a little paper in Evansville and that you had no intention of trying to invade the large paper field."[56]

Charles F. Mosher, a leading figure in the chain's central office, gave similar advice to the business manager of Scripps's Memphis *Press* when he faced attacks from the *News-Scimitar*. "Personally, nothing will give me greater pleasure than to know that the News-Scimitar was making a good profit every month for its proprietors." The business manager should approach the *News-Scimitar*'s editor and explain this view. "Emphasize to him the fact that . . . we have no desire to cost the News-Scimitar a penny in any way." Not only were the Scripps newspapers benign, but they were also a guarantee that some other newspaper would not enter the market. "The News-Scimitar cannot occupy all of the afternoon field in Memphis," Mosher said. "The Memphis Press and the News-Scimitar, between them, will almost entirely occupy the afternoon field in Memphis. There will be nothing, therefore, to attract the attention of anyone else from the outside and induce them to consider entering Memphis."[57]

Scripps made proposals to divide newspaper markets in at least three other cities: St. Louis, San Francisco, and Cincinnati. In 1894 he told other St. Louis publishers that he would promise to keep the penny St. Louis *Chronicle* small (six pages or fewer) if they all agreed to keep their larger papers (eight to sixteen pages daily) at 2 cents.[58] The publishers, unwilling to leave Scripps alone in the penny newspaper niche, refused. In 1906 he offered to divide the San Francisco market with the other chief afternoon newspaper, the *Bulletin*. As he told one employee, "I am quite willing to make a contract with the Bulletin to the effect that the News will never print more than a four page paper and the Bulletin shall never reduce its price so long as there is no other formidable one cent newspaper in the field." Scripps indicated that he was willing to give a bond "for any amount of money from ten thousand to half a million of dollars" to secure such an agreement. In December 1906 Wasson approached the *Bulletin* with the offer, which was refused.[59]

During the 1880s and early 1890s Scripps and his managers—notably Milton A. McRae—attempted to prevent price reductions by the Cincinnati *Times-Star*, the chief competitor to Scripps's Cincinnati *Post*. In 1887, when the *Times-Star* dropped its daily price from 3 cents (12 cents a week) to 2 cents (10 cents a week), McRae successfully organized newsboys to put pressure on the *Times-Star* to rescind the price cut.[60] In 1889, however, the *Times-Star* returned to 2 cents, and by 1892 its owner was contemplating cutting its price to a penny. McRae met with the owner, Charles Taft, to convince him to keep the price at 2 cents, arguing that dividing the market between the *Post* (at 1 cent) and the *Times-Star* (at 2 cents) could be lucrative. He told Scripps, "I left him [Taft] on the most friendly basis with the thing settled for 1893, viz: that The Times Star shall remain a 2c paper and The Post shall go on as it is. The eight-page papers The Post has been issuing have been scaring him. Truly we have been fortunate in thus making our settlement with him, because we can both make more money by so doing . . . I showed him the folly of his attempting to enter the one cent field. I proved it to him by facts and figures."[61] Taft seemed content to leave his price at 2 cents. "I have been to no little pains to attain this end," McRae said.[62]

In 1895 the *Times-Star* finally reduced its price to a penny, and its circulation grew. Three years later Scripps offered an "agreement of cooperation" with Taft to divide the Cincinnati market: the *Post* would cost a penny, the *Times-Star* 2 cents, and the newspapers would pool a portion of their circulation receipts. Scripps outlined his plan to Atwood, his emissary to Taft: "My idea is that the arrangement would be such that each paper should gain from the other's increase of circulation or maintenance of same. . . . This pro-rating [of revenues] should be of such a nature as would make us desirous of having the Times-Star have the greatest possible circulation and vice-versa. I feel certain that there would be a very large increase of the net receipts from circulation to the joint interests by such an arrangement."[63] Atwood visited Taft and reported that he "seemed very much interested in the negotiation" and that he proposed a pooling of all receipts, from advertising as well as circulation.

Taft apparently thought that the *Post* and *Times-Star* could control the Cincinnati afternoon newspaper market through such cooperation. He said he could run the *Times-Star* so that "it should keep all two cent competition out of this field. He believed," Atwood reported, "a one cent six page Post would do the like in the one cent field. The morning papers were not to be feared and probably not to be taken into consideration." Taft also predicted that "there are barrels of money to be made in the afternoon newspaper field if it is properly managed." Negotiations continued over several months, although apparently no formal agreement was ever signed and no profit-sharing plan implemented. The *Times-Star* continued as a penny paper.[64]

Eliminating Competitors

In each case where Scripps either made a formal or informal proposal to divide the market (San Francisco, Cincinnati, Seattle, Spokane, and St. Louis) he confronted strong, well-established newspapers, some of which had larger circulations than his own. When he faced weaker newspapers, however, Scripps was far less accommodating. In Cincinnati and St. Louis, serious competition developed from other newspapers seeking to reach the working-class market during the 1880s and 1890s. Twice in Cincinnati (in 1888 and 1894) and once in St. Louis (in 1897) Scripps took steps to kill newspapers he saw as threats to his control of the working-class niche.

The first competitor was the Cincinnati *Telegram,* a penny afternoon newspaper established in 1884. It was never particularly strong, but Scripps and McRae estimated that it siphoned both readers and advertisers from Scripps's Cincinnati *Post.* In 1887 McRae told Scripps that the *Telegram* was losing money but still producing a credible product (four pages daily and eight pages on Saturdays). Scripps contemplated buying the *Telegram* and killing it in 1888 but instead financed its move from afternoons to mornings. He paid the *Telegram*'s owner $4,000 (in a secret agreement) to leave the evening field, and the owner promised to "do all in his power to enable the Post to get that portion of the Telegram's circulation which it cannot continue to hold as a morning paper." The *Post* picked up about half of the *Telegram*'s afternoon readers and advertisers, but the *Telegram* fared poorly in the morning field and died in January 1889 after just four months.[65]

The *Telegram* incident reflected Scripps's view that morning newspapers were not direct competitors with afternoon publications. On several occasions he and his lieutenants attempted to deflect competition within the afternoon field by urging new publishers to start morning rather than afternoon newspapers. In 1889 Scripps was successful in influencing the prospective proprietors of the new Cleveland *Times* to change their plans and launch it as a morning publication, but in 1904 Chase attempted unsuccessfully to induce the managers of a prospective afternoon newspaper to move to the morning field.[66]

The Cincinnati *Telegram*'s success as an afternoon newspaper in taking advertising and readers away from Scripps's *Post* convinced Scripps that such competitors should be killed before they could gain a toe-hold in the market. When a Cincinnati typographical union began to make plans in 1894 to start a 1 cent afternoon labor newspaper (to be called the *News*), the *Post* moved to preempt the market. The *Post*'s editor, Charles Mosher, reported that he had begun increasing its size to eight pages and had added substantially to its labor news. "When the paper finally appeared, after several postponements, the Post was giving all the live news of labor and had the lines laid so completely that we scooped the News in its own field right along, besides giving eight pages and all the news of the world. This condition of affairs has proven a bar to any progress and the paper has only been kept alive by the money appropriated by the Union." The *News* limped along for less than two months, dying in November 1894.[67]

There were several labor-affiliated newspapers in St. Louis during the 1890s, although only one was a daily. The 1 cent *Evening Journal,* established in 1896, provided extensive coverage to local labor meetings, as did Scripps's *Chronicle*.[68] It was also far less radical than other local labor newspapers—only slightly more so than the *Chronicle,* which gravitated toward the American Federation of Labor and Samuel Gompers rather than toward socialist labor views— and argued that both Gompers and the AFL merited respect.[69] The *Evening Journal* also provided general-interest content such as sports and news about society, cooking, and fashion. Consequently, it appealed to much the same audience as the *Chronicle.*

Even though its circulation and advertising revenues were quite small, the business manager of the *Chronicle* saw the *Evening Journal* as a competitor for working-class readers and resolved to destroy it before it became well established. It had not yet developed a broad advertising base, but rather depended heavily on a contract to print legal notices for the city of St. Louis, work that constituted 69.2 percent of the newspaper's total advertising lineage. That contract was lucrative enough to sustain the *Evening Journal* through its first year, and it moved into a new office in early 1897.[70] When the city's printing contract came up for renewal in 1897, Scripps's lieutenants approached the other St. Louis dailies in an effort to take the printing away from the *Evening Journal*, which, they thought, would die without that business. Although most of the other established dailies (the *Globe Democrat, Republic, Post-Dispatch,* and *Star-Sayings,* in addition to the *Chronicle*) did not want the city printing, the morning *Republic* ultimately made the lowest bid of that group. Yet the *Evening Journal* still submitted the lowest bid for the contract. After the other newspapers argued that its limited circulation (about three thousand) did not meet the legal requirement of a "general circulation medium," city officials ruled against the *Evening Journal* and the printing went to the *Republic.* The *Chronicle's* business manager told McRae about the conspiracy against the *Evening Journal,* saying that the "sole object of this move" was to get the printing away from it. A few weeks later the *Journal* moved to morning publication but quickly died after facing a newsboy boycott organized by the two other morning publications, the *Globe-Democrat* and the *Republic.*[71]

The Cincinnati *News* and the St. Louis *Evening Journal* represented a potential threat to Scripps's market segmentation strategy because their close ties to labor unions made them direct competitors for working-class readers. Scripps's newspapers in other cities did not face serious competition from union-affiliated publications, most of which were weeklies and unable or unwilling to provide general, non-labor news content (e.g., on sports, fashion, or comics).[72] In Seattle, Scripps's *Star* had close ties to the Central Trades Council, and the weekly labor newspaper (the *Union Record*) praised it as the true friend of the laboring class.[73] In Spokane, when union members became dissatisfied with the *Press* and threatened to start their own daily, the *Press's* editor, J. D. Lee, quickly moved to make peace. Lee told Scripps that he had arranged a meeting with local labor leaders and would "try my best to head off the opposition against the Press and will keep you posted as to the outcome." Lee offered to let the Spokane Trades Council produce its own news column for the *Press:* "We want you to accept this as an invitation to use our columns at any time you may desire. We would suggest that you appoint some one member from the council to handle this stuff, of course it must be brief and written in an argumentative way and we will run it over the signature of any one you direct."[74] The threat of a union daily was not carried out.

Competition from Hearst

Driving newspapers such as the Cincinnati *News* or the St. Louis *Evening Journal* out of business was not particularly difficult. Both were new, and their owners did not have enough capital to sustain substantial competition from

Scripps or other publishers. One other competitor for working-class readers, William Randolph Hearst, was not as vulnerable, however. Scripps said, "I consider Hearst is in general and particular, my only possible competitor."[75]

Hearst had substantial capital, spent money lavishly in starting newspapers, and aimed at the same working-class readers Scripps sought. Even though he seemed to gravitate to larger markets such as New York and Chicago while Scripps sought out smaller markets such as Seattle, Spokane, and Dallas, the prospect of fighting with Hearst was a constant source of worry in the Scripps organization after 1900.

Before 1908, Scripps and Hearst faced each other in just three markets: Chicago, San Francisco, and Los Angeles. In 1900 Scripps had just begun the Chicago *Press* on a very modest scale when Hearst began his heavily promoted Chicago *American*, which quickly preempted the working-class market Scripps wanted. As one of Scripps's lieutenants reported, "The American made its appearance on July 4. They have affected us quite a bit. We have lost but little as yet but they have seemingly blocked us. The American is rapidly filling the field intended to be filled by the Press. Some of those who subscribed for the Press are quitting to take the American. The circulation of the American is wonderful, almost as prominent in all parts of the city as any other paper and in many places more prominent."[76] Within a few weeks the *American* had a weekday circulation of 112,000 and a Sunday circulation of 200,000, whereas the little Scripps *Press*, following its owner's slow-growth policy, had fewer than 3,000 readers. Scripps killed the *Press*, lamenting that "Hearst is filling every crack and cranny of my proposed field."[77]

San Francisco and Los Angeles were quite different examples of Scripps-Hearst competition. In San Francisco, Hearst's morning *Examiner* was well established long before Scripps entered the market. The opposite was the case in Los Angeles, where Scripps bought the *Record* in 1895 and Hearst started the *Examiner* in 1903. In San Francisco, Hearst did not have particularly close ties to the working class or labor unions, so Scripps was not forced to battle for working-class readers. In Los Angeles, however, Hearst cultivated ties with the unions and attempted to position the *Examiner* as the chief rival to the unions' archenemy: the *Times*. Scripps's afternoon *Record* held its own, however, because the *Examiner* was a morning publication. E. H. Bagby, business manager of the *Record*, said that a Hearst afternoon publication would have hurt: "We would have been crippled seriously, because his mode of paper would be hard for the Record to compete with." Hearst's presence did not undermine the *Record*'s carefully cultivated ties to labor. Some union members told Bagby that they did not entirely trust Hearst and thought that he was "their friend only so far as he can help William Randolph Hearst, the organization of Hearst clubs and the furtherance of Hearst's particular beliefs among the masses."[78]

Conclusions

Scripps went to great lengths to avoid competition because it threatened the market segmentation and low-cost strategies he employed to build a national newspaper chain. Competition undermined these strategies in two ways. First, established newspapers might undermine his low-cost strategy by fighting new Scripps ventures, thus raising capital and operating costs, retarding circulation growth, and delaying profitability. Second, other newspapers might also try to reach working-class readers, providing a major threat to Scripps's market segmentation strategy. So he depended on secrecy and still hunts to avoid retaliation when his newspapers were young. Once they were established, he sought to share markets with upscale rivals while driving out labor-oriented publications.

Despite efforts at secrecy and obscurity, Scripps's ventures did not always escape retaliation from established newspapers. Secrecy was not always as extensive as it was in Portland. Scripps's visit to Pueblo, Colorado, in early 1906 alerted local journalists there that he was the backer of the Pueblo *Sun*, started later that year.[79] The young editors and business managers who headed the new Scripps newspapers did not always share his view that small, obscure publications were best. The Spokane *Press*'s first editor, George Putnam, followed company policy by not printing Scripps's name on the masthead, but Putnam bragged to a few too many people about his association with Scripps. Spokane readers might not have known of the newspaper's owner, but others in the newspaper industry—including William Cowles—did.[80]

Established newspapers in Tacoma, Evansville, Memphis, Terre Haute, and Denver all attempted to drive the little Scripps newspapers from the market by offering discounts or premiums both to readers and advertisers. In Seattle, San Francisco, Oklahoma City, and Spokane, rivals eventually lowered their prices to a penny. In most of those cities Scripps's newspapers endured despite the competition, nurtured by the chain's resources (such as the NEA, capital, and machinery) and able to operate on limited resources.

Scripps's real challenge came in competition from other working-class publications. On the one hand, he faced the commercial appeal of newspapers such as Pulitzer's *World* or Hearst's *Examiner;* on the other, he faced the more radical, politically oriented, socialist labor newspapers of the era. He did not want to fight with either style of journalism but wanted to monopolize the working-class audience. To that end, he helped kill several somewhat radical, worker-oriented newspapers in Cincinnati and St. Louis, demonstrating that his fervent opposition to monopoly did not always apply to himself. Yet he was unable to derail William Randolph Hearst, whom he saw as his chief competitor, and tried to avoid confrontations with him altogether. He killed the fledgling Chicago *Press* rather than battle Hearst, and his afternoon newspapers in San Francisco and Los Angeles did not pose a serious threat to Hearst's morning newspapers in those cities.

Scripps's efforts to avoid competition were often in vain in the long run. Battles for circulation and advertising were common among newspapers around 1900, and there was no reason for Scripps to suspect that he could avoid competition. In Denver, the other afternoon newspapers had been fighting with each other long before Scripps's *Express* made its debut. At first, the *Post* and *Times* ignored it, but eventually they battled it as vigorously as they battled each other.[81] In San Francisco, the Scripps *Daily News* quietly expanded while the afternoon *Bulletin* and *Post* fought each other.[82] They, too, eventually caught on to the *Daily News*'s success and attacked it.

Despite all of this, Scripps considered his still hunt a success. In many cases it bought time—allowing his newspapers to become established before retaliation began. Most new ventures became profitable fairly quickly, except for those in Spokane, Pueblo, Nashville, and Fresno—the last three were killed by 1910. All were established relatively cheaply for between $10,000 and $35,000. And some had acquired substantial circulation in their markets. Scripps contended that his newspapers in San Diego, Los Angeles, San Francisco, and Seattle all had a larger city circulation than did any of their rivals. The measure of their success, said Scripps, was that they had not only acquired such circulation but also had done so without others knowing about it. "By reason of our unostentatious methods and our avoidance of all publicity and brag and any kind of advertising, it is more than likely that none of these communities have any suspicion of our relative situation."[83]

Advertising Is
the Enemy

As you know, I recognize the advertiser as the enemy of the
newspaper.
—E. W. Scripps to J. C. Harper, August 5, 1907

IN 1903, THE MANAGER of Seattle's largest department store, the Bon
Marché, demanded that Scripps's Seattle *Star* allow him to censor articles that
might embarrass the store. E. F. Chase, the *Star*'s business manager, believed
that the Bon Marché manager wanted to suppress articles about lawsuits
against the store, fearing that they encouraged other lawsuits. When Chase
refused, the store withdrew its lucrative advertising patronage from the *Star*.
The news depressed Chase. As he told Scripps, "I am very sorry to lose them.
I believe it is a decided injury to the business not to have them."[1]

Scripps, in contrast, was grimly jubilant because the Bon Marché's boycott
proved once again what he long had maintained: Large advertisers were
trouble. "I know by long and bitter experience the character and makeup of
the big advertiser," he advised. "He is invariably a bully to the local newspaper." Scripps said that department stores started advertising in a newspaper
because it was sound business practice. Their high volume of advertising led
to demands for special treatment such as reduced rates and even the suppression of news. When those demands were refused, the big advertiser routinely
"tried to injure the newspaper by the sudden removal of his patronage." Scripps
told Chase that he had made the right decision in refusing the Bon Marché's
demands: "I wish to congratulate you."[2]

Scripps's attitude in this instance reflected his belief that big business was
corrupting the American press. He contended that most U.S. newspapers were
owned by millionaires or else dependent on subsidies from millionaires in the
guise of advertising revenues. The result was a press that reflected only the

views of the elites—"the employing or capitalist class"—with little knowledge or regard for "wager earners" who made up the vast majority of the nation: "Not one half of one percent of the people of the United States are engaged in that class of business which makes them patrons of the advertising departments of newspapers, and yet this small fraction of the community has more influence over the newspapers of the United States than all of the rest of the community put together."[3]

The result was a press that was timid, unable to inform or represent the public. "We are not so much afraid of the law of libel as we are of the ill will of the advertiser," Scripps complained. "We are not only bound to study the feelings of individual advertisers but in great political matters we are compelled to color all of our utterances to suit the real or fancied business necessities of men who sell articles at retail."[4]

Dependence on advertising had contaminated all the American press, Scripps thought. "Who amongst all of us older successful newspaper men have not been corrupted, whether we have been prosperous or otherwise, by being nourished and fed by that very class in the community whose only and one great object seems to be to subvert democracy?"[5] "I do not believe," he said, "that a newspaper publisher can serve honestly both the reading public and the advertising public."[6]

Throughout the newspaper industry there has been ample evidence that advertisers have come to dominate the press. Department stores, the largest advertisers in most American cities, actively—often successfully—worked to influence or suppress news and editorial opinion. Many editors were eager to flatter them with "news" articles.[7] Advertisers insisted on advertisements disguised as news ("reading notices"), dictated where their ads appeared ("position"), and demanded "puffs" promoting them and their products. They retaliated with boycotts when editors were not compliant.

Scripps believed that advertising-laden newspapers had become puppets of big business, ignoring or even opposing the interests of the masses. In contrast, he wanted to create newspapers that were "the servant of the common people and not of the money class and *especially not of the advertising public.*"[8] Consequently, he limited the amount and types of advertisements they accepted. His low-cost strategy made that possible by reducing production costs and thus the need for advertising revenue. Limited reliance on advertising also reflected Scripps's market segmentation strategy and kept his publications closer to the working class rather than to upscale, big business interests.

Growing Concerns about Advertising

During the early years of his journalistic career Scripps did not seem particularly worried about the role of advertising in the American press. His antagonism became pronounced in the middle and late 1890s, when he became convinced that advertising had become the proverbial tail wagging the dog. Scripps ordered far greater scrutiny of advertising in general. "We have come to the parting of the ways. We must choose . . . to make our profit by sale of paper mainly or by sale of advertising space altogether."[9]

Yet he recognized that his newspapers still needed advertising revenue. That would reduce start-up costs of new newspapers and thus allow capital to be invested in other beginning publications. As he told the editor of the Memphis *Press,* "I have only one reason for desiring a good advertising business in a new newspaper and that is that the more money that comes in from that source the less will be the total cost of establishing that property."[10] Scripps also allowed that advertising might be essential in some cases. "Where your local circulation cannot possibly be made to exceed seven or eight thousand," he told the editor of the Oklahoma City *News,* "fixed expenses or rent and mechanical labor are such as to make it impossible to conduct a profit paying paper without an advertising patronage."[11] Advertising in established newspapers also produced revenue that could be spent on improving the news product.

The challenge, as Scripps saw it, was to allow advertising without letting it control the newspapers. His formula for accomplishing that had several components: exhortations to employees, small newspapers, limited space for advertising, relatively high advertising rates, the preeminence of editors, emphasis on circulation revenues, and a refusal to do favors for advertisers.

Exhortations to Employees

Scripps urged that employees be fearless and independent of advertising. He told W. D. Wasson, editor of the San Francisco *News,* that it must follow the general Scripps policies "directly, definitely, and decisively, and without regard to its effect upon our circulation or advertising business."[12]

Scripps's lieutenants reinforced this view. When W. P. Strandborg became editor of the Seattle *Star,* the newspaper's business manager (and chief representative in dealings with advertisers) stressed the importance of independence. "You will not be biased or influenced in the editorial treatment of local or general affairs on account of any money making proposition," Chase told him. "In other words, you are to give no consideration whatever to the effect that may be produced on an advertiser, or class of advertisers by any certain line of policy. You will have only one aim in view . . . larger circulation than any other Seattle paper."[13] B. H. Canfield, Scripps's western regional editor in 1908, told the editor of the Los Angeles *Record* to ignore advertising considerations when producing that newspaper. "I know that the Record is in a serious—perhaps dangerous—condition because of its lack of advertising. . . . Nevertheless, I insist on the enforcement of the rule. And enforce it clear to the hilt, too! Any campaign, crusade or line of editorial policy undertaken with one eye on the advertising situation is something directly contrary to every principle for which the Record stands."[14] In 1908, when the Evansville *Press* faced a local advertising boycott, Jacob C. Harper, that publication's superintendent, told its business manager, "I would sooner lose every line of advertising in the paper than, for a day, to knuckle down or submit to any dictation from our advertising patrons."[15]

Even the appearance of giving into advertising pressure worried Scripps. The business manager of the Fresno *Tribune* was replaced in 1908, shortly after a merchant boycott and W. H. Porterfield's urging the necessity of a better manager. Scripps worried that the firing might look like capitulation to advertising pressure and told Porterfield, "If the advertisers of the City of Fresno ever get it into their heads that you removed Evans because of the opposition of the larger advertisers of that town, the greatest of all possible misfortunes will have happened for the Tribune."[16]

Small Newspapers

All newspapers established during Scripps's major phase of expansion (1899–1906) had four pages, although several grew to eight after becoming well established. He was convinced that small (usually four-page) newspapers were one method for reducing advertisers' power and believed that small publications, with limited production costs due to their size, could subsist primarily on circulation revenues. Larger newspapers had far higher production costs (for news-gathering, paper, and printing) and required far more revenue than circulation alone could produce—thus becoming dependent on advertising. The larger the newspaper, the greater its dependence on advertising. As Scripps said, "The fact is that the smaller a newspaper is, the less room it has for advertising, and the more it makes on the sale of its paper, and the less it depends upon advertisers for its receipts, the more fearless and independent it can be as a journal."[17] When Progressive leaders in Colorado wanted a larger Denver *Express,* one of Scripps's lieutenants responded that it could be more faithful to reform principles by remaining a four-page newspaper. Harper told

Judge Ben B. Lindsey that larger publications were heavily dependent on advertisers and thus frequently could be compromised politically.[18]

Limiting Advertising Space

Unlike many in the U.S. newspaper industry, Scripps imposed sharp restrictions on the volume of advertising he allowed. It was never to exceed half of a newspaper's space—ideally, only 40 percent. R. F. Paine urged the managers of the Evansville *Press* to limit advertisements to eight columns (out of twenty-eight) during that newspaper's first year. The prospectuses of several other ventures begun in 1906 proposed reserving between twenty and twenty-two columns daily for news, leaving ten to twelve for advertising.[19]

More important, Scripps limited the size of individual advertisements. None were full-page, and few were larger than forty column inches (slightly bigger than a quarter of a page). The prospectus of the Pueblo *Sun* banned advertisements larger than forty inches, the proposal for a newspaper in Salt Lake City called for a thirty-inch limit, and the Terre Haute *Post* and the Denver *Express* each had a twenty-inch limit. The prospectuses of the Dallas *Dispatch* and the Nashville *Times* promised to "discourage too extensive use of its space by a few large advertisers."[20]

Limiting large advertisements and holding to four pages purposely excluded department store advertising. That was intentional, as Scripps told the editor of the Tacoma *Times*. "No small part of the value of my scheme and method of small papers is the fact that patronage of this class of customers is eliminated." Some department stores were willing to countenance four-page newspapers but balked at small advertisements. Those in Dallas, Denver, and Oklahoma City refused to advertise in Scripps's newspapers because of the limit.[21]

Not only did large advertisers try to influence content, but it was also the case that advertising was not all profit. Production costs associated with advertising could be high. Department stores, for example, usually demanded rates lower than small-scale advertisers, thus reducing profit margins. They also wanted advertisements to be changed daily in contrast to small ads that were changed infrequently, thus driving up composition costs.[22]

A high volume of advertising required extensive machinery and personnel, further raising costs. When E. H. Wells, editor of the Tacoma *Times,* wanted to buy a new press to expand and accommodate the demand for advertising, L. T. Atwood pointed out that the costs involved (a new press and increased expenditure for paper, news-gathering, and printing) were greater than anticipated revenues. The profit on additional pages (above the standard four-page newspaper) would be less than what could be realized on the simple four-page newspaper.[23] Scripps also refused to allow Porterfield to buy a new Linotype for the Sacramento *Star* in 1905. He had wanted to accommodate a one-year, twelve-thousand-inch advertising contract from a Sacramento department store until Scripps observed that the new machine (and related expenses for labor, electricity, and repairs) would run between $4,000 and $4,500. Total revenues, however, would be only $1,440, an arrangement that could be profitable only if the department store renewed or increased its advertising. The *Star* would be dependent upon the store's good will, and that was not independent journalism.[24]

Scripps preferred advertisements from small businesses that would not change their notices frequently. The prospectuses of the Dallas *Dispatch*, Nashville *Times*, and Oklahoma City *News* promised they would "cultivate a numerous clientele of small advertisers." The Cleveland *Press* reserved its last page—a popular space—for new and small advertisers.[25] Harper told H. J. Richmond, business manager of the Dallas *Dispatch*, "You know that we prefer a large number of small advertisers to a few big advertisers. The getting and holding of a larger number means more direct expense but the resultant advantage and security is very great. Coercive combination is almost impossible with a large number of advertisers."[26]

Increasing Advertising Rates

Scripps's newspapers not only refused advertising but also sought to control its volume by having high advertising rates compared to competitors. They all began, or attempted to begin, by charging nearly 20 cents per inch for advertisements. As advertising pressure grew, so did the rate. The rationale was that limiting the amount of space devoted to advertising made that space more valuable; advertisers would clamor for it and be willing to pay more. The strategy worked, at least to the extent that some newspapers were able to keep rates relatively high. In 1906, when the Sacramento *Star* was just a year old, its rate for classified advertisements was equal to that of the Sacramento *Union*, which had twice the circulation. The Portland *News* had an average rate of 24 cents an inch during its first year. Both the Spokane *Press* and the Tacoma *Times* raised rates when they faced high demands for advertising space. The Denver *Express*'s rate began at 25 cents per inch—relatively high for a new, four-page publication with limited circulation. As the volume of advertising increased so did the rate, climbing to 34 cents an inch in sixteen months.[27]

The Preeminence of Editors

Another strategy for maintaining the independence of Scripps newspapers from advertisers was the policy of vesting ultimate control in editors rather than business manager-publishers. In a departure from newspaper practices of the era, Scripps editors had control over the entire content of newspapers, including advertising. Harper told F. R. Peters, editor of the Evansville *Press,* that an "editor controls every line that goes into the paper, advertising as well as news. He should not permit his paper to be made the means of buncoing his readers."[28] Editors were also charged with the task of maintaining standards on news and advertising and avoiding all questionable advertisements that might undermine independence. Paine told Henry White, editor of the Sacramento *Star,* that the decision to accept or reject advertising "is a question wholly within Editor White's jurisdiction." No one (except Scripps, the controlling stockholder) could compel an editor to publish an advertisement.[29]

Scripps also attempted to keep news-gathering and advertising widely apart. The Newspaper Enterprise Association was created to be quite separate from advertising and general business concerns. As Harper observed, "It is so far removed from the business offices as to be less affected than some of our editorial staffs with business office considerations."[30]

Circulation Revenues

Independence from advertisers rested, too, on a steady supply of circulation revenues. Scripps said that newspapers should rely primarily on such revenue for operating revenues and profits, otherwise they could "have no independence from the selfish, greedy business or advertising public."[31] He believed that readers were far less likely than advertisers to withdraw patronage in disputes over content. Even if readers did boycott, they had far less economic clout than advertisers. Individual readers contributed about $3 a year to revenues, whereas individual advertisers might contribute hundreds or thousands. "One sulky advertiser can take more money out of a paper, as profits, than two thousand disgruntled readers," Scripps told one lieutenant.[32] Building revenues from readers was slower than from advertisers, but Scripps argued that it was much safer and more stable. "A business property then that depends on subscribers for its profit, must be one hundred times safer and sounder than that which depends on an advertiser," he told A. O. Andersson, editor of the Dallas *Dispatch.*[33]

New Scripps publications were dedicated to growth in circulation rather than in advertising. When the Evansville *Press* was established, Paine advised that "your aim now is circulation not advertising." A. R. Hopkins, founding editor of the Pueblo *Sun,* reported that "we are endeavoring to conduct the little paper as near as your plans as possible. We seem to be doing very well and circulation is going up every day. We have thus far paid little attention to the advertising." J. P. Hamilton, founding editor of the Denver *Express*, told Harper that once circulation had hit around two thousand, "advertisers are beginning to nibble. I have followed Mr. Scripps' advice about not seeking advertising, but simply going around and getting acquainted with the business men and telling them of our venture."[34]

The No-Favors Policy

Scripps newspapers refused to grant special favors to advertisers. In particular, Scripps dictated that his newspapers never promote (puff) an advertiser, never run advertisements disguised as news (reading notices), or never place advertising in special positions (e.g., at the top of the page or surrounded by reading matter). He intended that advertisers rely on his newspapers because they needed to do so, not because of favors bestowed. As he said, "If such an advertiser's business is gotten by making great concessions, by ardent solicitation, and by granting him all sorts of favors, such as the suppression of news that would give him offense and such as the publishing of puffs, of persons or business commendations, the inevitable result is that the editorial department of such a paper quickly becomes corrupted."[35] "I do not want advertising patronage as a result of kindly feeling. I want it to be the result of purely business considerations on account of the advertiser," Scripps told the editor of the Los Angeles *Record*.[36] Canfield reminded editors that reading notices were forbidden, and Paine praised Henry White, editor of the Sacramento *Star*, for refusing to disguise advertisements as news. "I think you are absolutely correct," he said, "in refusing to run paid theatrical puffs or any other reading matter business without the usual designation as ads by use of dashes, stars, etc."[37]

Special position in Scripps newspapers was not to be awarded as part of advertising contracts. Four-page newspapers in particular had few ideal positions to grant in the first place, and locking up those made composition and production difficult. When Andersson noted that the policy had resulted in lost advertising because Dallas advertisers were accustomed to position rights and that the rule had demoralized the advertising staff, Paine retorted that it was the staff's job to follow the owner's directions. If they could not do that, they should quit.[38]

The prospectuses of the Spokane *Press*, Tacoma *Times*, Denver *Express*, Dallas *Dispatch*, and the Oklahoma City *News* all included a ban on position advertising. LeRoy Sanders, editor of the *Times*, told Scripps that he had always avoided granting position privileges to advertisers. "I have insisted from the first that I would not prostitute the news for the benefit of the advertisers in the way of giving positions to ads. I have made my rule stick thus far but I have never known definitely just what authority I had in the matter of dictating relative to the character and position of ads."[39]

Independence in Practice—In practice, Scripps newspapers demonstrated a great deal of independence from advertisers. They refused a large volume of advertising, often did not carry advertisements from local department stores, and successfully withstood efforts by large advertisers to influence news and opinion. They also rejected advertising that ran counter to key editorial positions. In 1905, for instance, the Cincinnati *Post* rejected three advertisements from the Postum Cereal Company (maker of Grape Nuts): two advertised the cereal and a third attacked labor unions. The company insisted that the newspaper take all three advertisements or none. John Vandercook, the editor, told Scripps, "Of course, the Post printed none of them."[40] When the Standard Oil Company offered an advertisement defending itself from criticism by the Scripps newspapers, Paine quickly notified editors that company policy forbade its publication.[41] In 1906 Scripps newspapers refused advertisements from the Owl Drug Store chain, which also wanted to attack labor unions.[42]

Temperance was a major issue in Indiana during the early 1900s, and Scripps newspapers there refused liquor advertising so they would be free to report the views of both wets and dries with apparent even-handedness. The presence of liquor advertisements might have made opposition to prohibition seem economic rather than principled. The editor of the Terre Haute *Post* was told to avoid all liquor advertising so the *Post* could cover the issue without appearing beholden to liquor interests.[43]

In 1906 Harper instructed the editor of the Evansville *Press* to refuse renewal of an advertising contract from the Evansville Gas and Electric Lighting Company because such advertisements limited the newspaper's ability to discuss municipal lighting franchises. The advertisements "make an unfavorable impression upon me and are likely to do the same on others," Harper said. Paine objected to similar advertising in the Pueblo *Sun* and instructed its management to end them as quickly as possible.[44]

The high-spirited independence of Scripps's newspapers is probably clearest from the frequency of disputes with business interests and local chambers of commerce. Scripps publications faced advertiser-led boycotts on at least thirteen occasions in nine cities between 1899 and 1908.[45] Such boycotts originated in advertisers' ultimatums, which the newspapers refused. They weathered subsequent boycotts, and most continued to produce profits.

In Cincinnati and Cleveland, for example, theater owners tried to control the news columns of the *Post* and *Press*. Failing that, they withdrew their advertising. In 1896 the Cincinnati Theater Managers Association approached McRae and told him, "We were told that if the criticisms were not more moderate in character of tone that advertising would be withdrawn." The *Post* refused, and most of the advertising was withdrawn.[46] In 1901 the Cleveland *Press* faced similar problems when theater owners in that city demanded greater coverage of shows and the *Press's* editor refused. The theaters withdrew all their advertisements.[47]

Disputes with major merchants—usually the owners and managers of department stores—were common. Key Cincinnati department stores withdrew advertising from the *Post* in 1900 to protest its news policies. The Shillito Company refused to advertise in the newspaper because the *Post*—correctly—had noted that one of its employees had been exposed to smallpox. Mabley and Carew, one of the largest department stores in Cincinnati, withdrew its advertising because the *Post* reported on an elevator accident in the Carew Building.[48] The advertising returned, only to be pulled again in 1906 when the *Post* editorially attacked directors of a local gas company—one of whom was J. T. Carew, a partner in the store.[49]

In San Diego, the *Sun* had similar problems. The local real estate board boycotted it in 1906 because of the newspaper's assault on questionable business practices. The Los Angeles *Record's* pro-labor editorial stance also sparked protests and advertising boycotts. One department store told the *Record* in 1903 that key local merchants were "very displeased with the Record's attitude" on labor unions.[50] Scripps wrote to the director of the Los Angeles Merchants and Manufacturers' Association, F. J. Zeehandelaar, telling him that Scripps newspapers had a "duty" to address community issues involving "the lives of the rich and poor alike." He also made clear his resolve: "I am confident that the Merchant and Manufacturers of Los Angeles are far too intelligent to desire to exercise any influence whatever in the way of abridging or hampering the entire freedom of the press in discussing all matters of public concern."[51]

Similar battles erupted elsewhere. Seattle's largest department store, the Bon Marché, withdrew advertising from the *Star* when that newspaper's staff refused to give the store the right to edit all copy about itself. Chase told Scripps, "unless we would state that we would in the future refrain from printing news which they considered might injure them without first letting them see proof and cut out what they found objection to." That was impossible. As the largest store in Seattle "they have all the accidents and all the suits brought against them." The editor would "give them the safe fair treatment he did any small store or any individual who never advertised a dollar's worth and no different treatment." But they refused.[52] In St. Louis, the Barr Dry Goods Company, one of the largest in the city, withdrew its advertising from the *Chronicle* in 1906 when the newspaper refused to suppress a story on the arrest of a chauffeur employed by the president of the company—who was also the president of the St. Louis Advertisers Association. Milton McRae told Scripps that "Barr's advertising alone amounts of $8,000.00 per annum. No other newspaper in the city published the facts except the Star Chronicle, the editor refusing to suppress them."[53] In 1908, when the Evansville *Press* also faced an advertising boycott, Harper told the editor not to back down because "Evansville advertisers must know that they only buy a certain amount of space; that they cannot either purchase or influence the news or Editorial conduct of our paper."[54]

Non-advertising Newspapers—Despite great effort, Scripps found it difficult to inculcate his distrust of advertising. The chain's miserly approach to expenditures and its requirement of 15 percent profits made any source of revenue seem appealing to employees. Editors and business managers were also highly motivated to increase revenues and profits to generate dividends that would offset their low salaries. Advertising was a much faster route to profit than circulation. Wells said that "the idea of getting in all the money I could legitimately, at the earliest possible moment, has been strong in me, I will admit, for the insistent pressure to break even, a feeling that I should do so, made me turn to advertising receipts as the quickest source of revenue."[55]

Industrywide norms seem to have influenced Scripps editors and business managers. Few shared his preference for four-page newspapers. They enlarged their publications to eight pages as soon as they could and thus needed to increase advertising volume considerably. Both Scripps and Paine berated various editors for accepting too many advertisements.[56] Some editors wanted big advertisers; landing a department store advertisement was proof that merchants took a new newspaper seriously. Department store advertising was also valued at older and larger Scripps newspapers. The Cincinnati *Post* sought it in 1903 with a flyer that touted itself as "the people's paper."[57]

Some editors claimed that readers liked advertising and that Scripps's newspapers were losing potential customers because of their lack of department store ads. He rejected those views. "I have for the last dozen or more years been sickened with the din that has been poured into my ears to the effect that newspaper readers desire advertisements just as much as they do reading or news or other matter. My common sense and experience both rejected this proposal."[58]

Fairly constant supervision by Scripps and his central office was necessary to enforce his policies and rules on advertising. He came to believe that most newspaper managers could not successfully balance editorial integrity and advertising. Consequently, by 1904 he began to develop the idea of a non-advertising newspaper that would depend entirely on circulation revenue. After he had created a national telegraph news service in 1907, Scripps believed that a newspaper without advertising could be started successfully in the nation's largest cities—New York, Philadelphia, Boston, Baltimore, Chicago, St. Louis, and Pittsburgh—where large populations could produce substantial circulation revenues.[59] The project was delayed for several years, however; the first and only Scripps advertising-free project, the *Day Book,* began in 1911 in Chicago and died in 1917.[60] It was fearless, as Scripps wanted, but did not achieve mass circulation and never broke even. Its problems were many, including a lack of identity and Scripps's lack of energy to promote it. He had handed over many management responsibilities to his son, James, after 1908. In his late fifties and early sixties he did not have the fire that had driven the early expansion of his newspaper empire.

Conclusions

Advertisers had become important patrons of American newspapers by 1900. They provided the chief source of revenue, filled half or more of the nation's newspaper columns daily, and had impact on how news was defined.[61] That, Scripps believed, had robbed the American press of its vitality and ability to serve the public and democracy. The advertising-dominated press, he asserted, was a tool of the elites rather than the masses. Scripps realized that his newspapers, if true to his market segmentation strategy of serving the working class, would rile business interests. "My idea of a small paper . . . has always been based upon my clear understanding that a really independent newspaper serving the public must be fought by such 'interests,'" he said. Therefore, newspapers must be organized so that "under no circumstances could any combination of business men put it out of business."[62]

Although Scripps set out to create newspapers free from advertiser influence, corralling advertising was not easy. Newspapers—including his—relied on advertising to supplement circulation revenues. The low-cost strategy, which reduced start-up and operating costs, allowed him to lessen dependence on advertisers (compared to competitors) and adopt a series of rules that restricted the nature and size of advertisements.

Scripps did succeed in freeing his newspapers from extensive advertiser control, and they did not give in to advertiser demands over news. Moreover, they were able to continue publishing (and producing profits) despite more than a dozen advertising boycotts in the early twentieth century. The struggle was not easy, for Scripps was trying to counter a commercialism that permeated not only the press but also society at large. He had difficulty convincing editors that advertising was the enemy. Only constant vigilance kept his newspapers true to his policies.

An Advocate of the
Working Class

It shall be the first principle of this publication to be the organ, the
mouthpiece, the apologist, the defender and the advocate of the
working class.
—E. H. Wells to E. W. Scripps, July 1, 1903 (Prospectus, Tacoma *Times*,
1903)

IN MAY 1889 THE FOUR Scripps family newspapers—the Detroit *Evening
News,* Cleveland *Press,* St. Louis *Chronicle,* and Cincinnati *Post*—announced
plans to send a delegation of forty U.S. workers to the Paris International Exposition to study the state of European industry. The *Press* said that the trip
would provide invaluable ideas for industrial innovation, greater productivity,
and better working conditions. It was "no charity affair, no junketing party,
no purely pleasure excursion," but rather "a matter of business designed to be
instructive to those who go and to those who will read . . . the accounts of what
the forty discover in the way of new things in the industrial field, that is of
things new to Americans."[1]

In announcing this "Great Enterprise," the Scripps newspapers invited labor groups (particularly within their circulation areas) to help pick the delegates. What was needed were workers who represented "the most important
trades" and were known for "their sobriety and reliability, their capacity for
observation and their ability to convey to their fellow workmen, in plain but
clear and exact English, a fair conception of what they have seen and studied
in Paris and throughout Europe."[2]

The response was enthusiastic. Public officials, labor leaders, members of
the clergy, and economists endorsed the trip. Terence V. Powderly, the long-
time "Master Workman" of the Knights of Labor, called the enterprise "a very
laudable one," and Samuel Gompers of the American Federation of Labor
recommended one of the delegates ultimately chosen. Labor groups met to
nominate delegates—and voted their thanks to the Scripps newspapers for "the
interest shown our cause." Nominations flowed in; the Cincinnati *Post* received

more than three hundred for the ten delegates it chose. Farewell speeches from public officials and colorful parades with brass bands were part of the ceremonies as delegates left their hometowns and headed in mid-July to New York to catch their boat to Europe. While there, they visited key industrial centers (Liverpool, Birmingham, London, Antwerp, Essen, and Lyons) in addition to the Paris Exposition.[3]

All of this was reported in great detail in Scripps newspapers between May 4, when the trip was announced, through October 1889. Articles described the details of the trip and also provided a broad view of American labor, including discussions of the needs and interests of U.S. workers and profiles of the hard-working individuals (mechanics, dressmakers, railroad engineers, and others) chosen as delegates. During these six months the ingenuity, hard work, and loyalty of American labor were common themes in Scripps newspapers.[4]

The ingenuity and hard work of Scripps newspapers were important themes in the coverage as well. Scripps publications promoted not only American labor but also themselves throughout the spring and summer of 1889. A Cleveland *Press* headline heralded "A Great Enterprise in Behalf of American Industries" and a "Most Novel and Important Journalistic Undertaking."[5] Other articles routinely carried praise for Scripps newspapers as the friend of the American worker. The governor of Ohio praised the trip and noted, "I am more particularly gratified that THE SCRIPPS LEAGUE should have the spirit and generosity to undertake it."[6] One labor leader said although the government should have sponsored the trip, "it is exceedingly pleasing to me to know, however, that THE SCRIPPS LEAGUE has taken up the matter."[7]

Self-promotion by newspapers was fairly common in the late nineteenth century but seldom on this scale. In an age when American newspapers were calling attention to themselves by offering prizes in a wide array of contests, the Scripps "Workingmen's Expedition" stood out for its ambition, price tag, and explicit pro-labor point of view. Most other U.S. newspapers of the era offered more modest contests, with books, maps, or lithographs (worth a few hundred dollars or less) as prizes. The Scripps League, however, spent more than $25,000—a huge amount for such a cost-conscious company—to send the forty delegates, reporters, and organizers on the trip.[8] Coverage praised organized labor at a time when many newspapers (and Americans) found collective bargaining and strikes to be anathema; few newspapers solicited the advice of trade unions in the way the Scripps League did.

The Workingmen's Expedition was the brainchild of E. W. Scripps during his short presidency of the Scripps family newspapers and of Milton McRae. They saw the expedition as a good way to emphasize their ties to the working class. McRae predicted that the venture would "tickle every faction of organized labor." Mindful of the cost, he cautioned that "everything that we [do] in connection with it ought to pay us a revenue" through increased circulation or advertising. Another employee told Scripps that the Paris trip would be popular with workers and "strengthen you with the masses generally."[9]

Unlike most publishers of his era, Scripps saw working-class readers as a lucrative market. The newspaper industry ignored them, he claimed, leaving that market uncontested. Filling it could be very profitable.[10] Substantial revenues could be gained from circulation alone if newspapers were run cheaply enough. Even though workers lacked the purchasing power of the upper classes, their numbers made them a significant consumer group and thus of value to advertisers. In 1903 Scripps told the circulation editor of his Los Angeles *Record* that "the wage earning class is by far the largest purchasing class of Los Angeles, and however much the advertisers may respect the carriage trade, and desire it, they are absolutely dependent upon the basket trade, and dinner pail brigade, for their prosperity."[11]

The desire to reach working-class readers influenced content in all of the Scripps newspapers, beginning with the Detroit *Evening News*. There, Scripps learned from his older brother James that working-class journalism could be popular and lucrative. He followed that formula in his first editorship at the Cleveland *Press* and in creating his newspaper chain, providing extensive and sympathetic coverage of working-class issues and concerns. Most prospectuses for Scripps newspapers established after 1900 pledged allegiance to the "common people" and promised to serve as the "organ, mouthpiece, the apologist, the defender and the advocate of the wage earning class."[12]

Scripps's devotion to the working class reflected his personality, ideals, and business acumen. Poor as a youth, he had a deep distrust of the rich. He particularly opposed predatory wealth—elites exploiting the masses. Ruthless tycoons such as John D. Rockefeller drew his rage. Beyond that, he also was an entrepreneur who recognized that serving the working class was probably the most efficient way to build a newspaper chain. Serving an untapped portion of the overall newspaper market would be far easier and cheaper than creating publications identical to those already operating.

Changes in the Nature of News

Scripps newspapers reflected the changing definitions of news in the last half of the nineteenth century. By midcentury, newspapers had begun to move away from political advocacy and the party patronage that supported it. As Jeffery Rutenbeck has shown, the trend accelerated in the 1870s and beyond.[13] Newspapers began to adopt a more neutral, fact-based approach to news, and advocacy was increasingly relegated to an opinion (or editorial) page. The need to attract readers placed greater emphasis on making news more interesting, and the result was content far more sensationalistic than most of the political advocacy common earlier in the century.

Although newspapers became ostensibly more neutral, they still wielded substantial power in choice of topics. The notion of a press as a watchdog on society's institutions (particularly on government) spurred the "journalism of exposure." The press published articles that exposed malfeasance or corruption and called for reform, at least implicitly. Scripps's newspapers promoted working-class interests in that way. One editorial, "The Press Is the Modern Searchlight," described this style of journalism:

> The lime light of publicity is the great discoverer and the great deterrent of evil. The old scriptures are true today as thousands of years ago. Men love darkness rather than light because their deeds are evil. And when the searchlight of the newspaper is thrown upon their deeds, what a scatterment and a terror! . . .
>
> The searchlight is turned upon the predatory raid of the millionaire and he quails before it. It flashes into the light of public scorn the looters of great insurance companies and blasts and ruins whole families. . . . And now it is turned upon the corporations that are monopolies and now upon the graft and corruption of the railroads. All hail the searchlight![14]

The "searchlight" philosophy led to articles calling attention to the exploitation of children:

NEARLY TWO MILLION AMERICAN
CHILDREN ARE INDUSTRIAL SLAVES[15]

to impure food:

WATERING OF MILK IS
SHOWN BY CITY'S TESTS
Violations of Pure Milk
Law are Discovered
By New Inspector and
Warnings Will Be
Given Offenders[16]

and to unfair wages:

STORY OF POVERTY OF STREET CAR MEN
For Seven and One Half Days Work the Employe of
the Franchise Grabbers Receives the Princely
Wage of $13.50.[17]

In addition to this "journalism of exposure," Scripps newspapers relied on explicit advocacy—in editorials, editorial cartoons, and even news articles—to provide content that would resonate with working-class readers.

The Content of Scripps Newspapers

Scripps's market segmentation strategy produced newspaper content that fell into three general areas: advocacy of the rights of the common people, support for Progressive Era reform legislation, and close alliance with labor unions. Editorials, editorial cartoons, and news articles addressed each area.

The Common People

In 1904 E. W. Scripps told the editor of the San Francisco *Daily News* that "every page and every article" should reflect the interests of the common people. "Hook yourself tight and close to the heart of the common people. Be always with them and of them."[18] In practice, Scripps newspapers were eager to advocate policies that might benefit the lower classes in society and quick to defend them when threatened by the arrogance, greed, or selfishness of the rich.

Advocating the interests of the common people was a chief characteristic of Scripps's short but highly successful tenure as editor of the Cleveland *Press* (1878–80). The *Press* advocated extended hours for that city's public library, arguing that working-class readers—who could not easily afford to buy books—could only go there in the evening or early morning.[19] Under Scripps, the *Press* also exposed overpriced school books, calling them "a well-planned swindle of the people which falls with terrible severity upon . . . poor parents."[20] In addition, readers were warned that the fee-driven justice system in Cleveland often sacrificed the interests of working-class defendants. Scripps defended these attacks on injustice because it was the duty of the press "to educate and inform the masses of workingmen as to what is best to their interests."[21] Such devotion to the working class apparently was successful, because the *Press*'s circulation grew rapidly. In April 1879, when it was only six months old, Scripps claimed that circulation doubled that of its afternoon competitors.[22] The newspaper was enlarged that month but still turned down advertisements because of a lack of space.[23]

Scripps believed that his embrace of the common people was the basis for his success. Years later, he told a lieutenant that his Cleveland *Press* experiences had taught him that it was "not only profitable but pleasant and honorable to advocate the laboring class."[24] Throughout his career, his newspapers served as advocates for the common people: They raised money for orphans, the poor, and families whose homes had been burned; printed designs for inexpensive "workingmen's homes"; and engaged in a wide variety of crusades—for safety measures in theaters to prevent disasters from fires, free textbooks for public school children, protection of city water supplies, and cheaper gas, electricity, coal, and water.[25] Many of these crusades were popular with the readers Scripps wanted to reach. E. H. Wells, editor of the Tacoma *Times,* told him that he planned to start a crusade for cheaper gas in that city. A similar crusade when he was editor of Scripps's Seattle *Star* had boosted circulation by more than four thousand.[26]

Streetcars—In advocating the interests of the common people, Scripps newspapers paid significant attention to the price, safety, and quality of streetcar service. In most U.S. cities of the era, streetcar companies were privately owned but held government franchises allowing them to use the public domain (city streets) in exchange for providing a vital service (public transport).[27] It was a working-class issue for several reasons: Working-class people composed the vast majority of streetcar patrons; unlike upper classes (with private carriages or automobiles), they had no other way to get to work; and their often-meager incomes meant that streetcar fares constituted a major expense.

In 1888 the Cleveland *Press* argued that streetcar fares (5 cents for a single ticket but 4 cents if the customer bought $5 worth of tickets at one time) discriminated against common people.[28] By the early twentieth century, Scripps newspapers were advocating 3 cent fares. Articles focused on Thomas Johnson, mayor of Cleveland, and his long but ultimately successful battle for 3 cent car fares in that city.[29] In 1903 the Los Angeles *Record,* in a front-page editorial, argued that a reduction from 5 cent to 3 cent fares on that city's streetcars would have great value for the working class: "To the laboring man, the difference between $3 a month carfare, for two rides a day, and $1.80 a month for carfare, at 3 cents a ride, means everything. That little $1.20 will feed his family for a day, or a day and a half. It will buy his wife a new shirt waist. It will buy his boy a pair of shoes. . . . It will send the sick child into the country. It will help pay the rent."[30]

Scripps newspapers also crusaded for cleaner streetcars, increased service to avoid excessive crowding, slower speeds (arguing that speeding frequently led to fatal accidents), and wheelguards and cowcatchers.[31] They were quick to blame fatalities on the lack of such devices. The Cleveland *Press* described one crash in 1890:

BLOOD
On the Wheels and Track
Another Terrible and Sick
ening Motor Slaughter
An Italian Almost Cut in
Two on Euclid av.[32]

The article reported that "unguarded wheels" were the problem. The dead man—who was planning to get married in a few days—was "thrown under the wheels of the motor and mangled in such a horrible manner that the people who witnessed the accident were fairly sickened." In 1902 and 1903 the Los Angeles *Record* frequently ran a column entitled "Daily Victims" to list those injured or killed in streetcar mishaps.[33] A front-page cartoon in 1903 showed a speeding streetcar running down a female pedestrian. Headlined, "A Common Occurrence," the accompanying text cautioned, "The tragedy is repeated every day. Study the cartoon well. Your turn, reader, may be next."[34]

Enemies of the Common People—Scripps newspapers were at their most vibrant when battling enemies of the common people. In 1902, in a conference preparatory to the establishment of the Spokane *Press,* Scripps and that newspaper's prospective editor, George Putnam, agreed that it would be "the advocate and special pleader of the poor classes as *against the whole plutocratic and aristocratic combinations, political, economic and social.* "[35]

All Scripps newspapers embraced this battle against the "combinations"— the enemies of the common people. The chief culprit was often big business— greedy monopolies and trusts that sustained artificially high prices and thus reaped huge profits at the expense of the masses. Scripps's newspapers pilloried these malefactors, exposing their practices and seeking public outrage to force reform. They devoted an average of 63 percent of total business coverage to describing and attacking corruption and greed and examined monopolies and trusts in a wide variety of businesses, from railroads to beef and bread. Scripps's competitors, in sharp contrast, devoted an average of only 5.3 percent of their business coverage to those topics.[36]

Scripps publications exposed monopolies controlling supplies of coal, food, milk, and ice.[37] John D. Rockefeller was a favorite target for decades; his creation of the Standard Oil trust seemed to represent evil incarnate to Scripps's newspapers. When the U.S. government began antitrust proceedings against Standard Oil in 1906, they not only carried that news but also hoped for Rockefeller's scalp:

FIGHT IN OHIO BEGUN
AGAINST STANDARD OIL
Prosecution of Giant Corporation Is Preliminary
to Prosecution of John D. Rockefeller Individually.[38]

Scripps's Sacramento *Star* ran an article stressing how rich Rockefeller was. "John D's Income, Can You Grasp It?" alleged that Rockefeller's income amounted to $55.63 every minute—nearly four times the weekly wage of many laborers.[39]

Scripps newspapers dramatized the impact of trusts and monopolies on the masses by creating editorial cartoon characters—Mr. and Mrs. Common People—who were constantly at odds with greedy and grasping businesses. In one cartoon, "Modern Robbery of Mother Hubbard," Mrs. Common People (like Mother Hubbard) finds her family's larder bare, while a wolf ("Food Trust Wolf") says, "I Beat You to It." In another, Mrs. Common People is walking with "Low Priced Grocer" when thugs ("GROCERY TRUST") attack her escort. The headline reads, "GOOD OLD ROCKEFELLER METHODS IN THE GROCERY BUSINESS." Still another cartoon has Mr. Common People figuring a mathematics problem: The cost of living has increased 40 percent whereas wages have increased only 17 percent, leaving 23 percent to "Prosperity." An onlooker— a wealthy fat man labeled "The Trusts"—tells him that prices will continue to outstrip wages: "Cheer Up, the Worse Is Yet to Come!!" Another editorial cartoon depicts a picnic, where "THE TRUSTS" share a huge watermelon ("$180,000,000 Dividends") while Mr. Common People gets only a lemon.[40]

Reform

Scripps newspapers also devoted substantial attention to a wide array of reform measures that would increase the political or economic well-being of the common people. In particular, they supported the Progressive movement's effort to check the excesses of industrialization by wresting political and economic power from elites and returning it to the masses.[41] The goal resonated with the working class, which stood to gain much from the Progressive goals of municipal ownership of utilities, as well as pure food and drug legislation, limits on child labor, popular election of U.S. senators, and initiative, referendum, and recall. Scripps's newspapers publicized and endorsed much of the Progressive agenda—in particular, municipal ownership of utilities, pure food legislation, and a series of electoral reforms.

Municipal Ownership of Utilities—Municipal ownership of utilities may well have been the Progressive-era issue that the Scripps newspapers embraced most fervently.[42] Of all the reforms of that era, it likely had the most direct bearing on the day-to-day life of many workers. Rapid urban growth in the late nineteenth century had created demand for a wide variety of services—sewers, paved streets, water, electricity, and public transport. Corporations dominated these services, securing lucrative contracts (franchises) from city governments, often operating as monopolies, and frequently providing poor but high-priced service.[43] All citizens were forced to pay inflated prices for daily necessities such as water or electricity, an injustice that was most pronounced for those with limited incomes—the working class.

Advocates of municipal ownership believed it would lower the costs of basic services. Unlike private companies, municipally owned utilities did not need to pile up huge profits to please stockholders. One Scripps editorial concluded that municipal ownership would eventually be widespread in the United States "and the people will wonder why they tolerated a condition that made of a few men millionaires, gave to the public so little and charged them so much for it."[44] Another emphasized the success of municipal ownership both in Europe and in the United States:

HOW MUNICIPAL
OWNERSHIP WORKS
Europe Seems to Find It a Pretty
Good Thing, Take It by
and Large.[45]

Still other articles reported that municipal ownership of utilities worked well in other cities. It was cheaper than private ownership as well as safer, graft free, and less likely to encounter labor problems. A three-part series (from the Newspaper Enterprise Association) on the topic concluded that "where it fails it is the fault of men, not the system."[46]

Scripps's newspapers defined the issue as a contest between the common people and private companies seeking to profit from daily necessities such as electricity and water. Given those competing interests, public ownership was inevitable.[47] One editorial argued that municipal ownership was essentially democratic.[48] Others urged both city ownership of local utilities and federal ownership of irrigation systems to speed population in the West.[49]

In Los Angeles and San Diego, Scripps newspapers gave extensive coverage and support to local efforts to create municipal water companies. The *San Diegan-Sun* supported plans to buy water-bearing lands and organize a municipal water company in 1905, arguing that such action would produce a large supply of cheap water and free the city from reliance on private companies.[50]

In 1902 the Seattle *Star* strongly supported a ballot measure allowing the city to generate its own electricity. Articles and editorials supported the argument that municipal ownership would produce cheaper power.[51]

Pure Food Legislation—Scripps newspapers also focused on the pure food controversy, a prominent issue early in the twentieth century. Muckrakers such as Upton Sinclair provided riveting and shocking evidence that producers blithely sold tainted food to unsuspecting consumers, and the clamor for reform ultimately led to the Pure Food and Drug Act of 1906.[52] In the years before the new law, reformers documented abuses and created momentum for government regulation. Like electricity or water rates, it was an issue that pitted the common people against self-serving corporations, and the Scripps chain covered it extensively. Typical headlines were:

SICKNESS AND DEATH LURKS IN NEARLY
HALF OF THE NATION'S MILK SUPPLY[53]

and

INDECENCY AS WELL AS
FILTH IN PACKING HOUSES
Woman Detective Tells of
Abuses in Chicago Slaugh-
ter Pens—Case of a Man
Who Fell into a Vat.[54]

As part of the pure food campaign, Scripps newspapers focused on the quality of milk, warning readers that preservatives such as formaldehyde could injure or kill infants.[55] A Los Angeles *Record* article was headed:

BABIES BEING EMBALMED ALIVE BY USE OF
FORMALDEHYDE IN MILK.[56]

The front-page article included an editorial-like recommendation from the *Record* that the local board of health hire a "practical chemical expert" to analyze "the use and abuse of food preservatives." Articles and editorials also explored the various suggestions made by reformers, with particular emphasis on inspections by local health officials and stiff punishment for anyone selling tainted food.[57]

Electoral Reform—The belief that corporate interests controlled government spurred proposals to make government more responsive to the people. These included direct election of U.S. senators as well as initiative, referendum, and recall. A thirteen-part series of articles from the Newspaper Enterprise Association in early 1906 attempted to show that thirteen U.S. senators were active agents for big business interests. An editorial, "The Men Who Rule the Senate and Misrepresent the People," accompanied the series. Other articles reported on reformers who advocated direct election of U.S. senators, and editorials also supported direct election.[58]

Scripps newspapers also publicized and supported other means of making government more democratic. The Los Angeles *Record* advocated recall legislation in 1904 and carried front-page articles and editorials supporting the recall of city council member J. P. Davenport in 1904.[59] Articles described the efforts of supporters of initiative and referendum proposals around the country, including the American Federation of Labor, and a Cincinnati minister who was devoting full time to the cause. The Seattle *Star* strongly supported a proposal to turn party nominations over to voters instead of to the parties themselves.[60] Other issues concerned such inequities in American society as child labor, trusts, and monopolies; support for business competition (Scripps argued that it lowered prices); greedy landlords; monitoring city services (such as street sweeping or health departments) to assure that tax dollars were spent wisely; and criticizing the country's legal system for favoring the rich over the poor.[61]

Organized Labor

News about organized labor—unions—was part of Scripps's market segmentation strategy. He distrusted most unions—referring to them as the "aristocratic class of labor"—but recognized their value to workers.[62] Unions, even with their faults, were the only check to predatory big business. Scripps also hoped that his chain's support for unions would translate into circulation growth among workers and waivers from some union rules on numbers of workers. "Our editorial and journalistic policy being such as it is," he said, "organized labor can serve us in many ways, and at the same time serve itself, and its natural inclination would be to do so."[63] Once established, his newspapers could expand beyond their labor union core readers.[64] He also hoped that substantial coverage of labor issues, coupled with other features, would allow his publications to prevent inroads by labor union newspapers.[65]

Editors of Scripps's newspapers befriended labor union members, hired union printers, and provided extensive and sympathetic coverage to labor issues. On average, they devoted nearly nine times more space to labor issues than did their competitors.[66] They also provided constant support for laborers. One editorial praised "common labor" for performing "the work which none others will do. . . . It is the highest type of true heroism to be found in all history."[67] At a time when many Americans opposed labor unions, Scripps newspapers strongly supported the right of workers to unionize and bargain collectively. An editorial in the Los Angeles *Record* in 1903 proclaimed, "We have ever believed that the workingman is the backbone of the country. . . . We believe that labor should receive its full proportion of the profits of labor, and to this end we endorse trade unions."[68]

During the 1880s Scripps's newspapers provided sympathetic coverage to the Knights of Labor. After the decline of that group, they gave extensive publicity to Samuel Gompers and the American Federation of Labor. More radical labor groups merited little or no coverage, however. Scripps publications opposed violence, but when it occurred they sought to blame the enemies of labor: Pinkerton detectives, ruthless managers, or strikebreakers.[69]

Scripps's newspapers thus focused much more on issues of everyday life in labor than did their competitors, who portrayed labor primarily in terms of agitation and violence. They also provided coverage on a wide range of union-related issues: strikes, working conditions (unsafe jobs or work sites and wages), political activity by unions, and Labor Day celebrations. Their competitors focused primarily on strikes. On average, Scripps newspapers in five representative cities—Portland, Sacramento, San Diego, Cincinnati, and Evansville—devoted only 21 percent of their coverage of labor to strikes and 79 percent to other labor issues such as working conditions, political activities by unions, union meetings, Labor Day celebrations, and the cost of living. Competitors in those five cities, in contrast, devoted an average of 71 percent of their labor coverage to strikes and only 29 percent to other labor-related issues (fig. 5; table 5, appendix 1).

Strikes—When strikes did occur, Scripps newspapers detailed workers' demands and provided sympathetic coverage. In 1887 the Cincinnati *Post* defended a streetcar workers' strike, saying "the employes are not demanding anything unreasonable." The Cleveland *Press* defended striking miners in 1900, editorializing that "their grievances are enough to rouse the most patient to revolt." When Seattle streetcar employees were on strike in 1903, the *Star* defended them in an editorial headlined "RAILWAY COMPANY CAN AND MUST END STRIKE." And during a Portland streetcar employees' strike in 1907, the *Daily News* published a letter from union leaders to the public ("The Carmen State Their Position") at the top of its first page: "We are struggling for the God-given right that every man has to belong or not to belong to a labor organization if he sees fit." During the long streetcar strike of 1907 in San Francisco, a

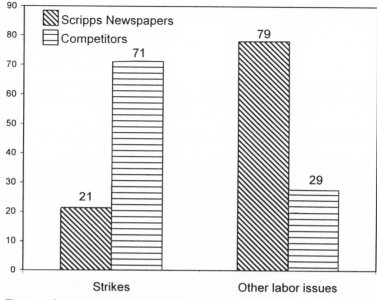

Figure 5. Coverage of Labor, by Percentage

Scripps reporter posed as a replacement worker and wrote a series ("My Experience as a Strike Breaker in San Francisco"), exposing corruption of management and strikebreakers and the callous disregard for public safety by both.[70]

Such sympathy was not usually forthcoming from most U.S. newspapers of the era. Contrasting coverage of a Pennsylvania miners' strike in 1902 is typical. The Seattle *Star* provided a much different interpretation of events than its afternoon competitor, the *Times*. The *Star* blamed authorities for strike-related violence, particularly after a deputy officer shot the son of a striking miner:

> BLOODSHED AND RIOT
> IN THE MINERS' STRIKE
> Deputy Officer Precipitates Trouble—Injunc
> tion May be Sought.[71]

In contrast, the Seattle *Times*, printing an Associated Press article, mentioned the shooting but attributed the violence to strikers:

> MEN IN UGLY MOOD
> Resent Shooting by Special Police
> Feared That Trouble May
> Break Out at Any Time
> Among Strikers.[72]

The *Times*'s article also carried accusations from the mine owners that "the mine workers [are] responsible for all the disturbances. . . . if the strikers wish to keep the peace they should prevent their sons from starting trouble." In San Francisco, the *Daily News* was the only newspaper in that city to support strikers during the 1907 streetcar workers' strike.[73]

Working Conditions—While competitors dealt with labor primarily by covering strikes, Scripps's newspapers paid attention to a wide array of union issues, including the length of the work day, work safety, and whether wages were keeping up with the cost of living. Articles publicized union demands for a reduction in work hours, and editorials supported that cause.[74] A *San Diegan-Sun* editorial endorsed the eight-hour workday, arguing that it would produce a "fairer equalization of the work of the world."[75] One article, "LABOR MORE DEADLY THAN LONG WARS," exposed unsafe working conditions and argued that work-related fatalities were much higher in the United States than in many other countries.[76]

The lag between wages and the cost of living also drew substantial attention from Scripps newspapers. The Cleveland *Press* editorialized that "wages need to be fair." Editorial cartoons illustrated how the "Common People" were squeezed by rising costs. One editorial, produced by the NEA, argued that the proverbial wolf was no longer at the door: "He has come inside. He has jumped up on the table, and he is sticking his red tongue into the faces of many a poor family."[77] The Newspaper Enterprise Association likewise produced a series of articles in late 1907 that focused entirely on the failure of wages to keep up with the cost of living:

COST OF LIVING INCREASED 40 PER CENT
BY TRUSTS WORKS AMAZING HARDSHIPS
UPON THE HONEST POOR OF NATION.[78]

Union meetings, where wages and other union concerns were discussed, received substantial coverage from Scripps newspapers, and editors routinely published articles covering local labor gatherings.[79] An official from the central office praised the editor of the Terre Haute *Post* for its labor column: "That is a good thing . . . I think it is the best thing you have done in recent months."[80] The editor of the Seattle *Star* said in 1903 that he ran labor notes because they were popular with readers.[81]

In addition to its regular "Labor Notes" articles, the *Record* published a column in 1903 and 1904 written by Francis Drake, president of the Los Angeles County Council of Labor.[82] In the column, Drake, who was paid by the

International Typographical Union and not by the *Record*, defended labor unions generally, argued that they raised wages for all workers, defended local strikers, and attacked labor's enemies in Los Angeles, particularly the *Times*.[83] Seventy-four Los Angeles labor leaders sent a letter to the *Record* in 1903, praising it for serving as a "daily newspaper through which to refute the malicious misrepresentations of the Los Angeles *Times*."[84]

Working women were likewise part of the target market, and their concerns also drew coverage. Wages were low and hours long. In 1887 the St. Louis *Chronicle* exposed the difficult working conditions many women faced:

WORKWOMEN'S WOES
Some Bold, Hard Facts About
Female Toilers
Fifty Cents Pay for 14 Hours' Work
Shop and Factory Oppression.[85]

Politics—Scripps newspapers viewed politics through the lens of working-class interests and evaluated candidates on their attitudes toward organized labor. When James Gillett ran for governor in California in 1906, Scripps newspapers condemned him as an enemy of labor. In "What Gillett Stands For," the Scripps Sacramento *Star* argued that he was an enemy of labor and a pawn of large corporations. Scripps's San Francisco *Daily News* published an article detailing Gillett's anti-labor record, describing him as "corporation controlled, as shown by his record in Congress and the circumstances of his nomination for Governor . . . he went to the Santa Cruz convention in a vessel manned by non-unionists and owned by labor crushers." In Congress, "he held back the anti-injunction bill and prevented a favorable report of it in spite of labor's pleas for its passage."[86]

The attacks on Gillett were well thought out. Just before Gillett's nomination, R. F. Paine, the chain's editor-in-chief, outlined the position Scripps's California newspapers would take if he was the Republican gubernatorial nominee. "We propose to show that he is the creature of 'the organization' and the corporations and that he has as such consistently opposed the measures favored by the workingmen in Congress."[87]

In cities where labor unions organized politically, such as Cincinnati, San Francisco, Sacramento, Portland, and Evansville, Scripps publications provided extensive coverage of political meetings and labor union political tickets.[88] In 1902 the Seattle *Star* covered a summer meeting of union members that laid the groundwork for the fall campaigns. Samuel Gompers began urging labor union members to organize politically in 1906, particularly to work to stop the election of anti-labor candidates.[89] The *San Diegan-Sun* urged local labor leaders to do likewise, arguing that labor political activity would help workers.[90] The Portland *Eastside News* printed the full platform of the local union labor party in early 1907.

When the San Francisco *Daily News* refused to support Eugene Schmitz, the mayoral nominee of the local labor union party, Scripps and his managers worried that the newspaper would lose union support and circulation. Paine told the editor, W. D. Wasson, to be careful about antagonizing unions: "I cannot tell, at this distance, what I would do in your place but it seems to me that, if I did not support the organized laborites out and out, I would be pretty liberal in notices of their meetings, presenting in a news way Schmitz's side of the case, without committing the paper outright to his support."[91] A year later, when Mayor Schmitz was accused of graft, Scripps ordered Wasson to be friendly toward him, assume his innocence, and generally ignore the topic as much as possible to avoid antagonizing unions.[92]

Labor Day and Other Labor Issues—The first Monday in September had become the focus of labor celebrations in the late nineteenth century, and Scripps's newspapers featured extensive coverage of that day's festivities.[93] The Cincinnati *Post* praised the local Labor Day parade in 1887 and defended the "new holiday," saying that "procession and the speeches . . . showed the public that the time has come when workingmen will take a more active part in politics and will insist upon reforms in the interest of workingmen, and therefore, in the interest of the whole country."[94] In 1900 the St. Louis *Chronicle* reported on:

THE GREATEST PARADE
of Brain and Brawn Ever
SEEN IN ST. LOUIS
Over 40,000 Members of Labor Unions
Marched Between Solid Lines
of Cheering Thousands.[95]

In other labor news, Scripps newspapers ran flattering articles on Gompers, and both publicized and endorsed unions' attack on Asian-American workers.[96] A 1903 NEA series—"Types of Union Labor"—explained what various workers (plumbers, compositors, brakemen or bakers) did in their jobs.[97] "What Trade Shall the Boy Learn?"—another NEA series in 1906—attempted to show young boys how to enter unions by serving as apprentices in a variety of trades, steamfitting, iron work, bricklaying, carpentry, printing, or as machinists.[98]

The printing-related employees of Scripps's newspapers were all unionized, and the newspapers themselves carried the union label and publicized the fact that most of their competitors did neither.[99] Editors had strict orders never to antagonize local labor unions. "It is not good business policy to have any differences or disputes with the Unions," Scripps told one manager, "only keep your temper and be careful all the time to avoid giving offense of organized labor." "Tact is the main thing needed," he informed the Seattle *Star's* business manager.[100] Milton McRae told the business manager of the *Kentucky Post* to avoid any disputes with unionized printers because "it is a fundamental principle of the concern to have no differences with union labor. That is, to permit strikes. Our plan is only to employ labor when it is profitable. It is unprofitable to permit labor disturbances."[101] Avoid strikes at all costs, Jacob Harper, the chain's attorney, told B. F. Gurley, editor of the Denver *Express*: "I caution you, though, under no circumstances to permit a walkout. We will pay the Union scale and submit to Union conditions and when unable to do so will cease business, but we will not permit ourselves to be put in a position of antagonisms. . . . So whatever you do, do not permit a walk out, even if you should have to submit to the present outrageous demands."[102] Scripps's newspapers always accommodated union wage demands and refused to join with other publishers in fighting unions.[103]

Support from Labor—The extensive and sympathetic coverage given to labor by Scripps's newspapers paid great dividends. On more than one occasion, editors found that strong support boosted circulation substantially. In 1894 the Cleveland *Press's* coverage of Eugene V. Debs's trial for helping organize a strike against the Pullman Railway Company pushed circulation to a record seventy-seven thousand. The managing editor reported that the coverage "doubtless . . . cost us the good will of many moneyed men but it did not weaken the paper."[104] The *Press* gave a great deal of attention in 1899 to the working conditions and demands of striking streetcar employees, and again editors reported that circulation had grown as a result.[105] The business manager of the Los Angeles *Record* reported in 1901 that the newspaper's support for local "laundry girls" had also boosted circulation greatly.[106] Strong support for striking streetcar workers likewise produced circulation gains for the San Francisco *Daily News* in 1907 that more than offset cancellations due to the coverage.[107] When the Seattle *Star* published anti-Japanese articles in 1900, editor E. H. Wells reported, "The Japanese articles which we have published have done us great good among the laboring men and have brought results." He added that the local labor union newspaper (a weekly) had recommended the *Star* to union members as "the only paper in Seattle that was genuinely interested in labor."[108]

Conclusions

Market segmentation was one of Scripps's key strategies in starting newspapers. He saw potential for success in serving readers ignored by most other newspapers and wanted his publications to serve "those who have no other mouthpiece": the working class.[109] Wasson said that he fought for the "interests of that great mass of the people who depend upon their toil for a livelihood. . . . In a word, we are taking care of the men and women who struggle for a living."[110]

Market segmentation had direct influence on content. Scripps newspapers paid a great deal of attention to working-class issues and provided far more news about labor—including strikes, wages, hours, political organization, and other events—than did their competitors. They also dealt more frequently with the everyday concerns of the working class. Editorial cartoons routinely portrayed the tribulations of Mr. and Mrs. Common People, and Scripps newspapers exposed trusts and monopolies that gouged working-class consumers. They also defended collective bargaining and strikes, supported government regulation of basic industries (food and transportation) and government ownership of basic utilities (electricity and water), and advocated greater political power for the common people through initiative, referendum, recall, and direct election of public officials. The common denominator was content that was consonant with Scripps's market segmentation strategy.

This style of news and advocacy won support for Scripps newspapers among the workers. R. F. Paine reported that the San Francisco *Daily News* was "derided by its rivals, loved by the poor people," and Wells wrote that local union leaders had gone "out of their way" to support the Seattle *Star*.[111] The Los Angeles *Record*, too, was called "the only paper that dares to speak for organized labor."[112]

"Is It Interesting?"

A good newspaper is one that will sell.
—E. W. Scripps to George H. Scripps, January 18, 1888

Among men who manufacture anything for the public, or sell the public anything, none succeed, as far as I know, unless they find out what the people want and give it to them.
—E. F. Chase to R. F. Paine, March 27, 1908

IN LATE 1879 the Cleveland *Press* discontinued its daily short story. Reporters and editors were tired of the somewhat frivolous bits of fiction that had been a staple of the newspaper throughout its first year of operation and agreed that the space would be far better used for news. Before long, however, readers began to complain. Customers stopped by the newspaper's office—"a much grieved throng of subscribers, both male and female, who demanded the continuation of the short stories."[1] Regional circulation agents also wrote in to demand the return of short stories, calling them the most popular part of the newspaper. Many women also sent letters of complaint.

As the *Press* admitted, the protest caught reporters and editors by surprise: "All this was mortifying in the extreme to the editorial writers, reporters and paragraphers, and they failed not freely to express their contempt for the 'low order of minds' which preferred 'such slush' as they called it, to the superior scintillations, weighty opinions and graphic descriptions of local affairs, the original products of the brains of the aforesaid editors, reporters and paragraphers."[2] "Humiliating as the situation was," the newspaper's editor—E. W. Scripps—returned the short stories to daily publication. Paying attention to readers' interests was good business. Short stories—so popular with women readers—caused the *Press* "to find its way into households, where the ladies and young people of the family read them, and from there they go through the rest of the paper."[3] High-brow material was worthless if no one read it.

The incident, and others like it at the Cleveland *Press*, shaped Scripps's notions of what constituted good newspapers. He told his sister Annie that readers "would rather have two columns of a sensational murder than a recipe for a panacea which would cure them of every ailment bodily and mentally existing." Every article needed to be interesting. "I can't afford to publish matter for only a few to read. Sticking types cost money. So does printing papers, so does the mailing of the papers, so does everything connected with the work and I must make every line of space count."[4] He told his older brother James that the Cleveland editorship had taught him the elements of success. "I learned that success did not so much lay in having everything in the paper as in having every thing that was in the paper good. I had rather my reader would feel certain before opening my paper that he was going to be *entertained* than that he was going to be *instructed.*"[5]

Creating interesting news became one of Scripps's central goals. He criticized the early issues of the St. Louis *Chronicle* (which he started in July 1880), saying that the average person "is too apt to fall asleep before he has read through even the editorial column."[6] Scripps attributed the great growth of the Cincinnati *Post* in 1883 to extensive and sometimes melodramatic coverage of a local boy evangelist—a story more dignified Cincinnati newspapers shunned. "Some of the editorials in the Post were prayers, some were sermons," he wrote—but all attracted readers.[7] In later years he maintained that the true test of an editor was his ability to provide content that pleased readers, many of whom read newspapers "largely to pass time or to kill time."[8]

As his newspaper chain grew, Scripps's lieutenants echoed and enforced his views. In 1908 one manager told the editor of the chain's Terre Haute *Post* to "cover the things that the people want to read."[9] B. H. Canfield, Scripps's western regional editor, maintained that "anything that was dull" had no place in a Scripps newspaper. Decisions about newsworthiness "should be based solely on the answer to the question, 'Is it interesting?'" Each article and picture "should be so bright, clever, and interesting that each editor would WANT to print it because it was good, live copy."[10]

That definition of newsworthiness was also widespread in the U.S. newspaper industry of the era. In 1897 the editor of the Buffalo *Times* argued that successful publications studied customers' tastes "with the same care that a successful merchant does," printing items that readers would enjoy.[11] Newspapers increasingly offered content to attract diverse readers: women's news (fashion, cooking, and society), history, short stories and serialized fiction, human-interest stories, and news of leisure activities (theater, sports, and music). As the Pittsburgh *Leader* bragged in 1898, "No matter in what you are interested, you will find the subject of your hobby duly exploited . . . in fact, whatever you most like to read, you will find the Leader's departments are the most carefully prepared, the most complete and the most interesting."[12]

Scripps refined this general notion of "whatever you most like to read" by focusing on one particular market segment: the working class. News and advocacy about working-class issues were part of that effort, but Scripps insisted that they should be presented in an appealing style. Moreover, readers would want other types of content to amuse or provoke them. To accomplish that, Scripps created small newspapers with many short articles. He also insisted on plain language and "sensational matter," large doses of humor, graphics, illustrations, feature articles, a deemphasis on politics, and an emphasis on human interest and content specifically geared toward women. How readers read these newspapers is not known. It is doubtful that every reader read every line. Some kinds of content (such as cartoons, features, and human-interest editorials) seem to have attracted the most attention. It is clear, however, that Scripps's market segmentation strategy directed both the subject matter and format of content in his newspapers.

Small Newspapers and Many Short Articles

The philosophy of Scripps newspapers was that a typical working-class reader, after a hard day's work, wanted the news in a concise, easy-to-read format. Scripps said that his San Francisco *Daily News* had succeeded because it was "a little one such as tired men can read quickly and such as ease-loving women can get through without too great effort." On another occasion, he said that workers wanted to get the news "with as little labor as possible."[13]

Most Scripps newspapers began as small-sheet, four-page publications and went to eight pages only after they were well established. Even at eight pages they were smaller than the blanket-sheet ten- and twelve-page newspapers published by competitors. That small size was seen as a marketing advantage. As the Los Angeles *Record* proclaimed in 1896:

> Little men sometimes
> have much more in
> them than big men.
> The Record is small in
> size but big with news.[14]

In 1879 many news items in the Cleveland *Press* were only one sentence long:

> The Park Theater Company are at the Weddell.
> Youngstown has sixty-six lawyers.
> A new Mormon temple is building at Logan, Utah.
> An extra session of Congress seems inevitable.[15]

On Monday, December 13, 1886, the *Press* called attention to its condensed version of the weekend's news:

THE NEWS OF TWO DAYS
Where It Can Be Read at a
Glance
Without Wading Through Several
Columns of Padded Space. What
Happened in Ohio over Sunday
Told in a Few Words.

Condensing news received consistent attention from Scripps and his managers. Tired workers, he said, wanted just the key points in an article rather than extensive detail, and he urged editors and reporters to condense the news as much as possible. Good writing would "make it impossible to have a twenty-five word item in the paper where a twenty-four word item would cover the same ground." He told one editor that readers expected long editorials to be dull and so ignored them. R. F. Paine, editorial superintendent of the Scripps newspapers in the early twentieth century, told the editor of the Tacoma *Times* that readers preferred short articles, and "I would condense more than ever."[16] Articles in Scripps newspapers were substantially shorter than those published by competitors. The average length of those on the front page was 30.5 column lines, whereas the average length of competitors' front-page articles was 77.1 (table 6, appendix 1).

Coverage of a 1905 New York state investigation into the insurance industry demonstrates how Scripps publications condensed news. Sen. William W. Armstrong chaired the investigation, which spanned three months (October-December) and attracted considerable national attention.[17] The nation's leading telegraph news services covered the hearings, and most newspapers devoted a good deal of space to the sensational hearings that uncovered fraud, nepotism, and shoddy business operations in some of the country's largest companies. Scripps's newspapers took their coverage from the chain's telegraph news service, the Scripps-McRae Press Association, which used a special correspondent.

Condensing characterized coverage of the Armstrong Committee hearings, too. Scripps's Sacramento *Star* devoted an average of sixty-two lines each to the coverage of four witnesses at the hearings; its two competitors published an average of 149 lines per person (table 7, appendix 1). The coverage in all three newspapers basically provided the same key ingredients. The *Star* provided only a bare overview of the testimony, whereas its rivals included more detail and quoted extensively from the actual testimony, sometimes in question-and-answer format. That same pattern also occurred in the Seattle and San Diego newspaper markets. In Seattle, for example, Scripps's *Star* covered the testimony of one insurance company employee in twenty lines and said that the employee had provided "all kinds of figures" but detailed none. In contrast, the other two Seattle newspapers did provide figures. The *Post-Intelligencer* used 88 lines and the *Times* 104.[18]

Simple Language

Small newspapers and short articles meant that working-class readers did not have to wade through a mountain of detail; simple language meant that they would easily grasp what they were reading. One Scripps editor said that short, simple words were best "not only to save space but also to make the meaning plainer to the man on the street, the man with the pail who quit school at twelve or thirteen. I would use 'pm' instead of 'afternoon' . . . ; 'aid' instead of 'assistance'; . . . 'wounds' instead of 'lacerations'; 'chances' instead of 'opportunities'; . . . 'taken' instead of 'transported.' "[19] Scripps maintained that most common people cared little about "polished style." A short, plainly worded statement of the news—"no matter how incomplete or non grammatical or how badly worded"—was better than the "most elaborate, most complete and most elegant article that could be produced by the brightest minds." The best reporters were ones with minimal training or experience. "I have learned that a cub reporter is more valuable to a newspaper than a skillful well trained reporter," Scripps said, "not because he is cheaper but because his writing is more natural, and more easily understood."[20] Most Scripps newspapers had a higher proportion of cubs than their competitors, primarily because salaries were low.

Managers within the Scripps chain advised editors on how to maintain a working-class touch. J. C. Harper, the chain's chief attorney and superintendent of the Denver *Express,* told that newspaper's editor to spend some time soliciting new readers door to door to get a better sense of the interests of average people.[21] He worried that the *Express* "at times . . . contains articles of a length and character that would interest chiefly the intellectual rather than the masses." In 1905 Paine ordered H. N. Rickey, editor of the Cleveland *Press,* to rely more extensively on the Newspaper Enterprise Association to sustain the working-class orientation of that publication. Paine worried that Rickey was "edging away from the masses, getting far above the level of the vast majority of readers." Paine specifically complained about "deep, literary and scientific editorials" and the "preference of high class serial stories over short love-sick ones."[22]

Vivid Language

Scripps maintained that "sensational matter is absolutely necessary to a newspaper" and defined sensationalism as "that kind of matter which produces some sensation of humor, of indignation or gratified curiosity or any other sort of sensation.[23] Frequently headlines provided the kind of eye-catching phrases that may have created a sensation. In 1889, for example, a Cleveland *Press* headline introduced an article about a recent murder:

SCREAMS
That Quivered on the
Night Air
Were the Pitiful Appeals
of Pearl Crall
As She Struggled in the Grasp
of a Ravisher
The Heinous Crime Occurred
Near Franklin—av.
How the Brute Fled after
Leaving His Victim.[24]

In its Armstrong investigation coverage, the Sacramento *Star* covered the same news events as its competitor, the Sacramento *Bee*, but in Scripps fashion featured far more vivid headlines. One detailed the testimony of an insurance executive:

PAYNE FROTHS
AT CHARGE
And Declares That He Is an Honest
Man in Every Particular
Gives Detail of His Virtue.[25]

The *Bee*, however, had a far more prosaic headline for an article covering the same testimony:

Says the Statements
of Wells Are False.[26]

Humor

Humor played a big role in capturing readers' attention. As Scripps said, "I have learned that men and women like to laugh better than they do to cry and that for steady appearance in a newspaper, humor is far more acceptable than heroics. I have learned that even a jolly rascal is a more acceptable companion to the average human being than a long faced stupidly honest man."[27] The

Newspaper Enterprise Association supplied humorous material to Scripps publications, and editors had orders to use it. Columns of jokes and witticisms appeared almost daily.[28] Jokes were short: "'How do you think you're going to like the new cook?' asked Smithers. 'I like her immensely,' replied Mrs. Smithers. 'She knows her business.' 'Good. And I suppose that before the week is ended she'll know the whole neighborhood's business.'"[29]

Humorous cartoons were also staples of Scripps newspapers, particularly after NEA's establishment. One regular series was "Mr. Skygack from Mars," in which a Martian, observing earthlings, continually misunderstands simple things. Concerning a bride and groom at their wedding, Mr. Skygack reports, for example, "Saw Pair of Earth Beings (Male and Female) brought before high official of tribe—pair was probably guilty of some serious crime judging from emotions depicted on faces—attendant eager throng stood expectantly by listening to official's reprimand."[30]

The NEA's prime cartoon character in its early years was the blustering misanthrope Everett True. In "Everett True Goes to the Market," a vendor tries to sell him "fine cantaloupes, fresh from the ranch," but Everett sees through him. Squashing the cantaloupes on the vendor, he shouts, "Try to fool me, and unload your lot of rotten cantaloupes! You brazen throat imposter!!! Fresh, are they? They look it!!!"[31] Everett True was forever at war with those who walked too slowly, spoke to him on streetcars, and sang off-key, as well as with wailing children and other irritations. Unlike most polite or self-controlled persons, he routinely vented his rage on the source of his irritation. According to Paine, Everett True was the NEA's most popular feature.[32]

The NEA also produced a large number of illustrated humorous columns. One, "Diana's Diary," a regular between 1906 and 1908, focused on the hapless Diana Dillpickles, a sweet but incredibly naive young woman who routinely became caught up in enthusiasms, whether belief in a guru-like preacher, physical culture, a get-rich-quick scheme for selling potato mashers, or romance. Diana would be on the verge of quitting her job as a clerk to pursue a new life (as the wife of a rich English nobleman or a Pittsburgh steel magnate) only to discover that she had been misled. The rich noblemen, physical culturalists, and gurus all turned out to be fakes who had duped the hapless Diana.[33] "Platonic Penelope" concerned another hapless young woman, always in search of platonic relationships with men but always disappointed by those who wanted much more.[34] Other illustrated humorous columns included "Bump Talks" by Professor Bumptarara (a spoof of phrenology), "A Bit of Vaudeville" (the comic misadventures of Osgar and Adolf, who spoke in fractured German-English), and rural wisdom in "Jabberings of John Jimpsonweed."[35]

MR. SKYGACK FROM MARS

He Visits the Earth as a Special Correspondent and Makes Wireless
Observations in His Notebook.

Mr. Skygack mistakes a wedding for a judicial hearing and assumes that the bride and
groom have been summoned before a "high official of the tribe" for a reprimand. (Seattle *Star*, Feb. 29, 1908, 4)

MR. SKYGACK FROM MARS

He Visits the Earth as a Special Correspondent and Makes Wireless
Observations in His Notebook.

Mr. Skygack mistakes a man in a bath for a deranged person sitting in a tub of hot
soup. He reports that he left quickly, "fearing enactment of some shocking tragedy."
(Seattle *Star*, Jan. 25, 1908, 4; Sacramento *Star*, Jan. 25, 1908, 2)

The Outbursts of Everett True

Everett True, one of the NEA's most popular cartoon characters, reacts in typical fashion to a bothersome insurance salesman. (Seattle *Star*, Nov. 29, 1905, 5)

OUTBURSTS OF EVERETT TRUE

When a cashier in a restaurant hesitates to accept a worn coin, Everett erupts, noting that the cashier had given him the same coin the day before. (Seattle *Star*, Feb. 3, 1908, 4)

OUTBURSTS OF EVERETT TRUE

Easily irritated, Everett is outraged when another restaurant patron talks too much.
(Seattle *Star*, Feb. 12, 1908, 4)

THE OUTBURSTS OF EVERETT TRUE

Everett takes the direct approach in getting rid of guests who have outstayed their welcome. (Seattle *Star*, Oct. 21, 1905, 3)

Illustrated News

Extensive use of graphics (photographs, cartoons, and drawings) was another way in which Scripps newspapers attempted to present news in a way that would interest working-class readers. As he said, "Pictures are more easily understood and read than words." A newspaper could "better afford to leave out of its columns, a half a dozen items covering the most important news of the day than it can afford to leave out one really good cartoon or other picture." On another occasion Scripps compared newspaper reading to travel and graphics to beautiful scenery, arguing that even a traveler who wanted a short cut ("a brief item of news") still wanted an scenic route (illustrated news).[36] Paine told the editor of the San Francisco *Daily News* that "art" (photographs, cartoons, or other illustrations) made newspapers "brighter looking when picked up for perusal at the fireside" and thus more popular with working-class readers. He also stressed that the art used was not decorative; it needed to convey information.[37] Milton McRae told the editor of the Dallas *Dispatch* to use smaller headlines and make room for more illustrations because "you will find them more profitable."[38]

Scripps newspapers began to illustrate articles with drawings during the late 1880s, and line drawings appeared in the Cleveland, Cincinnati, and St. Louis publications throughout the 1890s. The use of photographs became common after 1900. During the late nineteenth century, Scripps publications relied upon an informal process of sharing illustrations. That ended in 1902, however, when Scripps established the Newspaper Enterprise Association, an "Illustrative and News Enterprise Bureau." Paine, the first manager of the NEA, announced that the service would produce "at least three first class [editorial] cartoons, on general events, per week," portraits of celebrities, and photographs to accompany non-local news (supplied by the wire services) and features (also supplied by the NEA). The NEA began with a $400 per week budget in 1902, a year later the budget was running $1,000 per week, and by 1907 it was nearly $2,000 a week.[39]

In 1905 Leroy Saunders, editor of the Tacoma *Times,* reported that he used NEA illustrations extensively. They were popular with readers and gave the *Times* "a metropolitan aspect which goes a long way towards their success."[40] W. H. Porterfield reported that NEA editorial cartoons were particularly popular with readers of the *San Diegan-Sun* and Sacramento *Star.*

Counting illustrated news, humorous cartoons, and illustrations accompanying serialized stories, Scripps newspapers devoted about a quarter of total non-advertising content to artwork, compared to an average 5 percent by competitors (fig. 6; table 8, appendix 1). Even though the competitors published

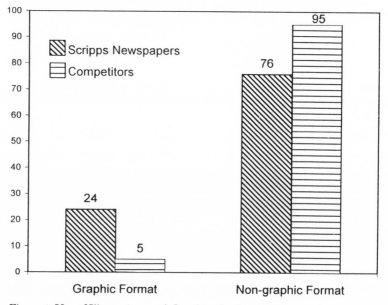

Figure 6. Use of Illustrations and Graphics, by Percentage

larger newspapers (eight, ten, or twelve pages daily), most produced fewer column inches of graphic material than did Scripps publications.

The NEA's illustrations allowed Scripps's newspapers to present much of their extensive coverage of the 1905 New York state investigation into the insurance industry in visual form—a typical use of graphics. In the last three months of 1905, for example, the Los Angeles *Record* published fifteen photographs or line drawings and ten editorial cartoons on the topic.[41] The photographs depicted leading insurance company executives and committee members and staff (particularly chief counsel Charles Evans Hughes), and editorial cartoons illustrated some of the key points of the case. "And They're Still Milking It" portrays one of the chief criticisms of the insurance industry: nepotism. "Thumbs Down!" simplifies the issues even further, with sympathetic figures of the Common People and Justice against the bloated Insurance Trust.

Illustrations—sometimes used with photographs, sometimes standing alone—drew attention to news. One article on U.S. Sen. John Dryden's proposal for federal control of the life insurance industry was illustrated with three large sticks ("The Insurance Big Stick," likely inspired by Theodore Roosevelt's much-publicized nostrum). Another on the testimony of an insurance industry lobbyist before the Armstrong Committee included his picture surrounded by an oversized question mark.[42]

AND THEY'RE STILL MILKING IT

Here, in a comment on nepotism in the insurance industry, "Paw McCurdy" (Richard McCurdy, president of Mutual Life Insurance Company) milks that industry for his family's benefit. (Seattle *Star*, Nov. 17, 1905, 4)

Thumbs Down

"The Common People" tell Justice to slay the bloated Insurance Trust, evoking Roman gladiatorial contests. (Sacramento *Star*, Oct. 8, 1905, 1; *San Diegan-Sun*, Oct. 10, 1905, 1; Seattle *Star*, Oct. 13, 1905, 1)

Feature Articles

Attempts to print news first—getting a scoop on competitors—were a major characteristic of newspaper competition in the late nineteenth century. Editors could produce special editions of their newspapers (extras) and make money from the public's desire for news about a disaster such as the Johnstown Flood, a prizefight, or the death of a president. During the 1880s and 1890s Scripps newspapers engaged in the battle for scoops. By the turn of the century, however, they began to recognize that such a battle was expensive and never-ending. Readers seemed far more interested in whether the news was interesting than whether it was a scoop. "Ordinarily, a news scoop now-a-days means a scoop for only a few minutes," Paine noted in 1905. "You can steal news facts but *it is different to steal their treatment, and so editors have been paying more attention to the treatment, which means more feature matter.*"[43]

Feature matter included articles that derived from current news events—the news behind the news. In the coverage of the Armstrong Committee's investigation, Scripps newspapers paid substantial attention to the news event itself—the cross-examination of insurance executives. In addition, they provided feature matter by giving readers a glimpse of key players. One feature, a character sketch of Charles Evans Hughes, was headed HUGHES—HE HAS FRENZIED INSURANCE FINANCIERS ON THE HIP and described the noted attorney as "a man of average height and build as New York well-groomed lawyers go, he would not be picked out on the street. . . . He seems five feet eight inches, straight, thin, boney. . . . When he speaks the crowd looks at his teeth. They look away to his deep set blue eyes, to his long sharp, quisitorial nose—a Greek nose without the wide, delicate, sensitive nostrils, to his high forehead—a splendid forehead, though not broad like Daniel Webster's."[44] "THE HOME OF A POOR MAN" examined one insurance company president's claim that he was poor by describing the luxury of his country home: "The country homes of few of the wealthiest men in the nation display more regal splendor than Mr. McCall's country place at West End, N.J. . . . The towering white mansion with its red tiled roof and green blinds stands upon a high eminence. From the far countryside it appears more like a big exposition building, or institution, than the home of one man, his wife and two sons. . . . It is said that the place cost $1,000,000. The stable alone cost $150,000."[45] The article, which carried three photographs, also noted the luxurious landscaping (done by "expert landscape artists") and a crew of forty servants, including "nine men who do nothing but work upon the lawns and flowering shrubbery."

Two other features focused on some of the larger issues related to insurance in the United States. The first was written by Henry George, Jr., son of the late reformer, and reflected the NEA's desire to produce "semi-news stories by famous people."[46] George's article covered the huge payments that insurance companies made to the Republican National Committee in 1896, 1900, and 1904. "If this whole business is not robbery," he asked, "what is it?"[47] Another article, by the Rev. Hugh O. Pentisost ("famous psychologist, author, political economist and criminal lawyer") was headlined *"thieves!"* and contained his contention that many insurance executives were "just plain ordinary thieves."[48]

These "semi-news" stories written by well-known people were common throughout the year in Scripps newspapers. In 1906 Sen. Knute Nelson from Minnesota contributed "I Remember My First Fourth," and on July 4 of that year the Newspaper Enterprise Association produced an article in which famous men and women (Anthony Comstock, Marie Dressler, Lew Fields, and Rose Pastor Stokes) answered the question "What's the Best Thing to Do on the Fourth?" Other prominent Americans (Eugene V. Debs, Harry Thaw, Carrie Nation, Anthony Comstock, Adm. George Dewey, and others) were asked "Why Are You Thankful?" for Thanksgiving 1907.[49]

Politics and Human-Interest Content

Scripps wanted his newspapers to focus on topics that would be interesting to readers. In practice, that meant placing less emphasis on more traditional definitions of news (government and politics, courts, accidents, and business) than their competitors did. Instead, they devoted proportionately more space to content dealing with leisure and entertainment. Five Scripps newspapers devoted an average of 49.4 percent of total space to traditional news (government, politics, and business); the average for competitors was 76.1 percent. Those same five newspapers devoted an average of 40.8 percent of their total space to content dealing with leisure activities (vaudeville, fiction, sports, comics, and jokes) and content for women. Competitors devoted an average of 19.9 percent of total space to such content (fig. 7; table 9, appendix 1).

The decision to deemphasize more traditional types of news (such as politics) came from Scripps's belief that the age of partisan journalism had ended and that readers had only a limited tolerance for news about politics.[50] In the first issue of the Cleveland *Press* on November 2, 1878, he proclaimed "We have no politics. . . . We are not republican, not democratic, not greenback and not prohibitionist. We simply intend to support good men and condemn bad ones, support good measures and condemn bad ones, no matter what party they

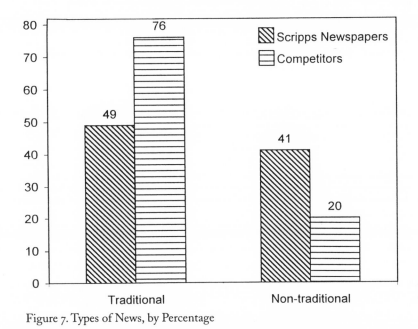

Figure 7. Types of News, by Percentage

belong to. We shall tell no lies about persons or policies for love, malice or money." Scripps claimed that political independence made his newspaper a better news medium. "No matter how honorable the editors of the partisan papers may be personally, they are forced to do the dirty editorial work dictated to them by party interests," he wrote in 1879. Such independence was good business because "we are in the newspaper business for the same purpose as that of most other people who go into business—to make money. The independent newspaper is always a more profitable concern than the party organ, no matter how successful the latter may be."[51]

Political independence suited the business needs of the growing chain by allowing individual newspapers to exploit local market conditions. In Spokane, where conservative Democrats had a strong tie to the older newspapers, the Scripps publication printed a weekly column from local Progressive Republicans. In Seattle, where political and press alliances differed, the Scripps *Star* gave space to local Democrats. In Nashville, where Democrats were the entrenched status quo, the Scripps newspaper gave space to local Republicans. Scripps's newspapers did not endorse these partisans but rather stated that the space had been donated to assure that independent voters had access to all political arguments. When H. B. Clark helped establish Scripps's San Francisco *Daily News* in 1903, he said it would be Democratic if one of its chief afternoon competitors (the *Post*) remained Republican. In St. Louis, where Scripps's chief competitor, Joseph Pulitzer's *Post-Dispatch,* was an independent Democratic publication, the editors treated local Republicans "at least with great consideration."[52]

Scripps newspapers did not avoid politics, however. They covered elections and ardently advocated a wide array of political causes but limited coverage following his dictum that "politics as a rule are not interesting."[53] In 1906 he told his Denver editor that people generally did not think or talk a great deal about politics, government, or crime, so it made no sense for a newspaper to devote a vast amount of space to such content.[54] "I have always thought that a newspaper should not fight all the time," Canfield wrote in 1908, "that there should be periods when, after it had accomplished certain things, it should turn its attention to other matters."[55] Instead of politics and other traditional types of news, Scripps newspapers emphasized content that would appeal to human interest—news about leisure activities such as plays and sports. One lieutenant advised that one "red hot story" was better than twenty other items.[56]

Even editorials dealt with human-interest topics, with inspirational homilies on subjects such as the need to laugh, the "transforming power of kindness," or the "disease" of worrying. The NEA was the prime supplier of such editorials. Paine, who wrote many, said that they spoke to the heart rather than to the mind.[57] One, "Don't Apologize for Yourself," urged readers to be proud of themselves; still others praised the power of positive thinking. According to "A Science of Living," "bad tempers, unhealthy consciences, irritable natures and so on are the germs from which disease springs." "Mind and Health" argued that optimism is the foundation for good health:

> Have you not noticed that the pessimist is always an invalid? He may be upon his feet and moving about, but he is never free from ailments and complainings. . . . Pessimism is as destructive a force in one's health as it is in one's purpose and performance The pessimist seeks the shadows and wilfully deprives himself of the life-giving sunshine. The sun, the flowers, the trees and the green each smile at him in vain. . . . Can one thus out of harmony with the forces of life hope for health? Never. Health is harmony. Discord is ill health. Optimism—happy, buoyant, wholesome optimism—counts more for health than do all the rest of the laws of hygiene.[58]

"Laugh and the World Laughs with You" maintained that "good humor is the saving grace of daily life," and "Only a Dog" examined the devotion of dogs to their owners: "The man who has the love of a dog is higher than a king. TO HIS DOG, MAN IS A GOD." The range of topics was broad—courage, health, values, human success, hobbies, the pursuit of happiness, and the appreciation of a pretty day.[59] Editorials did not ignore political issues but featured politics less often and human-interest topics more than did competitors. Human-interest editorials represented an average of 53.2 percent of all editorial space in five Scripps newspapers, compared to an average of 3.6 percent for competitors (table 10, appendix 1).

Other human-interest stories included a series of articles on Alaska by a traveling Scripps reporter in 1889, pieces on how electricity and gravity operate, and "person-on-the-street" interviews, as well as pieces about pets and unusual local surnames in St. Louis (there were Bitters and Sweets, Highs and Lows, Longs and Shorts).[60] One article produced by the Newspaper Enterprise Association in 1905 attempted to explain "What a Billion Dollars Means" to illustrate the magnitude of the indemnity Japan was demanding from Russia following the Russo-Japanese War: "But suppose you decide to tackle the debt yourself. If your income is $19,000 a year—and the great majority of incomes are much below that—it would take you a million years to pay it, to say nothing of the interest. And you'd have to go without eating besides. . . . It amounts to about $20 for every square mile on the earth's surface. The receipts of the Louisiana Purchase exposition were about $10,000,000. It would take then, one hundred expositions of that kind to earn such an indemnity."[61]

Scripps newspapers published many articles about odd events or unusual people. One described a young woman who disguised herself as a man and worked as a circus-wagon driver for six years before being discovered. A typical story in the "Interesting People" series of 1905 concerned "Twins, though Born in Separate Years" (one sister was born shortly before midnight on December 31, 1834, and the other after midnight on January 1, 1835). Another in the series described "a famous fat boy" in England, who weighed 312 pounds at age fourteen. Still others discussed a young waitress who wed a millionaire, a prosperous businessman who deserted his wife and six children for a seventeen-year-old stenographer, and a Lutheran church in Pennsylvania that paid one red rose for rent each year.[62]

"The Woman's Angle"

Scripps and his managers maintained that news of interest to women was of particular importance because they were more loyal customers than men. Paine wrote that "the woman in a house who swears by a paper is worth five men who buy it on the street." On another occasion he informed an editor, "You had better have one woman in a home demanding your paper than ten men buying it on the street." He also told Scripps that "hardly an item of importance goes into the Cleveland Press without some thought as to whether it can not be given a twist or a side light to catch the women's interest."[63]

W. D. Wasson, editor of the San Francisco *Daily News,* said that he had tried to interest women readers, "knowing that if women readers liked the paper they would have it whether their husbands wanted it or not.[64] When the *Daily News* sponsored a contest in 1905 on "Why I Read the Daily News," most respondents were women, further reinforcing the view that interesting content was necessary for them.[65] "I ran across a statement the other day to the effect that women are most interested in things that excite their imagination and credulity," Paine wrote in 1905. "Cannot you [an NEA editor] get something on this line out of fortune telling and the voodoo doctors of the south?" In 1906 he urged the new editor of the Kansas City *World* to provide "more matter of especial interest to women daily."[66]

Scripps newspapers regularly published articles to interest women, for example, "Of Special Interest to Women," "What's a 'Model Husband'? (Proper Conduct of a Man toward Woman in Married Life as Suggested by Women Writers)," "Shall a Girl Marry Beneath Her?" ["No! Marry your equal and keep your step upward"], and "Symptoms of Insincerity—How Can Girls Tell True from False Men."[67] Some were attributed to the fictional Cynthia Grey, whose work appeared regularly. "Do you love?" her "Twelve Reasons for Love" began, "Are you going to marry? Then you must give twelve reasons for your love. A recent authority on love and matrimony says, 'Don't marry unless you can take a pencil in hand and write down twelve substantial reasons for loving that particular person.' Can you give twelve reasons?"[68]

Scripps newspapers also sponsored contests that were designed to attract the attention of women. In 1903 women constituted virtually all of the respondents to "What Is a Kiss?" a Los Angeles *Record* contest. The Seattle *Star* ran a contest on "Do the Women Tell Bigger Lies Than the Men Do?" in 1905, which led to a flood of responses from women. A few months later, the *Star* ran another contest asking women if they would marry their husbands again, given the chance (most said they would), and in 1906 the *San Diegan-Sun* ran a contest on "The Ideal Woman."[69]

Short stories were another staple geared toward women. Scripps told one editor that women "always read the short stories" even if they read nothing else in the paper. "It was on account of the short story that the women always complained to her husband for failing to bring the paper home." The NEA produced the column-long stories, and editors had orders to carry one daily.[70] During the week of November 15, 1905, for example, the NEA distributed nine: "The Watch That Grandfather Wore," "A Week with Cousin Helen," "His Duty as a Guardian," "Her Two Lovers," "Moonlight on the Mossy Graves," "Under the Old Apple Tree," "The Tattered Stocking," "And He Played the

Tambourine," and "The Two White Roses." The NEA also produced serialized stories and poetry.[71]

Such attention to women readers was not unusual; most U.S. newspapers of the era also ran articles on fashion and recipes. The rationale for doing so was primarily economic; it met the interests of advertisers who wanted to reach women consumers.[72] But Scripps newspapers differed from competitors by making a particular effort at providing content of interest to working-class women. Articles about them and how to run a household on a limited income were common. Cynthia Grey's series "Home," for example, was a guide to penny-pinching ways. One article advised working-class women how to dress well without spending large sums of money on clothes.[73] In another article, she warned husbands "IT'S YOUR FAULT IF YOU SPOIL YOUR WIFE": "Young man, you have won her. Now don't spoil her. If you have been honest she has married you with her eyes open to the fact that you are poor. She is willing to make the best of your poverty; she is willing to skimp and pinch. Let her help." On another occasion Grey compared rich people with the poor and concluded, "Sometimes we poor folks are much happier." Other articles gave advice on how to cook cheaply and prepare Thanksgiving dinner for as little as $2 or $3 for a family of eight.[74]

Unlike other newspapers of the era, Scripps publications acknowledged that many women worked. One NEA article reported that more than 20 percent of American women worked outside of the home.[75] Articles focused on women who worked as boilermakers, blacksmiths, carpenters, roofers, or brakemen; still others were telegraph operators, butchers, tailors, charwomen, stenographers, and clerks. An NEA series in 1903 described the jobs of women who worked as suspender makers and overall makers, and another series in the Portland *Daily News* was headlined "Talks with Women Who Work."[76]

Other NEA editorials stressed that many women worked outside the home but few if any received adequate wages. One, "Workingwomen's Wages," reported that unmarried working women had a difficult time: "The woman who is alone and has no other means of support than the pay for her honest work walks thorough life on thin ice. Her's is a hard, cheerless and almost hopeless lot."[77] Another editorial attacked job discrimination and described a railroad that refused to promote any woman beyond the job of stenographer:

Nature has shut women out of certain occupations, but has given them as good brains as are possessed by men. With good brains and a fair show there is nothing to keep a woman stenographer from climbing. She can enter the pulpit and achieve success. She can become an employer of labor; a banker, a manufacturer, a farmer, florist, landscape gardener, painter, musician. She can so shape her affairs and guide her ambition as to enter a thousand walks that pay better and contain more fame than the place at a typewriter. She can do these things for she has done them.

As yet another editorial argued, a woman deserved a good job, good pay, and the "right to do whatever work she chooses and to receive a salary commensurate with that work."[78]

Catering to women's interests placed a premium on respectable newspaper content. E. F. Chase, supervisor of the Scripps Spokane *Press* in 1904, told its editor and manager to make it acceptable to women readers by running "only as much of the sayings and doings of the demi-monde and the tenderloin in general as is necessary to cover the news."[79] Scripps maintained that coverage of sexual vice was unprofitable because "these subjects should be avoided except in such cases as the editor feels that it is his duty to make an actual sacrifice on the part of the financial interests of his paper for the public good." It was Paine's opinion that 95 percent of women were highly moral, and thus newspapers needed to maintain a "tone of decency."[80]

Conclusions

In 1901 the Seattle *Star* sent postal cards to more than a thousand readers, asking for suggestions on how to improve the newspaper: "If there is a scarcity of news of any particular kind in which you are interested, please make the fact known. If there is news published of a character that does not interest you, make that fact known, too." A synopsis of the 140 replies appeared in the *Sun*. Most readers seemed to like its format of short articles, illustrations, feature material, and editorials.[81] The survey reflected E. W. Scripps's sense that his newspapers should work constantly to please readers. "It has always been a principle of mine that there was only one absolutely certain way of making a newspaper business succeed, and that was by making the most interesting paper possible," he told an editor in 1903.[82]

Coupled with his market segmentation strategy, Scripps's demand for interesting newspapers led to certain kinds of content. Editors attempted to make their publications easy to read by offering short stories in simple language so tired workers could follow the day's events without great effort. They also sought to entertain with jokes and cartoons and to make news interesting and easy to understand by heavy reliance on illustrations (photographs, line drawings, and editorial cartoons) and features. Up-beat inspirational editorials were common. Traditional news topics, such as government and business, were covered but shared page space with large doses of short stories, jokes, and articles on such leisure activities as vaudeville and spectator sports.

Compared to their competitors, Scripps newspapers had shorter articles, more vivid headlines, more jokes and illustrations, and more types of nontraditional content. All of that derived from Scripps's definition of a target audience. Content was crafted to reach working-class readers.

Scripps newspapers did not neglect serious political and social issues, and their advocacy for working-class issues and reform generally was apparent to anyone who could read. But they dealt with politics and other critical issues with an eye toward the reading habits and interests of the working class. From Scripps's point of view, doing so constituted good journalism and good business. How readers responded is a matter of speculation; correspondence between Scripps and his editors and other managers indicates that they were selective and paid the most attention to feature articles, cartoons, and human-interest editorials.

The Legacy of
E. W. Scripps

WHEN E. W. SCRIPPS DIED in 1926, *Editor and Publisher* called him a pioneer of American journalism who "had devoted his unique genius and the gigantic press power of its creation to fighting the battles of 'the forgotten man,' the worker without the prestige of wealth, political or social position."[1] He had established an empire of dozens of newspapers and founded both the Newspaper Enterprise Association and the United Press Associations. Moreover, he had influenced American journalism, creating the nation's first major newspaper chain while advocating independence in journalism. As one employee noted, "There was the freedom to write the truth as they saw it as reporters, and to discuss it fearlessly as editors, unhampered by business office expediency or by the private investments and personal interests of the owner."[2] It was "an extraordinary achievement for a man who started off in the historic American manner with small means and only a public school education."[3]

News for the Common People

Advocacy of working-class interests stemmed from Scripps's philosophy of journalism. The press should serve as the foundation of democracy, he said, because it could provide the information so vital to an enlightened electorate. "These United States are governed by many millions of voters who have no other possible means of informing themselves on the subject of legislation than the daily press," Scripps observed. "Doubted and even reviled as the daily press may be, on account of its shortcomings, still the government of the United States depends entirely upon judgments formed as a result of the contents of the daily newspapers."[4] In practice, he contended, the press had fallen far short of its duty to democratic society and become the tool of privileged elites, ignoring or even opposing the needs and interests of the masses. A press dominated by the few, representing the interests of the few, was not a press equal to the needs of democracy.

To counter the elitism of the American press, Scripps created newspapers that were the "friends, advisers, advocates and even the special pleaders of the ninety-five percent of the population that were not rich or powerful."[5] They were to be "an experiment, on the success of which depends a great deal of the future fortune of democracy. If we can prove that it is possible to publish . . . a daily newspaper that is almost reckless in its daring, in its loyalty to the common people, and defiant of the aristocratic masses, we will have set on foot the work of the emancipation of the press in this country. We will prove that newspapers can be owned and run by people who are not millionaires and without any subsidy (advertising) from the millionaire classes."[6]

That was Scripps's cause, his crusade. What he wanted was to send out "missionaries" among editors, journalism, and newspaper business managers nationwide to "PREACH THE GOSPEL of this new journalism and to direct many hundreds of young men's thoughts and energies to this new line."[7] The crusade would spread independent newspapers—ideally owned by Scripps—nationwide. "I have what you might call an ambition or an object in life, and that object is to create a great and independent and useful newspaper institution that will cover the United States and which will be of future great benefit and service to this country."[8]

Scripps's newspapers were stalwart supporters of organized labor when it had few friends and many enemies in the American press. They defended collective bargaining, strikes, and political activity by unions, advocated safer working conditions and the eight-hour day, and assailed monopolists and self-serving politicians who took advantage of the common people. In addition, they provided news and information in a way that would be accessible to workers. News was written for the laborer; articles and sentences were short and pictures plentiful. Scripps's newspapers did not avoid difficult or controversial topics, but they presented them in a way that increased the likelihood they could be read and understood. Editorial cartoons, for example, provided simplified but important information about serious political and economic issues.

The newspapers attempted to be interesting, too. They covered politics and government, long the traditional focus of American news, but gave them less space than did competitors. Political news was never neglected in Scripps newspapers, but it had its place and season. Most readers, Scripps believed, did not need or want a steady diet of business and political news; that sort of content reflected the tastes of reporters rather than the masses. Instead, Scripps newspapers focused on more entertaining fare: jokes and cartoons (featuring characters such as the enormously popular Everett True), advice columns from Cynthia Grey, news features, sports, and stories emphasizing oddities and bizarre events.

Scripps's decision to target working-class readers had a direct impact on the definition of news in his newspapers—and differentiated them from their rivals. Events and issues were evaluated according to their resonance with working-class readers. Speeches by labor leader Samuel Gompers, for instance, were highlighted, as were issues of particular concern to the working class, such as the cost of living or streetcar fares. Big businessmen such as John D. Rockefeller usually were portrayed in a negative light. Reports that drew little interest in the working class—such as business markets—did not appear. In contrast, Scripps's rivals did not define news through the eyes of labor.

Scripps contended that all newspapers were essentially shaping the news to reflect their markets. His stood out because they—unlike most of the U.S. press—did not implicitly or explicitly support political or business elites. Scripps contended that there was no such thing as a completely unbiased newspaper; all inevitably were subjective in how they defined news. He complained that most newspapers were cozy with traditional business and political interests. Through emphasis or omission their definition of news reflected a bias toward the status quo.

Independent Newspapers

Scripps recognized that working-class advocacy could invite attack from more conservative interests, and so he strove to keep his newspapers free from outside pressures. In particular he sought to limit dependence on advertising, reasoning that such business patronage often impinged upon a newspaper's ability to report the news and editorialize freely. Scripps believed that extensive dependence on advertising forced newspapers to please business elites and left them vulnerable to advertiser boycotts when they were not suitably submissive. As a result, Scripps—unlike most of his competitors—tried to emphasize circulation revenues over advertising revenues. He often started his newspapers with little or no advertising, and, once established, the publications limited the amount and size of advertisements they accepted. Advertising revenue offset production costs and kept sales prices low, but Scripps preferred the patronage of many small businesses rather than reliance on large ones.

Scripps was not the only contrarian of his era who rejected advertising, but the handful of publishers who actively tried to limit its influence and willingly turned down its revenues was very small. Most were all too eager to attract advertisers and even ran advertisements disguised as news (reading notices) and plugged advertisers in news columns. Scripps resisted the rising tide of commercialization and recognized that advertisers' influence extended far beyond their own notices and into the news columns themselves.

Scripps and Business Concerns

Scripps's great crusade to create independent, working-class newspapers involved not just purifying journalism but also making money. News for the "forgotten man" might be highly principled, but it also had to be profitable. As he said, "There is no good in a newspaper pretending to have courage and honesty without it being backed up not only by cash surpluses but by daily profit. The fool martyr who destroys himself and his newspaper for the sake only of being honest, can do no good to the country and can do much harm by teaching his fellows that honesty is a poor business policy."[9] The goal was good journalism, as Scripps reminded his employees, but "business success is an absolute necessary incident to the main object in view."[10]

Had the working-class newspaper not been profitable, Scripps would not have been its prophet. He had come to journalism first with a desire to make money—as a restless, ambitious entrepreneur. He soon learned that working-class journalism could be profitable. It exploited a reading audience ignored by most established newspapers of that era. Scripps's older brother, James, pioneered the working-class newspaper formula at the Detroit *Evening News*. E. W. Scripps's great genius was an ability to expand that model nationally, starting dozens of newspapers with limited capital.

Expanding his brother's model of journalism was not an easy proposition; Scripps did not start his career with a huge fortune. Yet he had luck, self-assurance, and entrée to the industry through his older brother's paper. Scripps's single share of stock in the Detroit *Evening News* provided the initial leverage for his entire career. He used that stock to finance his 30 percent interest in the Cleveland *Press,* and success there led to St. Louis and Cincinnati newspapers and to dreams of empire.

Even with dividends from two or three highly profitable newspapers, Scripps could create an empire only through the most rigid cost controls—represented by his low-cost and vertical integration strategies. Careful money management reduced start-up costs and allowed the establishment of many cheap newspapers rather than a few more grandiose ones. Economizing kept operating costs down, too, hastening profits that in turn could be funneled into new projects.

Cost controls were a necessary component of expansion; the ensuing chain further facilitated economizing. New Scripps newspapers got started with type and presses acquired cheaply from older properties, and chainwide newsprint purchases produced substantial savings. Content production through the Newspaper Enterprise Association and the telegraph news services provided a wide variety of copy, also chainwide, at a relatively low cost to each newspaper. Scripps showed that chains could be far more efficient economically than one-newspaper firms. Cost controls were a factor in remaining close to the working class. Scripps newspapers, priced at just a penny, were within the reach of everyone. He also restricted a key source of revenue from advertising. Only extensive economizing could keep his newspapers both cheap and relatively independent.

Newspaper Chains

During the early 1900s Scripps maintained that newspaper chains would soon dominate the industry because they could be far more efficient economically than one-newspaper firms. From his analysis of American business in the late nineteenth century he had concluded that competition necessitated economizing, which in turn spurred mergers. Only chain-affiliated newspapers would survive in the long run.

The creation of the newspaper chain was a logical and creative response to conditions in the industry around 1900. Intense competition and rising costs made it difficult for new newspapers to get started and endure, and Scripps's chain provided financial and journalistic resources to overcome some of those hurdles. His telegraph news service—sustained at first primarily by the chain—allowed him to circumvent the monopolistic practices of the Associated Press.

Some of the criticism of newspaper chains in the late twentieth century derives from the fear that they reduce competition. The Scripps chain, however, did just the opposite. It facilitated the establishment of newspapers and increased their ability to withstand attack from established publishers. Newspapers in the chain survived and thrived in cities where other publications had usually failed. In Seattle, for example, two newspapers (the morning Seattle *Post Intelligencer* and the afternoon Seattle *Times*) seemed to have a lock on the local market because a number of dailies had been started in the 1890s, only to fail quickly. It was because of the chain's resources that Scripps was able to establish and sustain a daily newspaper in Seattle.

In dozens of cities across the United States the Scripps chain introduced ideas and issues far different from most other newspapers. Unlike the vast majority of their rivals, Scripps newspapers brought substantive and sympathetic discussion of working-class and reform issues before the public—enriching public debate and discussion. The chain was the incarnation of reform, advocacy for the masses, and opposition to the excesses of big business. It is ironic that contemporary chains are often seen as the antithesis of reform and the embodiment of big business.

Scripps was a person of contradictions—the captain of industry (complete with estate and yacht) and at the same time a champion of workers. He defended the working class and welcomed unionized printers at all his newspapers but paid pathetically low wages to workers who had no union: reporters, editors, and business staff. While his publications railed against the rich and worried about the rising cost of living, some of his own employees had to borrow money from him to finance homes or meet medical expenses. He valued democracy but was himself an autocrat, tolerating no dissent within his family and business; contended that his sister, Ellen, was one of the greatest newspaper writers of the era but was loathe to hire women as reporters; and defended organized labor but helped kill newspapers that supported it.

Yet despite such contradictions, Scripps stands out from many of his peers. Unlike many, he attempted to create newspapers that served more than the elites. He also recognized that heavy dependence on advertising could be a Faustian bargain, with advertisers influencing far more than just the space they leased. Late in the twentieth century, television's dedication to the lowest common denominator and to the least offensive programming and magazines' use of "complementary copy"—articles that reinforce advertisers' pitches—all bear witness to Scripps's prescience.

E. W. Scripps and Modern Journalism

Despite the warm eulogies in publications such as *Editor and Publisher* and *Literary Digest,* Scripps did not succeed in reforming American journalism. His newspapers were far different from the norm—smaller, cheaper, and poorer. Most were the smallest publications in their cities. As markets later contracted, many failed (although clearly Scripps should not bear all of the responsibility for business failures in the 1930s or 1940s). Scripps's ideas about advertising never found favor with other publishers; the trend in American mass media was toward more advertising rather than less. Few newspapers championed the working classes as did Scripps, and fewer still tied themselves to a down-scale demographic audience. Modern Scripps-Howard newspapers are mainstream publications, not agitators against the status quo.

Scripps's legacy was limited because the business strategies he employed did not always serve his newspapers well in the long run. In particular, elements of his market segmentation and low-cost strategies reduced his newspapers' ability to compete in the media markets of the twentieth century. The market segmentation strategy led him to deemphasize advertising and emphasize circulation. That dependence on subscribers severely limited revenue, leaving Scripps's newspapers relatively poor. They were small during an era when readers appeared to enjoy the increasing bulk of most daily newspapers, and they lacked the resources to cover local stories as fully as their rivals. Competitor newspapers provided nearly three times as much local news as did Scripps newspapers, and his publications, as local news became increasingly important, were not well positioned to compete for readers' attention.

Although the deemphasis on advertising helped preserve the Scripps newspapers' independence, it also demonstrated his lack of understanding of readers and the changing nature of American society. Many readers seemed genuinely interested in getting commercial information, yet Scripps's interests extended only to news and not to advertising, which he flatly refused to believe that readers liked. In resisting advertising, Scripps was also battling the commercialization of American life and culture. However heroic that stance, he was never likely to succeed. What he failed to understand was that most Americans seem to prefer such business-subsidized media despite the inherent problems in such financing. After all, advertising patronage lowers the cost each consumer much bear. Although there are some well-known advertising-free publications (such as the newspaper *PM* and the reborn *Ms. Magazine*), they are few in number.

There is also little evidence that the working class as a whole understood or appreciated Scripps's style of journalism. In Los Angeles, San Francisco, and Chicago, the large Hearst newspapers, which had splashy crusades, plentiful advertising, and self-indulgent promotion, were far more popular than the small Scripps publications. Hearst's style of journalism seemed good enough for most working class Americans of that era. In each of those cities, the Hearst newspapers survived much longer than the Scripps newspapers. The problem may have been that Hearst was more attuned than Scripps to modern readers. Scripps viewed journalism primarily through his experiences at the Detroit *Evening News* and the Cleveland *Press;* as such, his notions about journalism were formed—and frozen—in the 1870s and early 1880s. Although he was highly creative in pioneering newspaper illustrations and photographs, he was less able to deal with other changes in the industry. He never understood the popularity of large newspapers, Sunday editions, or advertising.

In practice, Scripps's market segmentation strategy was not always evenly applied. In some cities, such as Cleveland and Cincinnati, his newspapers addressed themselves broadly to working-class concerns and prospered. In other cities, such as San Francisco, they tied themselves closely to labor unions and were unable to move beyond that segment of the working class. Scripps's estimate that his newspapers would serve "the ninety-five percent of the population that were not rich or powerful" was inflated.[11] Most seemed to aim at the bottom fifth or third of their markets.

The low-cost strategy limited the ability to compete because it tended to emphasize cost-cutting over quality. At times, economizing became the chain's chief goal rather than simply a means to an end. Scripps and his chief lieutenant—the chain's treasurer, Lemuel T. Atwood—devoted most of their attention to monthly profit-and-loss statements, judging each editor not by the quality of the news product but by his ability to generate profits within limited budgets. The editor who met the mandatory 15 percent profit requirement each month was a success, and little attention was paid to the news product unless it diverged greatly from the chain's general principles.

Apart from Scripps, the real power in the chain early in the twentieth century belonged to Atwood, who, as treasurer, wielded the power of the purse effectively, withholding crucial funding or equipment. While Scripps and Atwood gave orders, others—such chief editor Robert F. Paine—gave advice that was usually exhortatory rather than mandatory. Scripps worried at times that some of his editors produced newspapers distinguished primarily because of their cheapness. Nonetheless, his penny-pinching ways—which relied on small, inexperienced, and low-paid news staffs, cheap newsprint, and used presses—and emphasis on profits pushed his publications toward that outcome.

E. W. Scripps and the Newspaper Business

Although Scripps did not succeed in reforming journalism or even in creating a style of content that would long endure, he clearly influenced the structure of the industry by developing the first national chain. That structure still dominates the industry, characterizing about three-fourths of American dailies. By the late twentieth century newspaper chains operated in many ways as they did in Scripps's time—federations of centrally managed newspapers benefiting from common resources such as news features, jointly operated news bureaus, and national advertising bureaus.

Scripps's business activities also mark him as the prototype of the modern newspaper publisher—the "man of business, business over all."[12] Late in the twentieth century, American publishers would be engaged in much the same work as Scripps: establishing policy, planning, setting performance goals, marketing, providing fiscal oversight, trying to improve their product, and competing for consumers' attention and money.

During his long career, E. W. Scripps established or bought more than forty newspapers and created an international telegraph news service and a news features syndicate. Born poor on an Illinois farm, he created the nation's largest media company. He did not realize all of his goals: His chain was smaller than he had hoped, and he was unable to reform journalism and corral advertising. Still, he was one of the most astute newspaper businessmen of his era and developed the structure of newspaper operation that continues to endure and thrive.

Appendix 1

TABLES

Table 1. Percentage of Telegraph News According to City of Origin in Three Markets, 1907

	News from a City with a Scripps Newspaper	News from a City without a Scripps Newspaper	Column Inches
Sacramento *Union*	27.9	72.1	1,440.50
Sacramento *Bee*	19.8	80.2	1,689.00
Sacramento *Star* (Scripps)	50.8	49.2	234.25
San Diego *Union*	21.5	78.5	870.50
San Diego *Tribune*	16.9	83.1	735.75
San Diegan-Sun (Scripps)	39.1	60.9	226.75
Portland *Oregonian*	11.6	88.4	2,018.00
Portland *Evening Telegram*	10.7	89.3	2,034.25
Oregon *Journal*	11.8	88.2	1,141.00
Portland *Daily News* (Scripps)	44.3	55.7	293.75

Note: This table corresponds to figure 1.

Table 2. Sources of Non-Advertising Content by Percentages in Scripps Newspapers during First Week of Publication

	Pueblo *Sun*	Sacramento *Star*	Tacoma *Times*	Oklahoma *News*	Evansville *Press*
Local	18.2	28.4	19.2	15.7	17.0
Telegraph news services	17.6	19.7	18.6	24.3	9.6
NEA	64.2	51.9	62.2	59.9	73.4
Column inches	865.25	2,133.75	1,654.5	459.0	1,887.25

Sources: Pueblo *Sun*, Sept. 1–8, 1906; Sacramento *Star*, Nov. 21–26, 1904; Tacoma *Times*, Dec. 21–26, 1903; Oklahoma *News*, Oct. 4–10, 1906; Evansvillle *Press*, July 2–7, 1906.
Note: This table corresponds to figure 2.

Table 3. Reliance on Newspaper Enterprise Association for Selected Scripps Newspapers, 1907

	Percentage of Total Editorial Content	Column Inches
San Diegan-Sun	53.72	1,087.00
Portland *Daily News*	66.30	1,839.00
Sacramento *Star*	44.97	1,047.25
Seattle *Star*	32.80	1,221.25
Cincinnati *Post*	27.50	3,414.50
Evansville *Press*	62.70	2,336.75

Note: This table corresponds to figure 3.

Table 4. Percentage of Local, Non-Local Content in Three Newspaper Markets, 1907

	Local	Non-Local	Column Inches
San Diegan-Sun (Scripps)	25.4	74.6	1,087.00
San Diego *Union*	54.1	45.9	1,895.75
San Diego *Tribune*	47.6	52.4	1,398.25
Portland *Daily News* (Scripps)	17.6	82.4	1,839.00
Portland *Oregon Journal*	57.8	42.2	2,711.75
Portland *Evening Telegram*	47.0	53.0	3,881.75
Portland *Oregonian*	42.9	57.1	3,569.75
Sacramento *Star* (Scripps)	22.3	77.7	1,047.25
Sacramento *Bee*	34.2	63.8	2,564.00
Sacramento *Union*	38.3	61.7	2,333.75

Note: This table corresponds to figure 4.

Table 5. Coverage of Labor by Percentage in Five Newspaper Markets, 1907

	Strikes	Working Conditions	Politics	Labor Day and Other Labor Issues	Column Inches
Portland *Daily News* (Scripps)	25.40	29.4	19.6	25.4	241.00
Portland *Oregon Journal*	47.30	26.3	15.7	10.5	40.75
Portland *Telegram*	75.40	1.9	16.8	5.9	50.50
Portland *Oregonian*	91.80	0.0	4.6	3.6	42.75
Sacramento *Star* (Scripps)	15.40	49.5	28.2	6.9	80.75
Sacramento *Bee*	66.90	0.0	28.3	4.8	25.75
Sacramento *Union*	62.70	0.0	30.7	6.6	18.75
San Diegan-Sun (Scripps)	32.30	29.8	19.7	18.2	59.50
San Diego *Union*	83.70	0.0	8.2	8.1	15.25
San Diego *Tribune*	90.50	0.0	6.5	3.0	15.50
Cincinnati *Post* (Scripps)	12.70	36.6	8.6	42.1	205.75
Cincinnati *Times-Star*	73.10	0.0	0.0	26.9	36.25
Evansville *Press* (Scripps)	16.75	36.7	39.2	7.2	307.50
Evansville *Journal News*	47.30	0.0	17.1	35.3	27.50

Note: This table corresponds to figure 5.

Table 6. Average Length and Number of Page-One Articles in Four Cities, 1907

	Average Length (col. lines)	Average Number of Articles
Seattle *Star* (Scripps)	28.3	39.8
Seattle *Times*	70.4	15.3
Seattle *Post-Intelligencer*	50.3	26.6
Sacramento *Star* (Scripps)	29.6	33.6
Sacramento *Union*	59.6	16.0
Sacramento *Bee*	58.6	20.3
Evansville *Press* (Scripps)	41.3	30.5
Evansville *News and Journal*	95.4	14.6
Denver *Express* (Scripps)	23.0	41.2
Denver *Post*	98.2	12.3
Denver *Rocky Mountain News*	107.2	11.2

Table 7. Comparative Length in Column Lines of Articles
on Insurance Investigation, Sacramento, 1905

Testimony of	Sacramento *Star* (Scripps)	Sacramento *Bee*	Sacramento *Union*
James H.Hyde	90	182	271
Benjamin Odell	55	221	123
Chauncey Depew	52	84	77
Thomas F. Ryan	52	144	91

Sources: Sacramento *Star:* Nov. 14, 1905, 1 (Hyde); Nov. 16, 1905, 1 (Odell);
Nov. 16, 1905, 1, Nov. 17, 1905, 1 (Depew); Dec. 12, 1905, 1 (Ryan); Sacramento *Bee:* Nov. 14, 1905, 1 (Hyde); Nov. 16, 1905, 1 (Odell); Nov. 16, 1905,
1; Nov. 17, 1905, 1 (Depew); Dec. 12, 1905, 1 (Ryan); Sacramento *Union:* Nov.
15, 1905, 1, Nov. 16, 1905, 2 (Hyde); Nov. 17, 1905, 1 (Odell); Nov. 17, 1905,
3, Nov. 18, 1905, 1 (Depew); Dec. 13, 1905, 1 (Ryan).

Table 8. Content Format by Percentage in Five Newspaper
Markets, 1907

	Graphic Format	Non-Graphic Format	Column Inches
Portland *Daily News* (Scripps)	27.3	72.7	1,839.00
Portland *Evening Telegram*	17.4	82.6	3,881.75
Portland *Oregon Journal*	5.5	94.5	2,711.75
Portland *Oregonian*	5.4	94.6	3,569.75
Sacramento *Star* (Scripps)	29.0	71.0	1,047.25
Sacramento *Bee*	0.5	99.5	2,571.00
Sacramento *Union*	0.4	99.6	2,333.75
San Diegan–Sun (Scripps)	22.2	77.8	1,087.00
San Diego *Union*	3.5	96.5	1,895.75
San Diego *Tribune*	1.1	98.9	1,398.25
Cincinnati *Post* (Scripps)	19.9	80.1	3,414.50
Cincinnati *Times Star*	9.4	90.6	5,641.75
Evansville *Press* (Scripps)	25.9	74.1	2,336.75
Evansville *Journal-News*	8.1	91.9	3,243.50

Note: This table corresponds to figure 6.

Table 9. Patterns of Content by Percentage in Five Newspaper Markets, 1907

	Government, Politics, Business, Religion, Accidents, Deaths	Leisure Activities, Sports, Women, Comics, Society News	Column Inches
Sacramento *Star* (Scripps)	54.1	39.8	1,047.25
Sacramento *Bee*	74.9	24.1	2,564.00
Sacramento *Union*	82.5	14.8	2,333.75
San Diegan-Sun (Scripps)	55.1	39.3	1,087.00
San Diego *Union*	84.1	14.8	1,895.75
San Diego *Tribune*	76.2	20.3	1,398.25
Portland *Daily News* (Scripps)	46.2	47.3	1,539.00
Portland *Oregonian*	87.1	12.3	3,569.75
Portland *Oregon Journal*	75.2	19.9	2,711.75
Portland *Evening Telegram*	63.8	29.7	3,881.75
Evansville *Press* (Scripps)	37.1	45.5	2,336.75
Evansville *Journal News*	71.1	18.2	3,243.50
Cincinnati *Post* (Scripps)	54.4	32.5	3,414.50
Cincinnati *Times Star*	69.1	25.4	5,641.75

Note: Percentages do not total 100; not counted is content dealing with weather, historical features, divorce, insanity, and science and technology. This table corresponds to figure 7.

Table 10. Subject of Editorials by Percentage in Five Newspaper Markets, 1907

	Politics	Human Interest	Other	Column Inches
Sacramento *Star* (Scripps)	56.1	38.6	5.3	57.00
Sacramento *Bee*	81.6	1.3	17.1	81.75
Sacramento *Union*	87.8	0.0	12.2	139.75
San Diegan-Sun (Scripps)	51.4	42.7	5.9	51.50
San Diego *Union*	90.0	0.0	10.0	135.25
San Diego *Tribune*	90.4	0.0	9.6	146.25
Portland *Daily News* (Scripps)	40.7	53.8	5.5	110.50
Portland *Oregonian*	85.1	0.0	14.9	207.75
Portland *Evening Telegram*	89.7	2.7	7.6	186.50
Portland *Oregon Journal*	84.1	7.4	8.5	203.25
Evansville *Press* (Scripps)	11.2	83.1	5.6	88.50
Evansville *Journal News*	89.9	0.4	9.3	116.75
Cincinnati *Post* (Scripps)	38.2	48.1	13.7	106.00
Cincinnati *Times Star*	46.7	20.5	32.7	146.50

Appendix 2

A constructed week sample was created for 1907. All non-advertising content in the newspapers was coded according to subject and length. The original subject categories are below; the various tables and figures demonstrate collapsed versions of the categories.

Reliability: All categories had reliability above 93 percent.

Unit of measurement: The entire story (including headline), cartoon, or editorial.

Quantitative Content Analysis Codebook.
1. Subject

01. National politics: political issues (federal government, Congress, members of Congress, staff, bills, debates and proceedings, executive departments including cabinet, defense and armed forces, first family, national political parties), Supreme Court

02. U.S. foreign relations

03. Foreign politics: relations between and among foreign countries (where U.S. not clearly involved), wars, elections, governmental operations, heads of state

04. Foreign news (not political): general customs and culture

05. Foreign news: acts of nature (floods, earthquakes, disasters, famine), shipwrecks, accidents, deaths

06. Foreign news: society, art, culture, fashion, leisure (theater, books, sports, music)

07. Foreign news: disease (cholera, plagues)

08. Foreign news: business

09. Foreign news: crime, trials, police, arrests, jails

10. Foreign history

11. U.S. history: commemoration of U.S. historical events (Washington's Birthday, Civil War reminiscences, general U.S. history)

12. Natural history (U.S. or foreign): Ice Age, dinosaurs, etc.

13. State politics (other than home state of the newspaper): politics (legislatures, governors, state politicians); politics of cities outside home state (e.g., mayoralty election in a city outside home state)

14. Home-state politics (includes politics of cities in home state but not home city)

15. Local politics: home county, city, or suburbs (city council, mayor, agencies other than police, fire, hospital, and mental health)

16. General crime news: police, criminal court news not home county, home city, or suburbs, prisoners (current and past), jails, duels, police investigations, chases, arraignments, or trials in criminal cases, confessions, executions, general police news

17. Crime (home county, city, or suburbs): police and criminal court news, arrests

18. Civil court issues (lawsuits), not to include divorce cases, sanity hearings; general lawyers (unless concerning a crime), not home county, city, or suburbs

19. Civil court issues, home county, city, or suburbs

20. Accidents (fatal, not fatal) and hospitals: train wreck, explosion, boat sinking, carriage upset, injuries (not home county)

21. Accidents (fatal, not fatal) and hospitals: home county, city, or suburbs

22. Divorce, adultery, illicit love, romantic triangles, elopements, breach of promise, romance, etc.

23. Insanity, mental institutions

24. Suicides, attempted suicides

25. Fires, not home county, city, or suburbs

26. Fires, home county, city, or suburbs

27. Other local news, home county, city, or suburbs

28. General business and finance news, not home county, city, or suburbs: business, finance, railroads, mining, agriculture, real estate, general investment climate, shipping, trade, markets, crop news, fishing, ship and railroad schedules

29. Business and finance, home county, city, or suburbs (includes profiles of local businesses, business persons, bankruptcies)

30. Labor, not home county, city, or suburbs: working conditions, labor unions, labor talks, strikes

31. Labor (home county, city, or suburbs)

32. Science, education, technology, medicine: inventions, new technology, schools, school children, general health, drugs, general medical news, conventions or meetings in science, education, technology, or medicine

33. Disease, plagues, U.S.

34. Weather, U.S. (daily forecasts, weather reports, storms, etc.)

35. Religions, churches, charity, and philanthropy, denominational meetings, Vatican, philosophical or quasi-religious groups (e.g., Theosophical Society); charity

36. Deaths, serious illness: death from general causes (as opposed to accidents, crime), obituaries, wills, funerals, or reports on persons dying, not home county, city, or suburbs

37. Death, serious illness: Home county, city, or suburbs

38. Miscellany

39. Fashion, society news: parties, dances, reunions, general society, clothes, traveling

40. Recipes, cooking, news about the home: how to decorate, new homes, food

41. "Women's work": shopping, cleaning, cooking, volunteer work by women, women's groups, clubs, or auxiliaries

42. Women in unusual occupations (e.g., reporter, physician, minister)

43. Fraternal organizations (GAR, Masons, Odd Fellows)

44. General entertainment: theater, news, plays, reviews, interviews with actors, music (concerts, music festivals, music halls), lectures (Chautauqua, general lectures)

45. Reading and art: book reviews, news about books, writers, art, and artists

46. Other leisure activities (other than sports); vacations

47. Fiction, verse, news about fiction or verse

48. Hobbies, games (card games), pets, animals, zoos, circuses, animal protection groups

49. Sports and adventure: baseball, boats, boxing, golf, horse racing, walking, bicycling, tennis, hunting, misc., adventure (safaris, hunting, animal terror)

50. The newspaper itself: articles about the newspaper and general promotional articles

51. Newspaper coupons, premiums, contests, patterns, cut-out dolls, etc.

52. Indexes for the newspaper

53. Journalism in general (not this specific newspaper)

54. Editorials, editorial cartoons

55. Letters to the editor

56. Editorial page columns (but not editorials)

57. Articles for children (children's puzzles, literature)

58. Comics, jokes

59. Geek stories: Deformities, weird stories, two-headed people, mad-dogs, dwarfs, etc.

60. Miscellany

61. News of other states and cities, not home county, city, or suburbs and not political

62. Indians/Native Americans (traditions, culture); resettlement as part of national political news

63. Advice to the lovelorn

II. Business

(If the article, photograph, cartoon, etc., deals with business, what is presented?)

1. Excesses or corruption of business: evils of trusts, monopolies; need for regulation; investigations into business fraud or malfeasance; accusations of malfeasance

2. Honest business, explicit statement: business is good, honest

3. Routine business: ship arrivals, stock markets, etc.

4. Some combination of the above

5. Not applicable; no mention of business

III. Labor.

Does the article deal in any way with labor? labor unions?

1. Strike (pending, current, ending, ended; includes negotiations during a strike; any strike-related activities such as picketing, violence; profiles of workers during strikes)

2. Injunction against strike

3. Industrial accidents (e.g., worker hurt in accident on job)

4. Wages (not part of any of the above, e.g., wages low for workers; cost of living)

5. Labor political issues (labor union party, emphasis primarily on political activity; if other labor issues mentioned they are subsidiary to this point)

6. Other labor-related issues or events (e.g., union parade, meetings not strike related)

7. Not applicable; does not deal with labor

IV. Source of Article

1. Wire service (United Press Associations, Associated Press, etc.)

2. Newspaper Enterprise Association

3. Local

4. Other

5. Not clear, do not know

V. Photos, Illustrations

Is the article illustrated (photograph, line drawing)?

1. Yes—line drawing or cartoon

2. Yes—photograph

3. Yes, both line drawing, cartoon

4. Yes, other

VI. Length

Column inches of print: 000025 to 999999

VII. Length

Column inches of photograph: 000000 to 999999

VIII. Editorials: Subject

1. Local politics (city, suburbs)

2. Other politics (region, state, nation)

3. Human interest, moral uplift, inspirational message (work hard, save money, be wise)

4. Other

5. Not applicable (not an editorial)

IX. Origin of Article: Dateline.

If there is a dateline, what city?

1. Cleveland	2. Cincinnati	3. Covington, Ky.
4. St. Louis	5. Memphis	6. Nashville
7. Terre Haute	8. Evansville	9. Denver
10. Dallas	11. Oklahoma City	12. Pueblo
13. Los Angeles	14. San Diego	15. San Francisco
16. Fresno	17. Sacramento	18. Portland
19. Tacoma	20. Seattle	21. Spokane
22. Detroit	23. Columbus	24. Akron
25. Toledo	26. Berkeley	27. Kansas City
28. Des Moines	29. Other (specify).	

Notes

Introduction

1. The rise of a national economy required mass-marketing, so business came to rely on newspapers (through advertising) as a means of reaching consumers. The rise of cities created complex social settings where newspapers served as vital communications links.

2. Juergens, *Joseph Pulitzer,* xii.

3. Swanberg, *Citizen Hearst,* 90.

4. Ibid., 107.

5. Ibid., 524.

6. Lee, *The Daily Newspaper in America,* 214–15.

7. Swanberg, *Citizen Hearst,* 483–96.

8. Ibid., 484.

9. Lee, *The Daily Newspaper in America,* 722–23.

10. Owen, *Economics of Freedom of Expression,* 46.

11. *Printer's Ink,* May 28, 1890, 869–71.

12. Such pricing was not static; many of Scripps's competitors eventually lowered their prices.

13. E. W. Scripps to Ward C. Mayborn, Dec. 18, 1907, subseries 1.2, box 10, folder 4. (Unless otherwise indicated, all E. W. Scripps correspondence and documents cited in the following notes are housed in the E. W. Scripps Correspondence Collection, Alden Library, Ohio University.)

14. *Newspaper Maker,* April 12, 1900, 6.

15. E. W. Scripps to R. F. Paine, Jan. 16, 1906, subseries 1.2, box 6, folder 14.

16. Pittsburgh *Leader,* Jan. 21, 1898, 8.

17. *The Newspaper Maker,* Dec. 3, 1896, 4.

Chapter 1: The Struggle for Control

1. E. W. Scripps to H. B. Clark, Dec. 15, 1905, subseries 1.2, box 6, folder 11.

2. E. W. Scripps to Milton McRae, Oct. 9, 1900, subseries 1.1, box 4, folder 2.

3. E. W. Scripps to E. H. Wells, Sept. 11, 1900, series 2, box 4, letterbook 6, 1.

4. E. W. Scripps to H. B. Clark, Dec. 15, 1905, subseries 1.2, box 5, folder 11.

5. Trimble, *The Astonishing Mr. Scripps,* 11–13.

6. Kaplan, "The Economics of Popular Journalism," describes James Scripps's revolutionary approach to journalism and is particularly insightful.

7. Scripps, "Autobiography," series 4, box 11, 177.

8. Trimble, *The Astonishing Mr. Scripps,* 25.

9. Scripps, "Autobiography," series 4, box 11, 198.

10. Ibid., 231.

11. E. W. Scripps to Annie Scripps, Nov. 23, 1878, subseries 1.2, box 1, folder 1.

12. Scripps, "Autobiography," series 4, box 11, 243–47, emphasis added.

13. E. W. Scripps to Annie Scripps, Dec. 29, 1879, subseries 1.2, box 1, folder 1.

14. E. W. Scripps to Annie Scripps, Nov. 21, 1880, subseries 1.2, box 1, folder 2.

15. E. W. Scripps to Annie Scripps, Dec. 21, 1880, subseries 1.2, box 1, folder 2.

16. E. W. Scripps to George H. Scripps, Jan. 21, 1881, subseries 1.2, box 1, folder 3.

17. E. W. Scripps to Annie Scripps, Jan. 3, 1880, subseries 1.2, box 1, folder 2; William L. Collins to E. W. Scripps, Feb. 7, 1880, subseries 1.1, box 1, folder 2; E. W. Scripps to Annie Scripps, May 11, 1880, subseries 1.2, box 1, folder 2; Charles H. Fuller to E. W. Scripps, Dec. 14, 1880, subseries 1.1, box 1, folder 2.

18. E. W. Scripps to Annie Scripps, July 12, 1880, subseries 1.2, box 1, folder 2.

19. E. W. Scripps to Annie Scripps, July 12, July 18, 1880, subseries 1.2, box 1, folder 2.

20. E. W. Scripps to Annie Scripps, Dec. 12, 1880, subseries 1.2, box 1, folder 2.

21. E. W. Scripps to Annie Scripps, Oct. 21, 1880, subseries 1.2, box 1, folder 5.

22. Scripps ended up with 55 percent of the Cincinnati stock in 1883. Other stockholders were Ellen Scripps (5 percent), James (20 percent), and George (20 percent). Scripps, "Autobiography," series 4, box 11, 353; Memorandum, Oct. 10, 1883, subseries 1.2, box 1, folder 5; Trimble, *The Astonishing Mr. Scripps,* 91, 115.

23. E. W. Scripps to Annie Scripps, June 21, 1885, subseries 1.2, box 1, folder 6.

24. McRae, *Forty Years in Newspaperdom,* 17, 23, 38, 77.

25. E. W. Scripps to Annie Scripps, Nov. 23, 1878, subseries 1.2, box 1, folder 1; Scripps, "Autobiography," series 4, box 11, 354.

26. E. W. Scripps to Ellen B. Scripps, "Memorandum," March 16, 1901, subseries 1.2, box 4, folder 8.

27. E. W. Scripps, "A Summary of Men and Measures to Be Considered," Aug. 1889, subseries 1.2, box 2, folder 3.

28. In 1885 he had married Nackie Holtsinger. Their first child, James George Scripps, was born in 1886. Other children were John, Dorothy, Edward, Nackie, and Robert.

29. E. W. Scripps to M. A. McRae, Oct. 9, 1895, subseries 1.2, box 2, folder 10.

30. E. W. Scripps to J. C. Harper, March 13, 1899, subseries 1.2, box 3, folder 11; see also M. A. McRae to E. W. Scripps, Oct. 31, 1901, subseries 1.1, box 17, folder 14.

31. E. W. Scripps to E. H. Bagby, Nov. 17, 1905, subseries 1.2, box 6, folder 8.

32. E. W. Scripps to E. H. Bagby, W. H. Porterfield, E. H. Wells, E. F. Chase, J. P. Hamilton, and E. L. Rector, June 21, 1907, subseries 1.2, box 9, folder 3.

33. E. W. Scripps to M. A. McRae, March 13, 1899, subseries 1.2, box 3, folder 11.

34. E. W. Scripps to M. A. McRae, Dec. 14, 1900, series 2, box 4, letterbook 6, 223.

35. E. W. Scripps to L. T. Atwood, Nov. 10, 1906, subseries 1.2, box 8, folder 3.

36. E. W. Scripps to J. C. Harper, March 13, 1899, subseries 1.2, box 3, folder 11; E. W. Scripps to J. C. Harper, Jan. 15, 1901, series 2, box 4, letterbook 7, 79; E. W. Scripps to H. B. Clark, Jan. 23, 1906, subseries 1.2, box 6, folder 14.

37. E. W. Scripps to H. B. Clark, Dec. 15, 1905, subseries 1.2, box 6, folder 11.

38. New properties were the Seattle *Star*, Akron *Press*, Chicago *Press*, Spokane *Press*, San Francisco *Daily News*, Tacoma *Times*, Sacramento *Star*, Fresno *Tribune*, Denver *Express*, Evansville *Press*, Pueblo *Sun*, Terre Haute *Post*, Dallas *Dispatch*, Portland *News*, Oklahoma *News*, Memphis *Press*, Nashville *Times*. Acquisitions were: Des Moines *News*, Toledo *News-Bee*, Columbus *Citizen*, and Berkeley *Independent*.

Chapter 2: Expansion

1. The cities were Phoenix, Fresno, San Jose, Stockton, Portland, Salem, Walla Walla, Bellingham, Aberdeen, Vancouver, Victoria, Missoula, Helena, Fargo, Butte, Denver, Ogden, Salt Lake City, and Reno. Memoranda of Conference between E. F. Chase and E. W. Scripps, Miramar, Calif., April 28–30, 1905, subseries 1.1, box 5, folder 5.

2. E. W. Scripps to Annie Scripps, Nov. 21, 1880, subseries 1.2, box 1, folder 2.

3. E. W. Scripps to Annie Scripps, July 27, 1884, subseries 1.2, box 1, folder 6.

4. For instance, the St. Paul *Globe* bragged on July 27, 1885, that it was the first newspaper in that city with the news of Gen. U. S. Grant's death in 1885 (4). On November 7, 1884, the St. Louis *Republican* said it, among all St. Louis's newspapers, was "invariably first in carrying the intelligence of any great event to the waiting thousands of the great Mississippi Valley and the Southwest" (2).

5. E. F. Chase to H. B. Clark, July 17, 1900, subseries 3.1, box 6, folder 10; see also E. H. Wells to E. W. Scripps, July 3, 1900, subseries 1.1, box 16, folder 11; E. W. Scripps to E. H. Bagby, March 27, 1902, series 2, box 6, letterbook 10, 186, as well as Rosewater, *History of Cooperative News-Gathering in the United States;* Lee, *The Daily Newspaper in America;* Schwarzlose, *The Nation's Newsbrokers;* Blondheim, *News over the Wires;* Shaw, "News Bias and the Telegraph"; and Smith, "The Development of Monopoly Markets."

6. Pittsburgh *Leader*, April 7, 1898, 4.

7. Lee, *The Daily Newspaper in America*, 514–17.

8. The AP granted exclusive franchises to its members. These members could then block the supply of AP news to any new newspaper in their cities. McRae, *Forty Years*

in Newspaperdom, 112–15, 120–21; E. W. Scripps, "Autobiography," series 4, box 11, 500–521; E. W. Scripps to M. A. McRae, April 22, May 23, 1897, both in subseries 1.2, box 3, folder 6; M. A. McRae to E. W. Scripps, Nov. 17, 1900, subseries 1.1, box 16, folder 6.

9. Brief Memorandum of the Proceedings of the Editorial Advisory Board of the Scripps-McRae League, Sept. 30, 1896, subseries 3.2, box 3, folder 4; E. W. Scripps to R. F. Paine, April 13, 1897, subseries 1.2, box 22, folder 3; *Fourth Estate,* March 18, 1897, subseries 3.1, box 2, folder 10; E. W. Scripps to E. F. Chase, March 5, 1903, subseries 1.2, box 5, folder 1; "Publishers' Press, S.M.P.A and S.N.A.," subseries 3.1, box 21, folder 11; E. W. Scripps to R. F. Paine, April 19, 1905, subseries 3.1, box 18, folder 9; R. F. Paine to E. W. Scripps, Aug. 21, 1905, subseries 1.1, box 24, folder 7; E. W. Scripps to John S. Sweeney, May 16, 1906, subseries 1.2, box 7, folder 5; J. C. Harper to L. T. Atwood, July 23, 1906, subseries 3.1, box 21, folder 11; E. W. Scripps to L. T. Atwood, Aug. 21, 1906, subseries 1.2, box 7, folder 9; J. C. Harper to E. W. Scripps, June 25, 1907, subseries 1.1, box 26, folder 13.

10. Trimble, *The Astonishing Mr. Scripps,* 182.

11. For a list of clients in early 1898, see R. F. Paine to L. T. Atwood, May 9, 1898, subseries 3.1, box 3, folder 7.

12. Unlike the SMPA, the western Scripps telegraph company (SNA) did not have its own telegraph line ("leased wire"). As a result, its reports were often delayed by other messages on Western Union's lines.

13. SMPA, Nov. 15, 1897, subseries 3.1, box 57, folder 5; R. F. Paine to L. T. Atwood, May 9, 1898, subseries 3.1, box 3, folder 7; "Our Growth," 1902, subseries 3.1, box 11, folder 11; "Newspapers Serviced," 1904, subseries 1.2, box 5, folder 3; "Publishers' Press Association, Scripps-McRae Press Association and the Scripps News Association," 1906, subseries 3.1, box 21, folder 11.

14. E. W. Scripps to Milton A. McRae, April 4, 1900, series 2, box 3, letterbook 5, 240; R. F. Paine to E. W. Scripps, March 14, 1900, subseries 1.1, box 40, folder 12.

15. R. F. Paine to E. W. Scripps, March 26, 1900, subseries 1.1, box 40, folder 12. "The local connection is practically valueless, even if the paper persists in living. The S.M.P.A. has been with one editor and one reporter doing the big local work and receiving nearly nothing in return from the Democrat. It is pretty certain, too, that the A.P. gets benefit from the Democrat's connection with us. Altogether the situation has been unbearable." R. F. Paine to E. W. Scripps, March 22, 1900, subseries 1.1, box 40, folder 12.

16. R. F. Paine to E. W. Scripps, March 14, 1900, subseries 1.1, box 40, folder 12.

17. E. W. Scripps to J. C. Harper, June 2, 1900, subseries 2, box 3, letterbook 5, 471.

18. E. W. Scripps to R. F. Paine, April 16, 1906, subseries 1.2, box 7, folder 3.

19. E. W. Scripps to E. H. Bagby et al., Sept. 3, 1906, subseries 1.2, box 7, folder 10.

20. E. W. Scripps to H. B. Clark, Feb. 18, 1905, subseries 1.2, box 5, folder 4; H. B. Clark to E. W. Scripps, Oct. 8, 1900, subseries 1.1, box 15, folder 3.

21. E. W. Scripps to L. T. Atwood, March 19, 1903, series 2, box 8, letterbook 12, 225b.

22. E. W. Scripps to R. F. Paine, June 25, 1907, subseries 1.2, box 9, folder 3.

23. E. W. Scripps to B. F. Gurley, Sept. 5, 1906, subseries 1.2, box 7, folder 10; see also E. W. Scripps to L. T. Atwood, Oct. 23, 1905, subseries 1.2, box 6, folder 5; and E. W. Scripps Diary, 1906, subseries 1.2, box 7, folder 8.

24. A. O. Andersson and H. J. Richmond, "Dallas," Sept. 3, 1906, subseries 3.2, box 5, folder 12. Up to that time, the SMPA served Texas clients with a five-hundred-word report sent daily from Missouri. The AP had two reports, two thousand words and five hundred words, also sent from Missouri.

25. Ibid.

26. Ibid.

27. L. V. Ashbaugh to E. W. Scripps, Sept. 14, 1906, subseries 1.1, box 24, folder 12; L. T. Atwood to E. W. Scripps, Oct. 20, 1906, subseries 1.1, box 24, folder 14.

28. L. V. Ashbaugh to E. W. Scripps, Sept. 14, 1906, subseries 1.1, box 24, folder 12; J. C. Harper to E. W. Scripps, Sept. 29, 1906, subseries 1.1, box 25, folder 8.

29. R. F. Paine estimated it was losing about $1,000 a month in mid-1908. R. F. Paine to J. C. Harper, July 20, 1908, subseries 3.1, box 27, folder 10.

30. E. W. Scripps, "Subjects that I think the editors in chief should consider and decide upon," Nov. 16, 1908, subseries 3.1, box 28, folder 8.

31. R. F. Paine to J. C. Harper, July 20, 1908, subseries 3.1, box 27, folder 10. .

32. J. C. Harper to E. B. Scripps, Dec. 31, 1907, subseries 3.1, box 25, folder 13; "Memorandum on the Closing of the Nashville Times, Dec. 19th to 28th, 1907," subseries 3.1, box 25, folder 14; C. F. Mosher to Leonidas Polk, Dec. 21, 1907, subseries 3.1, box 25, folder 12.

33. E. W. Scripps to W. D. Wasson, Sept. 17, 1906, subseries 1.2, box 7, folder 10; W. D. Wasson to E. W. Scripps, Oct. 20, 1906, subseries 1.1, box 26, folder 5; E. W. Scripps to L. T. Atwood, Jan. 21, 1907, subseries 1.2, box 8, folder 9; E. W. Scripps to H. B. Clark, Jan. 12, 1907, subseries 1.2, box 8, folder 8; G. Warde McKim to E. W. Scripps, Jan. 23, 1907, subseries 1.1, box 27, folder 3; J. C. Harper to E. W. Scripps, Sept. 23, 1907, subseries 1.1, box 26, folder 13.

34. Scripps's newspapers were scooped on the *Bennington*, in part because of the lack of a leased wired and also because the San Diego staff did not make an extra effort to alert others (notably the Los Angeles *Record*) of the accident. Scripps, the SNA manager, and various Scripps editors criticized the *Sun* for this failure.

35. R. F. Paine to E. W. Scripps, Oct. 9, 1906, subseries 1.1, box 26, folder 1.

36. Milton A. McRae to E. W. Scripps, Oct. 3, 1906, subseries 1.1, box 25, folder 14.

37. A. O. Andersson to J. C. Harper, Nov. 16, 1907, subseries 3.1, box 28, folder 8.

38. E. W. Scripps to L. T. Atwood, Dec. 12, 1906, subseries 1.2, box 8, folder 5.

39. E. W. Scripps to L. T. Atwood, Nov. 15, 1906, subseries 1.2, box 8, folder 4.

40. E. W. Scripps to E. F. Chase, April 15, 1905, subseries 1.2, box 5, folder 5. See also E. W. Scripps to E. F. Chase, Feb. 17, 1906, subseries 1.2, box 6, folder 17: "I think personally I am prompted to hold on to the Press, because we need the Spokane field in our business of the Washington league." Spokane was an important agricultural and

railroad center as well as the gateway to the rich silver and copper mines of northern Idaho and western Montana. The mines not only made Spokane an important commercial center but also an important area for labor union activity. It was also the center of political power in eastern Washington.

41. E. F. Chase to E. W. Scripps, Feb. 24, 1906, subseries 1.1, box 24, folder 17.

42. E. W. Scripps to E. F. Chase, Feb. 17, 1906, subseries 1.2, box 6, folder 17.

43. E. H. Wells to E. F. Chase, June 22, 1905, subseries 3.1, box 18, folder 14.

44. Minutes of Conference between E. W. Scripps, Milton A. McRae, L. T. Atwood, and J. C. Harper, Miramar, Calif., Jan. 26, 1905, subseries 1.2, box 18, folder 1.

45. E. W. Scripps to W. H. Simms, March 3, 1906, subseries 1.2, box 7, folder 1; E. W. Scripps to L. T. Atwood, Aug. 21, 1906, subseries 1.2, box 7, folder 9; E. W. Scripps to John S. Sweeney, May 16, 1906, subseries 1.2, box 7, folder 5; Milton A. McRae to E. W. Scripps, Oct. 3, 1906, subseries 1.1, box 25, folder 14.

46. A. O. Andersson and H. J. Richmond, "Dallas," Sept. 3, 1906, subseries 3.2, box 5, folder 12.

47. C. H. Fentress to M. A. McRae, July 24, 1906, subseries 3.1, box 21, folder 11.

48. J. P. Hamilton to E. W. Scripps, March 9, 1906, subseries 1.1, box 25, folder 4.

49. Emmett N. Parker to J. C. Harper, Aug. 8, 1903, subseries 3.1, box 14, folder 6.

50. M. A. McRae to E. W. Scripps, June 6, 1902, subseries 1.1, box 19, folder 7; E. W. Scripps to Milton McRae, June 18, 1902, series 2, box 6, letterbook 10, 441.

51. E. W. Scripps to E. H. Wells, Oct. 25, 1905, subseries 1.2, box 6, folder 5.

52. Andriot, comp., *Population Abstract of the United States,* 1:619.

53. E. W. Scripps to L. T. Atwood, Sept. 15, 1906, subseries 1.2, box 7, folder 10. Scripps rejected Trinidad, Colorado, as a newspaper field, considering the population too small. E. W. Scripps Diary, July 1906, subseries 1.2, box 7, folder 8; E. W. Scripps to R. F. Paine, Sept. 18, 1906, subseries 1.2, box 7, folder 10.

54. H. Y. Saint to J. C. Harper, "Evansville, Indiana, as a Newspaper Field," April 1, 1904, subseries 3.2, box 5, folder 6.

55. A. O. Andersson and H. J. Richmond, "Dallas," Sept. 3, 1906, subseries 3.2, box 5, folder 12.

56. J. P. Hamilton to E. W. Scripps, March 9, 1906, subseries 1.1, box 25, folder 4.

57. M. A. McRae to Whom It May Concern, Jan. 14, 1907, subseries 3.1, box 23, folder 5.

58. C. H. Fentress to M. A. McRae, July 24, 1906, subseries 3.1, box 21, folder 11.

59. E. W. Scripps to W. D. Wasson, Sept. 17, 1906, subseries 1.2, box 7, folder 10.

60. James G. Scripps to E. W. Scripps, Jan. 13, 1906, subseries 1.1, box 26, folder 3; E. W. Scripps to W. D. Wasson, Sept. 17, 1906, subseries 1.2, box 7, folder 10; W. D. Wasson to E. W. Scripps, Oct. 20, 1906, subseries 1.1, box 26, folder 5; E. W. Scripps to L. T. Atwood, Jan. 21, 1907, subseries 1.2, box 8, folder 9; E. W. Scripps to H. B. Clark, Jan. 12, 1907, subseries 1.2, box 8, folder 8.

61. E. W. Scripps to L. T. Atwood, Oct. 7, 1904, subseries 1.2, box 5, folder 3; see also Memoranda of Conference between E. F. Chase and E. W. Scripps, Miramar, Calif.,

April 28–30, 1905, subseries 1.1, box 5, folder 5; E. W. Scripps Diary, 1906, subseries 1.2, box 7, folder 8.

62. R. G. Conant to H. B. Clark, March 2, 1905, subseries 3.1, box 18, folder 5.

63. M. Balthasar to J. P. Hamilton, May 30, 1905, subseries 3.1, box 18, folder 12.

64. Milton A. McRae to E. W. Scripps, Sept. 28, 1905, subseries 1.1, box 24, folder 4.

65. J. C. Harper to H. B. Clark, June 19, 1901, subseries 3.1, box 8, folder 11.

66. E. W. Scripps to L. T. Atwood, Oct. 23, 1905, subseries 1.2, box 6, folder 5; M. A. McRae to To Whom It May Concern, Aug. 7, 1906, subseries 3.1, box 22, folder 3 (capital for the Terre Haute *Post*); M. A. McRae to Whom It May Concern, Oct. 11, 1906, subseries 3.1, box 22, folder 10 (Dallas *Dispatch*); M. A. McRae to Whom It May Concern, Nov. 23, 1906, subseries 3.1, box 23, folder 2 (Memphis *Press*); M. A. McRae to Whom It May Concern, Nov. 6, 1906, subseries 3.1, box 23, folder 1 (Oklahoma City *News*); M. A. McRae to Whom It May Concern, Jan. 14, 1907, subseries 3.1, box 23, folder 5 (Nashville *Times*). For discussion of the "exploitation fund" and the "Newspaper Investment and Savings Society," see Minutes of Conference between E. W. Scripps, Milton A. McRae, L. T. Atwood, and J. C. Harper, Miramar, Calif., Jan. 26, 1905, series 1.2, box 18, folder 1; L. T. Atwood to M. A. McRae, July 25, 1906, subseries 3.1, box 22, folder 1.

67. Scripps paid $75,000 and McRae an additional $9,000 for control of the PPA. Scripps paid $35,000 for Fanita Ranch near San Diego. E. W. Scripps to H. B. Clark, Feb. 18, 1906, subseries 1.2, box 5, folder 4; E. W. Scripps to L. T. Atwood, Aug. 21, 1906, subseries 3.2, box 7, folder 9; E. W. Scripps to L. T. Atwood, Nov. 2, 1906, subseries 1.2, box 8, folder 3.

68. J. C. Harper to W. B. Colver, Oct. 27, 1908, subseries 3.1, box 28, folder 5.

69. Max Balthasar to J. Lee, April 9, 1904, subseries 3.1, box 16, folder 1.

70. M. A. McRae to E. W. Scripps, Oct. 20, 1906, subseries 1.1, box 25, folder 14: "Now you have told me that you are going to start a hundred [newspapers] before you die."

71. Associates advised Scripps against the deal; one said the newspaper was "on its last legs financially and the general expectation is that publication will soon be suspended. You COULD build it up, but the cost would be excessive." E. H. Wells to E. W. Scripps, Oct. 25, 1898, subseries 1.1, box 12, folder 5.

Chapter 3: Controlling Costs

1. E. F. Chase to H. B. Clark, Feb. 12, 24, 1899, subseries 3.1, box 3, folder 12; E. H. Wells to H. B. Clark, March 10, 1899, subseries 3.1, box 3, folder 13; E. H. Wells to E. W. Scripps, June 11, 1899, subseries 1.1, box 14, folder 10.

2. E. W. Scripps to E. H. Wells, Jan. 11, 1899, cited in "Special Called Stockholders Meeting," June 13, 1902, subseries 3.1, box 11, folder 1.

3. E. H. Wells to H. B. Clark, March 1, 1899, subseries 3.1, box 3, folder 13; E. H. Wells to E. W. Scripps, June 11, 1899, subseries 1.1, box 14, folder 10; E. H. Wells to

H. B. Clark, July 11, 1899, subseries 3.1, box 4, folder 10; E. H. Wells to H. B. Clark, Aug. 8, 1899, subseries 3.1, box 5, folder 1; H. B. Clark to E. W. Scripps, Nov. 12, 1899, subseries 1.1, box 13, folder 5; E. H. Wells to E. W. Scripps, Feb. 3, 1900, subseries 3.1, box 5, folder 13; E. F. Chase to H. B. Clark, April 28, 1900, subseries 3.1, box 6, folder 4.

4. Scripps, "Autobiography," series 4, box 11, 179; see also Kaplan, "The Economics of Popular Journalism."

5. Scripps, "Autobiography," series 4, box 11, 239–40.

6. Ibid., 138.

7. Ibid., 137; see also Kaplan, "The Economics of Popular Journalism," 67.

8. E. W. Scripps to Stanley Waterloo, June 2, 1880, subseries 1.2, box 1, folder 2.

9. E. W. Scripps to H. B. Clark, Feb. 14, 1901, series 2, box 4, letterbook 7, 293b; E. W. Scripps to W. P. Strandborg, June 4, 1903, subseries 1.2, box 5, folder 1.

10. E. W. Scripps to L. T. Atwood, Nov. 6, 1906, subseries 1.2, box 8, folder 3.

11. E. W. Scripps to R. F. Paine, Nov. 8, 1906, and E. W. Scripps to L. T. Atwood, Nov. 6, 1906, subseries 1.2, box 8, folder 3; E. W. Scripps to H. H. Hobbs, March 30, 1907, subseries 1.2, box 8, folder 13.

12. These expenses included editorial salaries; wire service and feature service costs; salaries for a Linotype operator, telegraph operator, composing room foreman, flatbed pressman, circulator, and advertising solicitor; and rent, telephone, fuel, power, and paper. "Tacoma Proposition," 1903, subseries 3.1, box 15, folder 5; E. H. Wells to E. W. Scripps, July 1, 1903, subseries 1.1, box 21, folder 14.

13. E. W. Scripps to J. P. Hamilton, March 30, 1906, subseries 1.2, box 7, folder 2. For Sacramento proposal, see W. H. Porterfield to E. W. Scripps, July 30, 1904, subseries 1.1, box 22, folder 4 and Oct. 5, 1904, subseries 1.1, box 22, folder 14; for Oakland, see W. D. Wasson to H. B. Clark, Dec. 31, 1906, subseries 3.1, box 23, folder 4; for Pueblo, see R. F. Paine to E. W. Scripps, Aug. 6, 1906, subseries 1.1, box 25, folder 1; for Salt Lake City, see R. F. Paine and H. B. Clark to E. W. Scripps, Oct. 2, 1906, subseries 1.1, box 26, folder 1; for Nashville, see Jay A. Gove and Ray G. Conant to E. W. Scripps, Oct. 25, 1906, subseries 1.1, box 24, folder 14; for Reno, see M. Balthasar to E. W. Scripps, Jan. 24, 1906, subseries 1.1, box 24, folder 15; and for Denver, see J. P. Hamilton to E. W. Scripps, March 27, subseries 1.1, box 25, folder 4.

14. E. W. Scripps to E. H. Wells, Nov. 28, 1903, subseries 1.2, box 5, folder 3.

15. E. W. Scripps to W. H. Porterfield, Aug. 22, 1905, subseries 1.2, box 5, folder 11.

16. E. W. Scripps to E. F. Chase, Aug. 17, 1902, series 2, box 7, letterbook 11, 137b; W. D. Wasson to H. B. Clark, Dec. 31, 1906, subseries 3.1, box 23, folder 4.

17. E. H. Wells to E. W. Scripps, Nov. 16, 1903, subseries 1.1, box 21, folder 14; E. H. Wells to E. W. Scripps, Dec. 12, 1903, subseries 3.1, box 15, folder 4; E. H. Wells to E. W. Scripps, March 6, 1905, subseries 1.1, box 24, folder 11; W. H. Porterfield to E. W. Scripps, March 1, 1907, subseries 1.1, box 27, folder 9; L. T. Atwood to E. F. Chase, Aug. 8, 1906, subseries 3.1, box 22, folder 3; E. W. Scripps to E. F. Chase, May 22, 1901, series 2, box 5, letterbook 9, 26–27; E. W. Scripps to E. F. Chase, Aug. 17, 1902, series 2, box 7, letterbook 11, 137b; E. W. Scripps to E. H. Wells, Aug. 22, 1902, subseries 1.2,

box 4, folder 19; Milton A. McRae to E. F. Chase, Sept. 5, 1902, subseries 3.1, box 11, folder 10.

18. E. F. Chase to E. W. Scripps, Jan. 28, 1901, subseries 1.1, box 17, folder 1.

19. E. H. Wells to E. W. Scripps, Feb. 14, 1901, subseries 1.1, box 18, folder 1.

20. E. W. Scripps to R. F. Paine, Jan. 26, 1906, subseries 1.2, box 6, folder 15; E. W. Scripps to J. C. Harper, Jan. 1, 1908, subseries 1.2, box 10, folder 4.

21. E. W. Scripps to Stanley Waterloo, June 2, 1880, subseries 1.2, box 1, folder 2; M. A. McRae to E. W. Scripps, March 28, 1902, subseries 1.1, box 19, folder 5; C. F. Mosher to H. L. S., July 22, 1910, subseries 1.2, box 12, folder 16.

22. E. H. Bagby to H. H. Hobbs, Oct. 6, 1906, subseries 3.1, box 22, folder 9.

23. George Putnam to L. T. Atwood, Oct. 6, 1902, subseries 3.1, box 11, folder 12; E. W. Scripps to L. T. Atwood, May 26, 1906, subseries 1.2, box 7, folder 5; E. W. Scripps to W. W. Thornton, June 29, 1907, subseries 1.2, box 9, folder 3; E. W. Scripps to E. F. Chase, April 18, 1907, subseries 1.2, box 8, folder 15.

24. E. W. Scripps to W. H. Porterfield, Sept. 21, 1906, subseries 1.2, box 7, folder 11; E. W. Scripps to W. H. Porterfield, April 4, 1906, subseries 1.2, box 7, folder 3.

25. E. W. Scripps to W. W. Thornton, June 29, 1907, subseries 1.2, box 9, folder 3.

26. E. W. Scripps to L. T. Atwood, H. B. Clark, and E. L. Rector, Dec. 22, 1906, subseries 1.2, box 8, folder 6.

27. E. W. Scripps to L. T. Atwood, Nov. 11, 1906, subseries 1.2, box 8, folder 3; E. W. Scripps to E. H. Bagby, Nov. 9, 1906, subseries 1.2, box 8, folder 3.

28. E. W. Scripps to Andrew C. Keifer, Feb. 18, 1907, subseries 1.2, box 8, folder 10; R. F. Paine to E. W. Scripps, Aug. 22, 1905, subseries 1.1, box 24, folder 7; E. W. Scripps to H. B. Clark, Aug. 24, 1905, subseries 1.2, box 5, folder 11; E. W. Scripps to E. F. Chase, March 5, 1907, subseries 1.2, box 8, folder 12; E. W. Scripps to M. A. McRae, Feb. 18, 1907, subseries 1.2, box 8, folder 10.

29. Kaplan, "The Economics of Popular Journalism," 67.

30. E. W. Scripps to R. W. Hobbs, Jan. 24, 1908, subseries 1.2, box 10, folder 6.

31. E. W. Scripps to W. D. Wasson, Sept. 25, 1905, subseries 1.2, box 6, folder 3; see also E. W. Scripps to E. F. Chase, Dec. 10, 1906, subseries 1.2, box 8, folder 5; and Scripps to M. A. McRae, Dec. 19, 1906, series 1.2, box 8, folder 6.

32. E. W. Scripps to H. B. Clark, May 6, 1906, subseries 1.2, box 7, folder 4.

33. E. W. Scripps to Paul Blades, Feb. 16, 1901, series 2, box 4, letterbook 7, 322–23; E. W. Scripps to E. F. Chase, May 15, 1901, series 2, box 5, letterbook 8, 290; E. W. Scripps Diary, 1906, subseries 1.2, box 7, folder 8.

34. Milton McRae to E. W. Scripps May 11, 1905, subseries 1.1, box 24, folder 2; E. W. Scripps to Paul Blades, Feb. 16, 1901, series 2, box 4, letterbook 7, 322–23; E. F. Chase to J. C. Harper, Feb. 1, 1908, subseries 3.1, box 26, folder 6.

35. The *East Side News* became the Portland *Daily News* about six weeks after it began publication. On the Spokane, Tacoma, and Seattle staffs, see E. H. Wells to J. C. Harper, 1908, n.d., subseries 3.1, box 26, folder 1. The Oklahoma City *News* had an editor and two reporters in 1908; see C. F. Mosher to W. B. Colver, Feb. 6, 1908,

subseries 3.1, box 26, folder 6. The Sacramento *Star* had an editor and two reporters, and the *San Diegan-Sun* had an editor and three reporters. Charles F. Mosher to R. B. Young, Oct. 27, 1908, subseries 3.1, box 28, folder 5.

36. J. P. Hamilton to E. W. Scripps, April 26, 1906, subseries 1.1, box 25, folder 1.

37. E. H. Wells to L. T. Atwood, Nov. 17, 1904, subseries 3.1, box 17, folder 5.

38. E. W. Scripps to Stanley Waterloo, June 8, 1880, subseries 1.2, box 1, folder 2.

39. E. F. Chase to E. W. Scripps, Dec. 21, 1900, subseries 1.1, box 15, folder 5.

40. George Putnam to E. W. Scripps, Jan. 26, 1904, subseries 1.1, box 22, folder 14.

41. L. T. Atwood to E. W. Scripps, June 10, 1891, L. T. Atwood to E. W. Scripps, Oct. 6, 1891, L. T. Atwood to E. W. Scripps, Nov. 5, 1891, and L. T. Atwood to E. W. Scripps, Dec. 11, 1891, subseries 1.1, box 4, folder 2; L. T. Atwood to E. W. Scripps, March 5, 1893, subseries 1.1, box 7, folder 2; Scripps-McRae League Report for 1893, Jan. 1894, subseries 1.1, box 7, folder 7; George A. Shives to L. T. Atwood, Oct. 5, 1894, subseries 3.2, box 1, folder 2; E. W. Scripps to W. P. Strandborg, June 4, 1903, subseries 1.2, box 5, folder 1.

42. R. W. Harris to E. W. Scripps, June 5, 1881, and Stanley Waterloo to E. W. Scripps, May 31, 1881, subseries 1.1, box 1, folder 3; H. B. Clark to E. W. Scripps, Jan. 20, 1900, subseries 1.1, box 14, folder 12; E. H. Wells to H. B. Clark, May 26, 1900, subseries 3.2, box 4, folder 4; E. H. Wells to E. W. Scripps, March 25, 1902, subseries 1.1, box 18, folder 8. See also E. H. Wells to E. W. Scripps, March 7, 1906, subseries 1.1, box 26, folder 6; E. H. Wells to E. W. Scripps, March 25, 1902, subseries 1.1, box 18, folder 8.

43. On staff raids, see H. B. Canfield to E. W. Scripps, Aug. 2, 1905, subseries 1.1, box 23, folder 8; E. H. Bagby to E. W. Scripps, Sept. 9, 1902, subseries 1.1, box 18, folder 6; and W. H. Porterfield to E. W. Scripps, May 6, May 8, 1901, subseries 1.1, box 17, folder 16. On salary levels, see R. F. Paine to L. T. Atwood, July 30, 1906, subseries 3.1, box 22, folder 1; M. A. McRae to E. W. Scripps, Jan. 3, 1904, subseries 1.1, box 24, folder 1; E. H. Wells to E. W. Scripps, April 10, 1907, subseries 1.1, box 28, folder 1; E. H. Wells to James G. Scripps, Sept. 7, 1908, subseries 3.1, box 28, folder 1; and J. C. Harper to E. W. Scripps, Sept. 19, 1908, series 1.1, box 28, folder 10.

44. R. F. Paine to E. W. Scripps, Sept. 21, 1906, subseries 1.1, box 26, folder 2.

45. W. H. Porterfield to E. W. Scripps, Feb. 12, 1906, subseries 1.1, box 26, folder 2.

46. E. W. Scripps to B. H. Canfield, July 29, 1905, subseries 1.2, box 5, folder 8; E. W. Scripps to R. F. Paine, Feb. 28, 1906, and E. W. Scripps to R. F. Paine, Feb. 28, 1906, subseries 1.2, box 6, folder 17.

47. E. W. Scripps to W. D. Wasson, Jan. 30, 1908, subseries 1.2, box 10, folder 7.

48. M. A. McRae to W. W. Thornton, Dec. 16, 1899, subseries 3.1, box 5, folder 9; M. A. McRae to W. W. Thornton, Jan. 8, 1900, subseries 3.1, box 5, folder 11.

49. Charles F. Mosher to L. T. Atwood, April 14, 1900, subseries 3.1, box 6, folder 3.

50. L. T. Atwood to E. W. Scripps, May 22, 1900, subseries 1.1, box 14, folder 11; E. W. Scripps to L. T. Atwood, April 24, 1907, subseries 1.2, box 8, folder 15; E. F. Chase to E. W. Scripps, Dec. 14, 1903, subseries 1.1, box 5, folder 5; J. P. Hamilton to E. F. Chase, April 20, 1904, subseries 3.1, box 16, folder 2; R. F. Paine, Circular Letter to

Western Editors, Aug. 9, 1906, subseries 3.1, box 22, folder 3; R. F. Paine to G. H. Tavenner, April 23, 1907, series 3.1, box 23, folder 12.

51. Seattle *Star*, Dec. 12, 1905, 1, and Dec. 13, 1905, 1, 11; Seattle *Times*, Dec. 12, 1905, 1, and Dec. 13, 1905, 1, 13; E. W. Scripps to R. F. Paine, Dec. 21, 1905, subseries 1.2, box 6, folder 12; R. F. Paine to E. W. Scripps, Dec. 22, 1905, subseries 1.1, box 24, folder 7; R. F. Paine to W. P. Strandborg, Dec. 26, 1905, subseries 3.1, box 20, folder 5; R. F. Paine to E. W. Scripps, Dec. 26, 1905, subseries 1.1, box 24, folder 7; E. F. Chase to H. B. Clark, Jan. 8, 1906, subseries 1.2, box 6, folder 13.

52. R. F. Paine to E. W. Scripps, Oct. 11, 1887, and W. H. Little to E. W. Scripps, Nov. 4, 1887, subseries 1.1, box 1, folder 5; John Ridenour to E. W. Scripps, June 12, 1888, subseries 1.1, box 1, folder 9; E. W. Scripps to E. F. Chase, March 5, 1903, series 2, box 8, Letterbook 12, 188b.

53. Scripps, "Autobiography," series 4, box 11, 240, 283.

54. E. W. Scripps to John Sweeney, July 11, 1887, subseries 1.2, box 2, folder 3.

55. Ibid.

56. E. W. Scripps to R. F. Paine, Aug. 11, 1890, and R. F. Paine to E. W. Scripps, Sept. 11, 1890, subseries 1.1, box 2, folder 5; L. T. Atwood to E. W. Scripps, Aug. 15, 1891, subseries 1.1, box 4, folder 2; Morton L. Hawkins to L. T. Atwood, July 12, 1892, subseries 3.1, box 1, folder 7; L. T. Atwood to C. F. Mosher, April 21, 1896, subseries 3.1, box 2, folder 4; Minutes of the Editorial Advisory Board of the Scripps-McRae League, June 30, 1896, subseries 3.2, box 3, folder 2; L. T. Atwood to Charles F. Mosher, June 21, 1900, subseries 3.1, box 6, folder 8; L. T. Atwood to H. N. Rickey, July 23, 1900, subseries 3.2, box 4, folder 6; L. T. Atwood to Chas. F. Mosher, July 23, 1900, subseries 3.2, box 4, folder 6; Plan for Reporting for the Scripps-McRae Newspapers, the Republican Convention at Philadelphia, June 19, 1900, and the Democratic Convention at Kansas City, July Fourth, 1900, subseries 3.2, box 4, folder 4; Memorandum of the Proceedings of the Editorial Advisory Board of the Scripps-McRae League, March 31, 1896, subseries 3.2, box 3, folder 2; Minutes of the Editorial Advisory Board of the Scripps-McRae League, July 30, 1896, subseries 3.2, box 3, folder 3.

57. L. T. Atwood to E. S. Wright, Aug. 2, 1900, L. T. Atwood to Henry Cabot Lodge, Aug. 4, 1900, L. T. Atwood to Eugene V. Debs, Aug. 2, 1900, and L. T. Atwood to Marcus A. Hanna, Aug. 2, 1900, all in subseries 3.1, box 7, folder 1; A. S. Johnson to L. T. Atwood, Sept. 23, 1901, subseries 3.2, box 4, folder 11; L. T. Atwood to Ralph H. Booth, Nov. 15, 1901, subseries 3.1, box 9, folder 9; Ralph H. Booth to L. T. Atwood, Nov. 19, 1901, subseries 1.2, box 4, folder 18; L. T. Atwood to Ralph H. Booth, Nov. 21, 1901, subseries 3.1, box 9, folder 1; L. T. Atwood to Editor, Grand Rapids Press, Dec. 23, 1901, subseries 3.1, box 9, folder 15; L. T. Atwood to R. F. Paine, Dec. 24, 1901, subseries 3.1, box 9, folder 16.

58. E. W. Scripps to E. F. Chase, E. H. Bagby and W. H. Porterfield, June 23, 1902, E. W. Scripps to Gentlemen, May 27, 1902, and "Proposed Plan of Illustrative and News Enterprise Bureau," May 27, 1902, all in series 2, box 6, letterbook 10, 468, 412, 414.

59. L. T. Atwood to E. W. Scripps, June 10, 1891, L. T. Atwood to E. W. Scripps, Oct. 6, 1891, L. T. Atwood to E. W. Scripps, Nov. 5, 1891, L. T. Atwood to E. W. Scripps, Dec. 11, 1891, and L. T. Atwood to E. W. Scripps, March 5, 1893, all in subseries 1.1, box 4, folder 2; Scripps-McRae League Report for 1893, Jan. 1894, subseries 1.1, box 8, folder 2.

60. L. T. Atwood to E. W. Scripps, March 14, 1891, L. T. Atwood to E. W. Scripps, March 14, 1891, L. T. Atwood to E. W. Scripps, April 11, 1891, L. T. Atwood to E. W. Scripps, June 10, 1891, L. T. Atwood to E. W. Scripps, Oct. 6, 1891, L. T. Atwood to E. W. Scripps, Nov. 5, 1891, and L. T. Atwood to E. W. Scripps, Dec. 11, 1891, all in subseries 1.1, box 4, folder 2; L. T. Atwood to E. W. Scripps, July 5, 1892, and L. T. Atwood to E. W. Scripps, Aug. 23, 1892, subseries 1.1, box 5, folder 1; Scripps-McRae League Report for 1893, Jan. 1894, subseries 1.1, box 8, folder 2.

61. Marlen E. Pew to R. F. Paine, July 1, 1907, subseries 3.1, box 24, folder 7.

62. In reality, it was even cheaper than that because Scripps sold the service to other newspapers, too. The full size of that client base is not known, so the average cost was computed just for the Scripps newspapers.

63. L. T. Atwood to R. F. Paine, April 15, 1903, subseries 3.1, box 13, folder 5.

64. A. R. Hopkins to R. F. Paine, April 12, 1907, subseries 3.1, box 23, folder 2.

65. Memoranda of Conference between E. F. Chase and E. W. Scripps, April 28–30, 1905, subseries 1.2, box 5, folder 5. The *Star* paid an average of $2.98 a column for local news and $1.14 for telegraph news. With thirty-eight weekly columns of NEA material, about twenty-six of local news, and twenty-four of telegraphic news, overall the *Star* paid an average of $1.31 per column for non-advertising content.

66. E. W. Scripps to E. F. Chase, Feb. 17, 1906, subseries 1.2, box 6, folder 17; E. W. Scripps to E. H. Wells, Oct. 31, 1906, subseries 1.2, box 8, folder 2.

67. E. W. Scripps to Paul H. Blades, July 16, 1902, E. W. Scripps to E. H. Wells, July 16, 1902, E. W. Scripps to Paul H. Blades, July 24, 1902, and E. W. Scripps to Paul H. Blades, July 24, 1902, all in series 2, box 7, letterbook 11, 42, 43, 56.

68. For analysis of Pueblo and Denver's usage of the NEA, see Diary of R. F. Paine, Trip Eastward, Nov. 6, 21, 1906, and Diary of R. F. Paine, Trip to Cheyenne, Denver, Pueblo, Kansas City, Nov. 6, 1906, both in subseries 3.2, box 5, folder 12.

69. J. C. Harper to W. C. Mayborn and F. R. Peters, Dec. 24, 1907, and Harper to A. O. Andersson, Dec. 27, 1907, both in subseries 3.1, box 25, folder 12.

70. E. H. Wells to J. P. Hamilton, subseries 3.1, box 15, folder 6.

71. E. H. Wells to E. W. Scripps, Feb. 1, 1906, subseries 1.1, box 26, folder 6.

72. The mats were produced at a centralized engraving plant in Cleveland. E. H. Bagby to F. D. Waite, Nov. 19, 1906, subseries 3.1, box 23, folder 2. As Paine described this process, "The mats for the art [illustrations, cartoons, photographs, etc.] will be on papier mache, when not electrotypes—the cuts being not over 12½ ems to the single column in width; the metal castings from these matrices to be done at your own expense, as per arrangements which you can make with firms in your city." Paine to Dear Sir, (circular letter on NEA), 1902, subseries 3.1, box 11, folder 5.

73. R. F. Paine to George Putnam, Nov. 18, 1902, subseries 3.1, box 12, folder 1. Paine was quoting a letter Putnam, the Spokane editor, had written to him.

74. R. F. Paine to W. H. Porterfield, June 17, 1902, subseries 3.1, box 11, folder 3; George Putnam to L. T. Atwood, Nov. 22, 1902, subseries 3.2, box 5, folder 2.

75. E. W. Scripps to R. F. Paine, Aug. 4, 1903, series 2, box 9, letterbook 13, 173.

76. E. W. Scripps to B. H. Canfield, May 20, 1903, subseries 1.2, box 5, folder 1; E. W. Scripps to H. B. Clark, Oct. 6, 1906, subseries 1.2, box 7, folder 12.

77. J. C. Harper to R. F. Paine, June 15, 1908, subseries 3.1, box 27, folder 7; W. H. Porterfield to E. F. Chase, May 4, 1908, subseries 3.1, box 27, folder 3; W. H. Porterfield to B. H. Canfield, Dec. 9, 1908, subseries 3.1, box 28, folder 11; W. H. Porterfield to Bensel Smythe, May 14, 1908, subseries 3.1, box 27, folder 3; E. H. Wells to J. C. Harper, 1908, n.d., subseries 3.1, box 26, folder 1.

78. E. F. Chase to H. B. Clark, July 23, 1900, subseries 3.1, box 6, folder 10; E. W. Scripps to H. B. Clark, Oct. 17, 1900, series 2, letterbook 6, 79; H. B. Clark to E. W. Scripps, Dec. 17, 1900, subseries 1.1, box 15, folder 3; H. B. Clark to E. W. Scripps, Jan. 10, 1900, subseries 1.1, box 15, folder 4.

79. H. M. Young to M. A. McRae, June 29, 1892, subseries 3.1, box 1, folder 7; M. A. McRae to E. W. Scripps, Nov. 8, 1892, subseries 1.1, box 5, folder 9; H. M. Young to George Shives, Dec. 16, 1898, subseries 3.1, box 3, folder 11.

80. E. W. Scripps to H. B. Clark, Jan. 9, 1907, subseries 1.2, box 8, folder 7.

81. The fifty-three-week year occurred in 1892, and McRae estimated that it would occur again in 1897. M. A. McRae to E. W. Scripps, Nov. 8, 1892, subseries 1.1, box 5, folder 9; E. W. Scripps to J. P. Hamilton, Feb. 4, 1907, subseries 1.2, box 8, folder 10.

82. R. F. Paine to E. S. Wright, July 10, 1899, subseries 3.1, box 4, folder 10; Charles F. Mosher to E. S. Wright, May 2, 1899, subseries 3.1, box 4, folder 3; L. T. Atwood to E. S. Wright, April 29, 1899, subseries 3.1, box 4, folder 3.

83. M. A. McRae to H. E. Terry, Oct. 31, 1899, subseries 3.1, box 5, folder 5.

84. Charles J. Stein to M. A. McRae, Sept. 12, 1900, subseries 3.1, box 7, folder 4; Charles J. Stein to M. A. McRae, Oct. 18, 1900, subseries 3.1, box 7, folder 6; L. T. Atwood to Charles F. Mosher, March 23, 1900, subseries 3.1, box 6, folder 2.

85. W. W. Thornton to M. A. McRae, March 29, 1900, subseries 3.1, box 6, folder 2.

86. M. A. McRae to E. W. Scripps, April 25, 1900, subseries 1.1, box 16, folder 4.

87. R. F. Paine to Will Strandborg, May 16, 1903, subseries 3.1, box 13, folder 9.

88. E. W. Scripps to Hyacinth Ford, Nov. 7, 1906, subseries 1.2, box 8, folder 3.

89. E. W. Scripps to J. P. Hamilton, April 25, 1907, series 1.2, box 8, folder 15.

90. E. W. Scripps to J. C. Harper, July 30, 1908, series 1.2, box 12, folder 3.

91. E. W. Scripps to H. B. Clark, Aug. 24, 1905, series 1.2, box 5, folder 11.

92. George A. Shives to M. A. McRae, May 9, 1898, series 3.1, box 3, folder 7.

93. H. M. Young to M. A. McRae, April 2, 1897, series 3.1, box 3, folder 1.

94. E. W. Scripps, "Notes and Topics to Be Taken Up with the Managers of the Young Eastern Papers," Jan. 25, 1907, series 1.2, box 8, folder 9.

95. L. T. Atwood to E. W. Scripps, Jan. 13, 1904, series 1.1, box 21, folder 5; E. W. Scripps to L. T. Atwood, Jan. 7, 1903, series 2, box 5, letterbook 9, 447.

96. L. T. Atwood to E. W. Scripps, Jan. 19, 1903, series 1.1, box 19, folder 13.

97. E. W. Scripps to R. F. Paine, Jan. 26, 1906, subseries 1.2, box 6, folder 15; Charles Stein to E. W. Scripps, March 6, 1901, subseries 1.1, box 18, folder 1; E. W. Scripps to H. B. Clark and W. D. Wasson, Nov. 9, 1904, subseries 1.2, box 5, folder 3; E. W. Scripps to E. F. Chase, July 24, 1905, subseries 1.2, box 5, folder 8; J. C. Harper to Ward C. Mayborn, July 9, 1906, subseries 3.1, box 21, folder 9.

98. E. W. Scripps to W. D. Wasson, Jan. 22, 1906, subseries 1.2, box 6, folder 14; E. W. Scripps to H. B. Clark, May 18, 1906, subseries 1.2, box 7, folder 5.

99. E. W. Scripps to George Putnam, April 28, 1903, subseries 1.2, box 5, folder 1.

100. E. W. Scripps to E. F. Chase, March 5, 1903, subseries 1.2, box 5, folder 1.

101. E. H. Wells to E. H. Bagby, Jan. 19, 1904, subseries 3.1, box 15, folder 8; E. H. Wells to J. P. Hamilton, Dec. 12, 1903, subseries 3.1, box 15, folder 4; E. H. Wells to J. P. Hamilton, Sept. 23, 1904, subseries 3.1, box 17, folder 1.

102. Charles F. Mosher to E. M. Lucas, Feb. 3, 1908, subseries 3.1, box 26, folder 6.

103. E. W. Scripps to E. L. Rector, March 13, 1907, subseries 1.2, box 8, folder 12.

104. E. W. Scripps to E. F. Chase, July 24, 1905, subseries 1.2, box 5, folder 8.

105. J. C. Harper to Dan Lehburger, April 4, 1908, subseries 3.1, box 26, folder 13.

106. E. F. Chase to E. W. Scripps, Dec. 21, 1900, subseries 1.1, box 15, folder 5; H. E. Rhoads to E. W. Scripps, Nov. 14, 1905, subseries 1.1, box 24, folder 8; J. P. Hamilton to E. R. Buck, Nov. 28, 1905, subseries 3.1, box 20, folder 2.

107. E. W. Scripps, "Unfinished Business," Feb. 10, 1900, subseries 3.2, box 4, folder 4; H. E. Rhoads to E. W. Scripps, Nov. 14, 1905, subseries 1.1, box 24, folder 8; E. W. Scripps to J. P. Hamilton, Oct. 26, 1906, subseries 1.2, box 8, folder 2; W. H. Porterfield to Ernest Reynolds, Nov. 14, 1895, subseries 3.1, box 20, folder 1.

108. E. W. Scripps, "Notes and Topics to Be Taken Up with the Managers of the Young Eastern Papers," Jan. 25, 1907, subseries 1.2, box 8, folder 9.

109. E. W. Scripps to Hyacinth Ford, Nov. 7, 1906, subseries 1.2, box 8, folder 3.

110. E. W. Scripps to E. H. Wells, Jan. 1, 1903, subseries 1.2, box 5, folder 1.

Chapter 4: Management

1. E. W. Scripps to E. H. Wells, Nov. 28, 1903, subseries 1.2, box 5, folder 3.

2. E. W. Scripps to E. H. Wells, Nov. 28, 1903, subseries 1.2, box 5, folder 3.

3. E. W. Scripps to H. N. Rickey, April 18, 1905, subseries 1.2, box 5, folder 5.

4. As JoAnne Yates writes, "Managerial control—over employees (both workers and other managers), processes, and flows of materials—is the mechanism through which the operations of an organization are coordinated to achieve desired results." Yates, *Control through Communication*, xvi.

5. Wren *The Evolution of Management Thought*, 88; Mackenzie, *Organizational Structure*, 166; Nelson, *Managers and Workers*, 9; see also Nelson, ed., *A Mental Revolution*, 7; Litterer, "Systematic Management," 461–76; Litterer, "Systematic Management: Design

for Organizational Recoupling," 375; Chandler, Jr., *Strategy and Structure*, 14, 21–27. "The philosophy of management that evolved . . . , later to be labeled *systematic management*, promoted rational and impersonal systems in preference to personal and idiosyncratic leadership for maintaining efficiency in a firm's operation. . . . Systematic management attempted to improve control over—and thus the efficiency of—managers, workers, materials, and production processes." Yates, *Control through Communication*, xvi.

6. E. W. Scripps to A. H. Hopkins, Dec. 8, 1903, subseries 1.2, box 8, folder 5.

7. E. W. Scripps to M. A. McRae, March 11, 1899 (emphasis added), subseries 1.2, box 3, folder 11; also see R. F. Paine to Will P. Strandborg, May 16, 1903, subseries 3.1, box 13, folder 9; E. W. Scripps to H. B. Clark and W. D. Wasson, Oct. 9, 1904, subseries 1.2, box 5, folder 3; E. W. Scripps to R. F. Paine, May 18, 1905, subseries 1.2, box 5, folder 6.

8. M. A. McRae to E. W. Scripps, Oct. 3, 1890, subseries 1.1, box 3, folder 8; M. A. McRae to E. W. Scripps, Nov. 8, 1892, subseries 1.1, box 5, folder 9; E. H. Wells to H. B. Clark, Aug. 15, 1899, subseries 3.1, box 5, folder 2; L. T. Atwood to E. W. Scripps, Sept. 28, 1899, subseries 1.1, box 12, folder 7; Synopsis of the Cleveland Press Report for Nov. 1899, Dec. 1, 1899, subseries 3.2, box 3, folder 7; E. W. Scripps to M. A. McRae, April 10, 1900, subseries 3.1, box 6, folder 4; E. W. Scripps to W. H. Porterfield, March 17, 1901, series 2, box 5, letterbook 8, 30–31 (quotation); L. T. Atwood to M. A. McRae, April 4, 1901, subseries 3.2, box 4, folder 9; Charles J. Stein to M. A. McRae, Oct. 31, 1902, subseries 3.1, box 19, folder 12; J. P. Hamilton to E. H. Bagby et al., March 29, 1905, subseries 3.1, box 18, folder 7; E. W. Scripps to M. A. McRae, April 23, 1905, subseries 1.2, box 5, folder 5.

9. The central office determined payment levels. L. T. Atwood to E. F. Chase, June 15, 1905, subseries 3.1, box 18, folder 13; Cabinet Meeting, July 10, 1905, subseries 3.2, box 5, folder 10; Charles J. Stein to W. W. Thornton, July 15, 1905, subseries 3.1, box 19, folder 3.

10. E. W. Scripps to W. W. Thornton, Jan. 16, 1906, subseries 1.2, box 6, folder 14.

11. E. W. Scripps to E. H. Bagby, Feb. 3, 1906, subseries 1.2, box 6, folder 16 (emphasis added); see also E. W. Scripps to L. T. Atwood, Jan. 12, 1907, subseries 1.2, box 8, folder 8; E. W. Scripps to H. B. Clark, E. F. Chase, E. H. Wells, and W. H. Porterfield, Feb. 21, 1907, and E. W. Scripps to L. T. Atwood, Feb. 21, 1907, subseries 1.2, box 8, folder 11.

12. L. T. Atwood to E. F. Chase, July 8, 1905, subseries 3.1, box 19, folder 2; see also E. W. Scripps to E. H. Bagby, Feb. 3, 1906, subseries 1.2, box 6, folder 16.

13. "Libel Judgments and Litigation Expenses," Cabinet Meeting, July 10, 1905, subseries 3.2, box 5, folder 10; L. T. Atwood to E. F. Chase, July 8, 1905, subseries 3.1, box 19, folder 2; see also L. T. Atwood to E. F. Chase, June 15, 1905, subseries 3.1, box 18, folder 13; E. W. Scripps to J. C. Harper and L. T. Atwood, Dec. 16, 1905, subseries 1.2, box 6, folder 11.

14. Jay A. Gove and R. G. Conant to E. W. Scripps, Oct. 25, 1906, subseries 1.1, box 24, folder 14.

15. Conference at Miramar, Calif., between E. W. Scripps, E. B. Scripps, and George Putnam, Aug. 17, 1902, subseries 1.2, box 4, folder 19; H. B. Clark to E. W. Scripps, March 4, 1903, subseries 1.1, box 20, folder 6; E. H. Wells to E. W. Scripps, July 1, 1903, subseries 1.1, box 21, folder 14; "Special Called Stockholders Meeting," June 13, 1902, subseries 3.1, box 11, folder 4, citing E. W. Scripps to E. H. Wells, Jan. 11, 1899; W. H. Porterfield to E. W. Scripps, Oct. 5, 1904, subseries 1.1, box 22, folder 14; Alfred O. Andersson and H. J. Richmond to E. W. Scripps, Sept. 3, 1906, and Robert W. Hobbs and E. S. Fentress to E. W. Scripps, Sept. 20, 1906, subseries 1.1, box 24, folder 14; R. F. Paine and H. B. Clark to E. W. Scripps, Aug. 6, 1906, subseries 1.1, box 25, folder 1; J. P. Hamilton to E. W. Scripps, March 27, 1906, subseries 1.1, box 25, folder 4.

16. E. W. Scripps to W. W. Thornton, April 18, 1905, subseries 1.2, box 5, folder 5; E. W. Scripps to E. H. Wells, Sept. 11, 1900, series 2, box 4, letterbook 6, 1.

17. E. F. Chase to E. W. Scripps, Oct. 12, 1899, subseries 1.1, box 13, folder 6; L. T. Atwood to E. W. Scripps, Jan. 8, 1901, subseries 3.1, box 7, folder 12; E. W. Scripps to E. H. Bagby, E. F. Chase, and F. D. Waite, Jan. 12, 1901, series 2, box 4, letterbook 7, 75; L. T. Atwood to E. F. Chase, Feb. 17, 1903, subseries 3.1, box 12, folder 11; E. H. Wells to E. W. Scripps, July 1, 1903, subseries 1.1, box 21, folder 14; E. L. Rector to L. T. Atwood, Sept. 14, 1906, subseries 3.1, box 22, folder 7; E. W. Scripps to J. P. Hamilton, Feb. 4, 1907, subseries 1.2, box 8, folder 10.

18. E. W. Scripps to L. T. Atwood, Jan. 12, 1907, subseries 1.2, box 8, folder 8; see also E. W. Scripps to E. H. Wells, April 25, 1905, subseries 1.2, box 5, folder 5.

19. E. W. Scripps to E. F. Chase, May 15, 1901, series 2, box 5, letterbook 8, 290; see also E. W. Scripps to E. H. Wells, April 25, 1905, subseries 1.2, box 5, folder 5; E. W. Scripps to W. H. Porterfield, Oct. 20, 1905, subseries 1.2, box 6, folder 5; E. W. Scripps to H. B. Clark, Jan. 15, 1906, subseries 1.2, box 6, folder 14; E. W. Scripps to W. D. Wasson, Jan. 22, 1906, subseries 1.2, box 6, folder 14; and E. W. Scripps to E. H. Wells, Feb. 8, 1906, subseries 1.2, box 6, folder 16.

20. Charles J. Stein to George Putnam, July 18, 1903, Putnam Papers, University of Oregon; E. W. Scripps to W. W. Thornton, Aug. 1, 1905, subseries 1.2, box 5, folder 9.

21. E. W. Scripps to L. T. Atwood, Feb. 17, 1903, series 2, box 8, letterbook 12, 141; L. T. Atwood to George Putnam, March 17, 1903, subseries 3.1, box 13, folder 2.

22. L. T. Atwood to E. F. Chase, Feb. 29, 1904, subseries 3.1, box 15, folder 11.

23. E. W. Scripps to H. B. Clark, Jan. 9, 1907, subseries 1.2, box 8, folder 7.

24. L. T. Atwood to E. H. Bagby, Jan. 15, 1902, subseries 3.1, box 10, folder 1; L. T. Atwood to E. W. Scripps, Jan. 19, 1903, subseries 1.1, box 19, folder 13; Atwood to Scripps, Jan. 27, 1904, subseries 1.1, box 21, folder 15; Charles J. Stein to L. T. Atwood, Feb. 3, 1905, subseries 3.1, box 18, folder 2; Charles Stein to E. W. Scripps, Jan. 12, 1906, subseries 1.1, box 26, folder 4.

25. E. W. Scripps to H. B. Clark and W. D. Wasson, Oct. 9, 1904, subseries 1.2, box 5, folder 3.

26. E. W. Scripps to L. T. Atwood, Feb. 12, 1901, series 2, box 4, letterbook 7, 265; E. W. Scripps to L. T. Atwood, Sept. 15, 1906, subseries 1.2, box 7, folder 10.

27. E. W. Scripps to E. F. Chase, Feb. 28, 1901, series 2, box 4, letterbook 7, 405; E. W. Scripps to E. H. Bagby, March 1, 1901, series 2, box 4, letterbook 7, 406.

28. E. W. Scripps to R. F. Paine, Sept. 23, 1905, subseries 1.2, box 6, folder 3; E. W. Scripps to E. H. Bagby, April 4, 1906, subseries 1.2, box 7, folder 3.

29. E. W. Scripps to E. H. Wells, April 25, 1905, subseries 1.2, box 5, folder 5.

30. E. W. Scripps to J. P. Hamilton, May 12, 1906, subseries 1.2, box 7, folder 5; see also L. T. Atwood to E. F. Chase, April 26, 1900, subseries 3.1, box 6, folder 4; E. W. Scripps to Paul H. Blades, March 8, 1900, series 2, box 3, letterbook 5, 187.

31. E. W. Scripps to E. H. Bagby, Jan. 12, 1901, series 2, box 4, letterbook 7, 59; J. P. Hamilton to E. H. Bagby, May 22, 1901, series 2, box 5, letterbook 9, 20; E. W. Scripps to E. F. Chase, July 10, 1902, and E. W. Scripps to E. H. Bagby, July 9, 1902, series 2, box 7, letterbook 11, 15b, 8; L. T. Atwood to E. W. Scripps, Jan. 8, 1901, subseries 3.1, box 7, folder 12; J. P. Hamilton to L. T. Atwood, Dec. 26, 1906, subseries 3.1, box 23, folder 3.

32. E. W. Scripps to E. H. Bagby, Nov. 15, 1902, series 2, box 7, letterbook 11, 445b.

33. Charles J. Stein to L. T. Atwood, July 23, 1903, subseries 3.1, box 24, folder 3.

34. E. H. Bagby to W. H. Porterfield, March 2, 1905, subseries 3.1, box 18, folder 5; E. W. Scripps to H. B. Clark, Jan. 24, 1906, subseries 1.2, box 6, folder 14; R. F. Paine to J. C. Harper, Oct. 15, 1906, subseries 3.2, box 22, folder 10; Diary of R. F. Paine, Portland, Tacoma, Seattle, Spokane Trip [Oct. 1906], subseries 3.1, box 22, folder 12; Diary of R. F. Paine, Trip Eastward, Nov. 6, 1906, subseries 3.1, box 23, folder 2; J. C. Harper to R. F. Paine, Sept. 29, 1905, subseries 3.1, box 19, folder 11; Diary of J. C. Harper's Trip West, Jan. 27–March 1, 1907, subseries 3.1, box 23, folder 7.

35. E. H. Wells to H. B. Clark, Aug. 20, 1899, subseries 3.1, box 5, folder 2.

36. Charles J. Stein to H. B. Clark, May 29, 1900, subseries 3.1, box 6, folder 6; E. W. Scripps to L. T. Atwood, July 30, 1900, subseries 1.2, box 4, folder 1.

37. E. W. Scripps to Paul H. Blades, March 31, 1900, and H. B. Clark to C. J. Stein, May 23, 1900, series 2, box 3, letterbook 5, 234, 398–99.

38. C. J. Stein to L. T. Atwood, June 11, 1903, subseries 3.1, box 13, folder 13; Charles J. Stein to E. W. Scripps, Jan. 12, 1906, subseries 1.1, box 26, folder 4.

39. L. T. Atwood to To All Concerned, Aug. 15, 1906, subseries 3.1, box 22, folder 4; C. F. Mosher to L. T. Atwood, Oct. 23, 1906, subseries 3.1, box 22, folder 12; C. F. Mosher to L. T. Atwood, Dec. 26, 1906, subseries 3.1, box 23, folder 4.

40. E. W. Scripps to J. C. Harper, Jan. 15, 1906, subseries 1.2, box 6, folder 13.

41. E. W. Scripps to R. F. Paine, Nov. 7, 1905, subseries 1.2, box 6, folder 7.

42. E. W. Scripps to H. N. Rickey, Sept. 6, 1905, subseries 1.2, box 6, folder 1.

43. W. H. Porterfield to E. W. Scripps, Oct. 28, 1905, subseries 1.1, box 24, folder 8.

44. E. W. Scripps to Raymond Buck, Feb. 8, 1906, subseries 1.2, box 6, folder 16.

45. E. W. Scripps to E. H. Bagby, Jan. 6, 1908, subseries 1.2, box 10, folder 5.

46. E. W. Scripps to H. B. Clark, May 24, 1906, subseries 1.2, box 7, folder 5.

47. W. H. Porterfield to R. F. Paine, April 5, 1905, subseries 3.2, box 5, folder 9; R. F. Paine to Max Balthasar, May 4, 1905, subseries 3.1, box 18, folder 10; E. W. Scripps to

W. H. Porterfield, Aug. 28, 1905, subseries 1.2, box 5, folder 12; R. F. Paine to Frank T. Searight, Sept. 22, 1905, subseries 3.1, box 19, folder 10; R. F. Paine to Mel Uhl, Sept. 25, 1905, subseries 3.1, box 19, folder 10; R. F. Paine to W. P. Strandborg, Sept. 27, 1905, subseries 3.1, box 19, folder 11; R. F. Paine to LeRoy Sanders, Oct. 19, 1905, subseries 3.1, box 19, folder 14 (quotation); B. H. Canfield to R. F. Paine, Oct. 30, 1905, subseries 1.1, box 23, folder 8; R. F. Paine to LeRoy Sanders, Oct. 19, 1905, subseries 3.1, box 19, folder 14; R. F. Paine to H. Y. Saint, Nov. 3, 1905, and R. F. Paine to Horace Brown, Nov. 6, 1905, subseries 3.1, box 19, folder 16.

48. R. F. Paine to E. H. Bagby, Aug. 27, 1902, subseries 3.1, box 11, folder 9.

49. R. F. Paine to E. W. Scripps, July 18, 1903, subseries 1.1, box 21, folder 9.

50. R. F. Paine to B. H. Canfield, July 19, 1905, subseries 3.1, box 19, folder 3.

51. R. F. Paine to W. H. Porterfield, Nov. 25, 1905, subseries 3.1, box 20, folder 2.

52. E. W. Scripps to W. H. Porterfield, Aug. 28, 1905, subseries 1.2, box 5, folder 12; E. W. Scripps to E. H. Bagby and B. H. Canfield, Sept. 12, 1905, subseries 1.2, box 6, folder 2.

53. E. W. Scripps to L. T. Atwood, Nov. 15, 1905, subseries 1.2, box 6, folder 8; R. F. Paine to Dear Sir, Aug. 9, 1906, subseries 3.1, box 22, folder 3; E. W. Scripps to W. H. Porterfield, Sept. 21, 1906, subseries 1.2, box 7, folder 11.

54. E. W. Scripps to W. H. Porterfield, Aug. 22, 1905, subseries 1.2, box 5, folder 11.

55. E. W. Scripps to W. H. Porterfield, Aug. 22, 1905, subseries 1.2, box 5, folder 11.

56. R. F. Paine to E. W. Scripps, Aug. 7, 1906, subseries 1.1, box 26, folder 1.

57. B. H. Canfield to E. W. Scripps, Aug. 2, 1905, subseries 1.1, box 23, folder 8; C. F. Mosher to R. F. Paine, Nov. 11, 1907, subseries 3.1, box 25, folder 7.

58. C. F. Mosher to R. F. Paine, Nov. 11, 1907, subseries 3.1, box 25, folder 7.

59. E. W. Scripps to W. H. Porterfield, Aug. 16, 1902, series 2, box 7, letterbook 11, 139.

60. E. W. Scripps to John Vandercook, March 15, 1905, subseries 1.2, box 5, folder 4. "I am not a socialist. I am not a philanthropist. . . . Nothing is farther from my thoughts than philanthropy." E. W. Scripps, "Profit Sharing Plan," Feb. 19, 1905, subseries 1.2, box 5, folder 4.

61. E. W. Scripps to W. W. Thornton, Aug. 1, 1905, subseries 1.2, box 5, folder 9.

62. E. H. Wells to H. B. Clark, Aug. 20, 1899, subseries 3.1, box 5, folder 2; E. F. Chase to H. B. Clark, April 17, 1900, subseries 3.1, box 6, folder 4; E. W. Scripps to E. H. Wells, Nov. 28, 1903, subseries 1.2, box 5, folder 3.

63. Dividends of Minority Stockholders, E. W. Scripps Finance Book, April 14, 1907 to Oct. 5, 1907, series 2, box 1, letterbook 1, 42, 47, 48, 54, 61, 65, 66, 71, 72, 77, 78, 83, 84, 92, 101, 102, 109, 110.

64. Ibid.

65. Atwood earned $3,153.24, Harper $3,093.54. Ibid., 42, 47, 48, 54, 61, 65, 66, 71, 72, 77, 78, 83, 84, 92, 101, 102, 109, 110, 114, 118, 122, 123, 129, 134, 141, 148, 155.

66. Ibid., 42, 47, 48, 54, 61, 65, 66, 71, 72, 77, 78, 83, 84, 92, 101, 102, 109, 110, 114, 118, 122, 123, 129, 134, 141, 148, 155.

67. This provision was usually part of the prospectuses for new papers. George Putnam to L. T. Atwood, Aug. 18, 1902, Putnam Papers, University of Oregon; E. F. Chase to L. T. Atwood, June 12, 1905, subseries 3.1, box 18, folder 13; M. Balthasar to E. W. Scripps, Jan. 24, 1906, subseries 1.1, box 24, folder 15; J. P. Hamilton to E. W. Scripps, March 27, 1906, subseries 1.1, box 25, folder 4.

68. L. T. Atwood to J. P. Hamilton, Sept. 15, 1904, subseries 3.1, box 16, folder 14; E. H. Wells to L. T. Atwood, Oct. 19, 1904, subseries 3.1, box 17, folder 2; L. T. Atwood to W. H. Porterfield, July 28, 1905, subseries 3.1, box 19, folder 3.

69. L. T. Atwood to E. W. Scripps, Jan. 7, 1903, subseries 3.1, box 12, folder 6; E. W. Scripps, E. H. Wells, and E. F. Chase, Jan. 10, 1903, subseries 3.1, box 12, folder 7.

70. E. W. Scripps to E. H. Wells, Jan. 1, 1903, subseries 1.2, box 5, folder 1.

71. W. P. Strandborg to E. W. Scripps, April 13, 1905, subseries 1.1, box 24, folder 10.

72. LeRoy Sanders to L. T. Atwood, Jan. 22, 1906, subseries 3.1, box 20, folder 7.

73. E. W. Scripps to L. T. Atwood, Feb. 25, 1907, subseries 1.2, box 8, folder 11.

74. E. W. Scripps to W. H. Porterfield, May 6, 1905, subseries 1.2, box 5, folder 6.

75. Articles of Incorporation of the Star Publishing Co., Aug. 23, 1900, subseries 3.1, box 7, folder 3; L. T. Atwood to E. W. Scripps, Oct. 18, 1902, subseries 1.1, box 18, folder 7.

76. Articles of Incorporation, San Diegan-Sun Co., Sept. 27, 1905, subseries 3.1, box 19, folder 11.

77. E. W. Scripps to W. W. Thornton, Aug. 1, 1905, subseries 1.2, box 5, folder 9.

78. E. W. Scripps to J. C. Harper, March 29, 1905, subseries 1.2, box 5, folder 4.

79. E. W. Scripps and H. Y. Saint, "Notes . . . of a Memorandum," Miramar, Nov. 17, 1903, subseries 3.1, box 15, folder 1.

Chapter 5: Avoiding Competition

1. E. W. Scripps Diary, July 24, 1906, subseries 1.2, box 7, folder 8; E. W. Scripps to E. F. Chase, Aug. 30, 1906, subseries 1.2, box 7, folder 9; Turnbull, *History of Oregon Newspapers,* 195.

2. E. W. Scripps to W. D. Wasson, May 19, 1906, subseries 1.2, box 7, folder 5.

3. "Price warfare has been shown to be a significant deterrent to new entry." Karakaya and Stahl, *Entry Barriers and Market Entry Decisions,* 18.

4. Cleveland *Press,* April 8, 1879, 1, April 10, 1879, 1, April 23, 1879, 1, Jan. 23, 1880, 3, Feb. 6, 1880, 3.

5. Cleveland *Press,* Nov. 15, 1878, 1, April 7, 1879, 1.

6. Cleveland *Press,* Aug. 9, 1879, 2; Trimble, *The Astonishing Mr. Scripps,* 60–61.

7. Cleveland *Press,* April 15, 1881, 1.

8. Cleveland *Press,* April 20, 1881, 1, April 21, 1881, 1, April 30, 1881, 2, May 2, 1881, 1; Trimble, *The Astonishing Mr. Scripps,* 80–87.

9. E. W. Scripps to B. F. Gurley, July 29, 1907, subseries 1.2, box 9, folder 5 (emphasis added).

10. E. W. Scripps to W. D. Wasson, May 19, 1906, subseries 1.2, box 7, folder 5.

11. E. W. Scripps to R. F. Paine, Sept. 2, 1905, subseries 1.2, box 6, folder 1.

12. Linda Lawson, *Truth in Publishing: Federal Regulations of the Press's Business Practices, 1880–1920* (Carbondale: Southern Illinois University Press, 1993).

13. E. H. Wells to E. H. Bagby, Jan. 19, 1904, subseries 3.1, box 15, folder 8; E. F. Chase to H. B. Clark, Feb. 12, 1899, subseries 3.1, box 3, folder 12.

14. E. W. Scripps to W. H. Porterfield, March 21, 1901, series 2, box 5, letterbook 8, 78–79.

15. Diary of R. F. Paine, Nov. 11, 1906, subseries 3.2, box 5, folder 12.

16. E. W. Scripps to E. F. Chase, June 7, 1905, subseries 1.2, box 5, folder 7.

17. H. B. Clark to E. W. Scripps, Jan. 20, 1900, subseries 1.1, box 14, folder 12; E. F. Chase to E. W. Scripps, Dec. 21, 1900, subseries 1.1, box 15, folder 5; E. F. Chase to E. W. Scripps, Jan. 25, 1902, and E. F. Chase to E. W. Scripps, March 18, 1902, subseries 1.1, box 18, folder 8. In 1906 Scripps described the process to McRae: "No letters even were addressed to me by the managers and editors of the [Seattle] paper from the office or through a stenographer with my name mentioned. When a stenographer took a letter, a blank was left in place of my name and the manager in sending the letter, wrote in my name and addressed the envelope himself." E. W. Scripps to M. A. McRae, Sept. 26, 1906, subseries 1.2, box 7, folder 11.

18. E. H. Wells to J. P. Hamilton, Oct. 18, 1901, subseries 3.1, box 9, folder 6; E. W. Scripps to E. F. Chase, Oct. 20, 1906, subseries 1.2, box 8, folder. Chase promised to keep the material safely locked up. E. F. Chase to E. W. Scripps, Oct. 26, 1906, subseries 1.1, box 24, folder 17.

19. E. W. Scripps to M. A. McRae, Sept. 26, 1906, subseries 1.2, box 7, folder 11.

20. M. A. McRae to E. W. Scripps, Feb. 10, 1905, subseries 1.1, box 24, folder 1.

21. H. B. Clark to L. T. Atwood, Jan. 19, 1903, subseries 3.1, box 12, folder 7.

22. E. W. Scripps to J. C. Harper, M. A. McRae, and L. T. Atwood, Dec. 18 and Dec. 20, 1901, subseries 1.2, box 4, folder 8; L. T. Atwood to E. W. Scripps, Oct. 19, 1905, and L. T. Atwood to E. W. Scripps, Oct. 21, 1905, subseries 1.1, box 23, folder 5.

23. E. W. Scripps to W. W. Thornton, and E. H. Bagby, Nov. 17, 1905, subseries 1.2, box 6, folder 8.

24. H. B. Clark to E. W. Scripps, March 17, 1904, subseries 1.1, box 22, folder 4.

25. H. B. Clark to E. W. Scripps, Feb. 4, 1904, subseries 1.1, box 22, folder 4. Clark told Atwood, "So far we are not replacing any other evening paper. We have not stopped a hundred Bulletins and Posts in all our circulation. The Bulletin has from twenty to twenty-five thousand carrier circulation; the Post possibly seven thousand carrier circulation." H. B. Clark to L. T. Atwood, subseries 3.1, box 15, folder 11.

26. J. C. Harper to F. W. Hunsicker and W. B. Kenny, June 26, 1906, subseries 3.1, box 21, folder 7; Jacob C. Harper to W. C. Mayborn, June 27, 1906, subseries 3.1, box 27, folder 7.

27. E. W. Scripps to E. H. Bagby, Aug. 19, 1902, series 2, box 7, letterbook 11, 159; E. W. Scripps to L. T. Atwood, Oct. 16, 1906, subseries 1.2, box 8, folder 1.

28. E. W. Scripps to E. H. Bagby, Aug. 19, 1902, and E. W. Scripps to E. F. Chase,

Aug. 19, 1902, series 2, box 7, letterbook 11, 159, 158; E. H. Wells to E. W. Scripps, July 1, 1903, subseries 1.1, box 21, folder 14; J. P. Hamilton to E. W. Scripps, March 27, 1906, subseries 1.1, box 25, folder 4; J. C. Harper to Ward C. Mayborn, July 9, 1906, subseries 3.1, box 21, folder 9.

29. J. C. Harper to Ward C. Mayborn, July 9, 1906, subseries 3.1, box 21, folder 9.

30. For San Francisco, see H. B. Clark to L. T. Atwood, Jan. 19, 1903, subseries 3.1, box 12, folder 7; H. B. Clark to E. W. Scripps, April 5, 1903, subseries 1.1, box 20, folder 6; H. B. Clark to E. W. Scripps, April 27, 1903, subseries 1.1, box 20, folder 4; and H. B. Clark to E. W. Scripps, July 8, 1903, subseries 1.1, box 20, folder 4. For Portland, see E. F. Chase to E. W. Scripps, Aug. 8, 1906, subseries 1.1, box 24, folder 17. For Pueblo, see E. L. Rector to H. B. Clark, Sept. 20, 1906, subseries 3.1, box 22, folder 7. For Nashville, see E. H.Bagby to H. H. Hobbs, Oct. 6, 1906, subseries 3.1, box 22, folder 9.

31. E. W. Scripps to R. F. Paine, Sept. 14, 1905, subseries 1.2, box 6, folder 2; E. W. Scripps to R. F. Paine, Aug. 28, 1905, subseries 1.2, box 5, folder 12.

32. E. W. Scripps to M. A. McRae, Aug. 30, 1905, subseries 1.2, box 5, folder 12; H. B. Clark to E. W. Scripps, Jan. 12, 1906, subseries 1.1, box 24, folder 16.

33. E. W. Scripps to H. B. Clark, May 26, 1906, subseries 1.2, box 7, folder 5.

34. E. W. Scripps to W. D. Wasson, Dec. 29, 1906, subseries 1.2, box 8, folder 6. Scripps offered a bond, pledging never to go over four pages an issue for the *Daily News* if the *Bulletin* would not drop its price. The offer was in vain. W. D. Wasson to E. W. Scripps, Dec. 28, 1906, subseries 1.1, box 26, folder 5.

35. J. C. Harper to R. F. Peters, July 24, 1906, subseries 3.1, box 21, folder 11; C. F. Mosher to L. T. Atwood, Oct. 23, 1906, subseries 3.1, box 22, folder 12; Diary of R. F. Paine, Nov. 23, 1906, subseries 3.2, box 5, folder 12.

36. R. F. Paine to E. W. Scripps, Aug. 6, 1906, subseries 1.1, box 25, folder 1; E. L. Rector to L. T. Atwood, Sept. 14, 1906, subseries 3.1, box 22, folder 7; J. P. Hamilton to M. A. McRae, Aug. 15, 1906, subseries 3.1, box 22, folder 4.

37. E. W. Scripps to W. D. Wasson, May 19, 1906, subseries 1.2, box 7, folder 5; R. F. Paine to H. B. Clark, April 17, 1906, subseries 3.1, box 21, folder 2; see also E. W. Scripps to R. F. Paine, May 9, 1906, subseries 1.2, box 7, folder 4.

38. E. W. Scripps to E. H. Wells, Oct. 19, 1905, subseries 1.2, box 6, folder 5.

39. M. A. McRae to E. W. Scripps, Oct. 3, 1906, subseries 1.1, box 25, folder 14; McRae to Messrs. Andersson and Richmond, Oct. 3, 1906, subseries 3.1, box 22, folder 9; E. H. Bagby to James G. Scripps, Sept. 2, 1905, subseries 3.1, box 19, folder 7; E. W. Scripps to John Vandercook, March 15, 1905, subseries 1.2, box 5, folder 4; E. W. Scripps to J. P. Hamilton, May 12, 1906, subseries 1.2, box 7, folder 5; R. F. Paine and H. B. Clark to E. W. Scripps, Oct. 2, 1906, subseries 1.1, box 26, folder 1.

40. Oklahoma City *News,* Oct. 1–Nov. 30, 1906.

41. E. L. Rector to L. T. Atwood, Sept. 14, 1906, subseries 3.1, box 22, folder 7; Pueblo *Sun,* Sept. 1–6, 1906; A. R. Hopkins to E. W. Scripps, Oct. 11, 1906, subseries 1.1, box 25, folder 10.

42. E. H. Wells to E. W. Scripps, March 17, 1903, subseries 1.1, box 21, folder 14.

43. For Tacoma, see E. H. Wells to E. W. Scripps, July 1, 1903, subseries 1.1, box 21, folder 14. For Nashville, see Jay A. Gove and Ray G. Conant to E. W. Scripps, Oct. 25, 1906, subseries 1.1, box 25, folder 14. For Dallas, see A. O. Andersson and H. J. Richmond to E. W. Scripps, Sept. 3, 1906, subseries 1.1, box 24, folder 14. For Oklahoma City, see E. S. Fentress and R. W. Hobbs to E. W. Scripps, Sept. 20, 1906, subseries 1.1, box 24, folder 14.

44. R. F. Paine to E. W. Scripps, Aug. 6, 1906, subseries 1.1, box 25, folder 1; R. F. Paine to E. W. Scripps, Sept. 25, 1906, subseries 1.1, box 26, folder 1; Charles F. Mosher to J. D. Snively, April 10, 1908, subseries 3.1, box 26, folder 14; E. W. Scripps to J. P. Hamilton, July 15, 1907, subseries 1.2, box 9, folder 5; Charles F. Mosher to L. T. Atwood, Oct. 22, 1907, subseries 3.1, box 25, folder 5.

45. Charles F. Mosher to L. T. Atwood, Oct. 23, 1906, subseries 3.1, box 22, folder 12.

46. E. W. Scripps to J. C. Lee, July 30, 1903, subseries 1.2, box 5, folder 1.

47. E. W. Scripps to W. D. Wasson, May 19, 1906, subseries 1.2, box 7, folder 5.

48. E. W. Scripps to George Putnam, Aug. 22, 1902, subseries 1.2, box 4, folder 19; E. W. Scripps to J. C. Lee, July 30, 1903, subseries 1.2, box 5, folder 1; E. F. Chase to John C. Lee, Oct. 12, 1904, subseries 3.1, box 17, folder 2; E. F. Chase to John C. Lee, Oct. 25, 1904, subseries 3.1, box 17, folder 3; E. F. Chase to John C. Lee and H. Y. Saint, Nov. 5, 1904, subseries 3.1, box 17, folder 4; J. C. Lee to E. F. Chase, Oct. 17, 1904, subseries 3.1, box 17, folder 2.

49. Paul Blades to E. W. Scripps, March 1, 1900, and Paul Blades to E. W. Scripps, March 11, 1900, subseries 1.1, box 15, folder 2; E. W. Scripps to H. G. Otis, May 23, 1900, series 2, box 3, letterbook 5, 393; E. W. Scripps to E. H. Bagby, March 30, 1901, series 2, box 5, letterbook 8, 148–49; E. W. Scripps to Paul H. Blades, July 31, 1901, series 2, box 5, letterbook 9, 191; H. G. Otis to E. W. Scripps, Feb. 5, 1904, subseries 1.1, box 22, folder 12; E. H. Bagby to J. P. Hamilton, Feb. 11, 1904, subseries 3.1, box 15, folder 10; R. F. Paine to B. H. Canfield, Dec. 10, 1906, subseries 3.1, box 23, folder 3.

50. E. H. Wells to E. W. Scripps, July 1, 1903, subseries 1.1, box 21, folder 14. For Dallas, see A. O. Andersson and H. J. Richmond to E. W. Scripps, Sept. 3, 1906, subseries 1.1, box 24, folder 14. For Oklahoma City, see E. S. Fentress and R. W. Hobbs to E. W. Scripps, Sept. 20, 1906, subseries 1.1, box 24, folder 14. For Nashville, see Jay A. Gove and Ray G. Conant to E. W. Scripps, Oct. 25, 1906, subseries 1.1, box 24, folder 14. For Denver, see J. P. Hamilton to E. W. Scripps, March 27, 1906, subseries 1.1, box 25, folder 4.

51. E. W. Scripps, "Notes and Topics to be Taken Up with the Managers of the Young Eastern Papers," Jan. 25, 1907, subseries 1.2, box 8, folder 9.

52. E. W. Scripps to E. F. Chase, Feb. 13, 1903, subseries 1.2, box 5, folder 1.

53. E. F. Chase to E. W. Scripps, Dec. 2, 1902, subseries 1.1, box 18, folder 9; H. B. Clark to E. F. Chase, Dec. 5, 1902, subseries 1.1, box 18, folder 7; E. W. Scripps to E. F.

Chase, Dec. 27, 1902, series 2, box 8, letterbook 12, 50; E. W. Scripps to E. F. Chase, Feb. 13, 1903, subseries 1.2, box 5, folder 1.

54. E. W. Scripps, "Memoranda of My Trip East—May 9th, 1904, to July 23rd, 1904," series 2, box 42, personal letterbook B, 299b.

55. Ibid.

56. J. C. Harper to W. C. Mayborn, June 17, 1907, subseries 3.1, box 24, folder 5.

57. Charles F. Mosher to R. B. Young, April 3, 1908, subseries 3.1, box 26, folder 13.

58. E. W. Scripps, Concerning the S.M.L., May 16, 1894, subseries 1.2, box 2, folder 9.

59. E. W. Scripps to M. Balthasar, March 7, 1906, subseries 1.2, box 7, folder 1; W. D. Wasson to E. W. Scripps, Dec. 28, 1906, subseries 1.1, box 26, folder 5; E. W. Scripps to W. D. Wasson, Dec. 29, 1906, subseries 3.1, box 23, folder 4.

60. M. A. McRae to Board of Directors, July 1, 1887, subseries 1.1, box 1, folder 5.

61. M. A. McRae to E. W. Scripps, Nov. 5, 1892, subseries 1.1, box 5, folder 9.

62. M. A. McRae to E. W. Scripps, Oct. 11, 1892, series 1.1, box 5, folder 8.

63. M. A. McRae to E. W. and Geo. H. Scripps, Sept. 4, 1895, subseries 1.1, box 9, folder 1; Charles Stein to M. A. McRae, Oct. 9, 1896, subseries 3.1, box 2, folder 6; E. W. Scripps to L. T. Atwood, Oct. 2, 1898, subseries 1.2, box 3, folder 10.

64. L. T. Atwood to E. W. Scripps, Oct. 10, 1898 (first quotation), and L. T. Atwood to E. W. Scripps, Nov. 16, 1898 (second quotation), subseries 1.1, box 11, folder 8; Adams, "Secret Combinations and Collusive Agreements," 199–201; see also Adams, "Market Subordination and Competition."

65. M. A. McRae to Board of Directors, July 1, 1887, subseries 1.1, box 1, folder 5; E. W. Scripps to John Sweeney, Feb. 23, 1889, subseries 1.2, box 2, folder 2; Memorandum between L. A. Leonard and E. W. Scripps, 1888, subseries 1.2, box 2, folder 1; M. A. McRae to E. W. Scripps, Dec. 28, 1888, subseries 1.1, box 1, folder 8; M. A. McRae to E. W. Scripps, March 5, 1890, subseries 1.2, box 3, folder 6.

66. E. W. Scripps to John Sweeney, Aug. 3, 1889, subseries 1.2, box 2, folder 2; E. W. Osborn to E. W. Scripps, Dec. 10, 1889, subseries 1.1, box 2, folder 8; E. F. Chase to E. W. Scripps, Aug. 8, 1904, subseries 1.1, box 22, folder 5; E. W. Scripps to W. H. Porterfield, March 15, 1907, subseries 1.2, box 8, folder 12.

67. E. W. Scripps to John Sweeney, Feb. 23, 1889, subseries 1.2, box 2, folder 2; C. F. Mosher to L. T. Atwood, Nov. 3, 1894, and C. F. Mosher to L. T. Atwood, Nov. 3, 1894, subseries 3.2, box 1, folder 2; M. A. McRae to E. W. Scripps, Nov. 5, 1894, subseries 1.1, box 8, folder 3.

68. St. Louis *Evening Journal*, June 23, 1896, 1, June 29, 1896, 1, July 4, 1896, 3.

69. St. Louis *Evening Journal*, July 14, 1896, 1.

70. E. W. Osborn to M. A. McRae, May 29, 1897, subseries 3.1, box 11, folder 2. During the week of January 24, 1897, only 26.4 percent of the newspaper's space was devoted to advertising (out of 224 columns); of the 58.8 columns devoted to advertising, 69.2 percent came from the city contract.

71. E. W. Osborn to M. A. McRae, May 29, 1897, subseries 3.1, box 11, folder 2; *Evening Journal,* May 26, 1897, 2; St. Louis *Journal,* June 18, 1897, 4.

72. There were few daily labor papers before the 1910s. See Shimmons, "The Labor Dailies," 85–93.

73. The *Union Record* was a weekly newspaper until 1918, when it became a daily. O'Connell, "The Seattle *Union Record,* 1918–1928."

74. J. C. Lee to E. W. Scripps, March 21, 1904, subseries 1.1, box 22, folder 9; J. C. Lee, Editor of Spokane *Press,* to Spokane Trades Council, March 16, 1904, subseries 3.1, box 15, folder 12.

75. E. W. Scripps to H. B. Clark, June 29, 1907, subseries 1.2, box 9, folder 3.

76. E. J. Cull to M. A. McRae, July 19, 1900, subseries 3.1, box 6, folder 10.

77. E. J. Cull to M. A. McRae, July 19, 1900, subseries 3.1, box 6, folder 10; E. W. Scripps to M. A. McRae, July 18, 1900, subseries 1.2, box 4, folder 1.

78. E. H. Bagby to M. A. McRae, March 14, 1904, subseries 3.1, box 15, folder 12.

79. R. F. Paine to E. W. Scripps, Sept. 14, 1906, subseries 1.1, box 26, folder 1.

80. Milton A. McRae, "Survey of the Spokane, Wash., Newspaper Field," Sept. 22, 1903, subseries 3.1, box 14, folder 11.

81. B. F. Gurley to J. C. Harper, May 6, 1908, subseries 3.1, box 27, folder 2; J. C. Harper to E. W. Scripps, July 20, 1908, subseries 1.1, box 28, folder 10; B. F. Gurley to J. C. Harper, Nov. 30, 1908, subseries 3.1, box 28, folder 9; J. C. Harper to B. F. Gurley, Dec. 7, 1908, and J. C. Harper to D. Lehrburger, Dec. 7, 1908, subseries 3.1, box 28, folder 10.

82. H. B. Clark to B. H. Canfield, July 24, 1905, subseries 3.1, box 19, folder 3.

83. E. W. Scripps to W. B. Colver, Dec. 29, 1906, subseries 1.2, box 8, folder 6.

Chapter 6: Advertising Is the Enemy

1. E. F. Chase to E. W. Scripps, Aug. 5, 1903, subseries 1.1, box 20, folder 6.

2. E. W. Scripps to E. F. Chase, Aug. 10, 1903, Putnam Papers, University of Oregon.

3. E. W. Scripps, "Non-Advertising Newpaper Scheme," Nov. 2, 1904, subseries 1.2, box 5, folder 3.

4. Ibid.

5. E. W. Scripps to Jacob Harper, Oct. 8, 1907, subseries 1.2, box 9, folder 10.

6. E. W. Scripps to Jacob Harper, Aug. 5, 1907, subseries 1.2, box 9, folder 6.

7. *Newspaper Maker,* Nov. 19, 1896, 3; *Profitable Advertiser,* June 15, 1893, 12; Boston *Globe,* Feb. 8, 1885, 3; Chicago *Herald,* Dec. 17, 1893, 14, May 6, 1895, 40; Cincinnati *Tribune,* Sept. 16, 1893, 3; St. Louis *Republic,* May 5, 1899, 4; Hower, *A History of Macy's,* Table 20; *Chicago Dry Goods Reporter,* March 25, 1899, 53.

8. E. W. Scripps to L. T. Atwood, March 4, 1907, subseries 1.2, box 8, folder 12 (emphasis added).

9. E. W. Scripps to R. F. Paine, Dec. 18, 1899, series 2, box 3, letterbook 4, 370.

10. E. W. Scripps to H. H. Hobbs, Jan. 4, 1908, subseries 1.2, box 10, folder 4.

11. E. W. Scripps to R. W. Hobbs, March 23, 1908, subseries 1.2, box 10, folder 12.

12. E. W. Scripps to William D. Wasson, Feb. 17, 1908, subseries 1.2, box 10, folder 9.

13. E. F. Chase to W. P. Strandborg, April 28, 1903, subseries 3.1, box 13, folder 7.

14. B. H. Canfield to K. J. Murdoch, Dec. 8, 1908, subseries 3.1, box 28, folder 11.

15. J. C. Harper to F. R. Peters, Feb. 17, 1908, subseries 3.1, box 26, folder 7.

16. E. W. Scripps to W. H. Porterfield, Oct. 15, 1907, subseries 1.2, box 9, folder 10.

17. E. W. Scripps to W. H. Porterfield, Oct. 16, 1910, subseries 1.2, box 13, folder 3.

18. J. C. Harper to Judge Ben B. Lindsey, Oct. 20, 1908, subseries 3.1, box 28, folder 4.

19. E. W. Scripps, "Notes and Topics to be Taken Up with the Managers of the Young Eastern Papers," Jan. 25, 1907, subseries 1.2, box 8, folder 9; R. F. Paine to J. C. Harper, July 14, 1906, subseries 3.1, box 21, folder 10; E. S. Fentress and R. W. Hobbs to E. W. Scripps, Sept. 20, 1906, and Jay A. Gove and R. G. Conant to E. W. Scripps, Oct. 25, 1906, subseries 1.1, box 24, folder 14; Diary of R. F. Paine, Nov. 23, 1906, subseries 3.2, box 5, folder 12.

20. H. B. Clark and R. F. Paine to E. W. Scripps, Aug. 6, 1906, subseries 1.1, box 25, folder 1; R. F. Paine and H. B. Clark to E. W. Scripps, Oct. 1, 1906, subseries 1.1, box 26, folder 1; Diary of R. F. Paine, Nov. 23, 1906, subseries 3.2, box 5, folder 12; E. W. Scripps to J. P. Hamilton, July 15, 1907, subseries 1.2, box 9, folder 5; A. O. Andersson and H. J. Richmond to E. W. Scripps, Sept. 3, 1906 (first quotation), E. S. Fentress and R. W. Hobbs to E. W. Scripps, Sept. 20, 1906, and J. A. Gove and R. G. Conant to E. W. Scripps, Oct. 25, 1906 (second quotation), subseries 1.1, box 24, folder 14; E. W. Scripps to J. P. Hamilton, July 15, 1907, subseries 1.2, box 9, folder 5; Charles Mosher to L. T. Atwood, Oct. 22, 1907, subseries 3.1, box 24, folder 5; W. H. Porterfield to George S. Smith, March 11, 1908, subseries 3.1, box 26, folder 9; Charles Mosher to J. D. Sniveley, April 10, 1908, subseries 3.1, box 26, folder 14; R. F. Paine to E. F. Chase, July 13, 1908, subseries 3.1, box 27, folder 9.

21. E. W. Scripps to E. H. Wells, March 6, 1907 (quotation), subseries 1.2, box 8, folder 12; E. W. Scripps to J. P. Hamilton, July 15, 1907, subseries 1.2, box 9, folder 5; Charles Mosher to L. T. Atwood, Oct. 22, 1907, subseries 3.1, box 25, folder 5; R. W. Hobbs to Charles F. Mosher, May 28, 1908, subseries 3.1, box 27, folder 5.

22. W. H. Porterfield to H. E. Rhoads, Feb. 23, 1909, subseries 3.1, box 29, folder 6.

23. L. T. Atwood to E. H. Wells, Dec. 14, 1904, subseries 3.1, box 17, folder 6.

24. E. W. Scripps to W. H. Porterfield, Aug. 22, 1905, subseries 1.2, box 5, folder 11.

25. E. W. Scripps to M. A. McRae and L. T. Atwood, April 7, 1900, series 2, box 3, letterbook 5, 260; E. F. Chase to E. W. Scripps, Sept. 20, 1900, subseries 1.1, box 15, folder 5; E. F. Chase to E. W. Scripps, Nov. 7, 1900, subseries 1.1, box 16, folder 11; A. O. Andersson and H. J. Richmond to E. W. Scripps, Sept. 3, 1906, and E. S. Fentress and R. W. Hobbs to E. W. Scripps, Sept. 20, 1906, subseries 1.1, box 24, folder 14; Jay A. Gove and R. G. Conant to E. W. Scripps, Oct. 25, 1906, subseries 1.1, box 24, folder 14; J. C. Harper to H. J. Richmond, Oct. 10, 1908, subseries 3.1, box 28, folder 3.

26. Jacob Harper to H. J. Richmond, Oct. 10, 1908, subseries 3.1, box 28, folder 3.

27. W. H. Porterfield to E. W. Scripps, Dec. 13, 1906, subseries 1.1, box 26, folder 2; Charles F. Mosher to R. F. Paine, Nov. 12, 1907, subseries 3.1, box 25, folder 7; E. H. Wells to J. P. Hamilton, Dec. 3, 1904, subseries 3.1, box 17, folder 6; George Putnam to L. T. Atwood, March 12, 1903, subseries 3.1, box 13, folder 1; Charles F. Mosher to R. F. Paine, Nov. 11, 1907, subseries 3.1, box 25, folder 7; J. C. Harper to A. O. Andersson, Oct. 1, 1908, series 3.1, box 28, folder 3. Not all of the small Scripps newspapers were successful in getting advertising rates to increase rapidly. The advertising rate of the Oklahoma City *News* began at 23 cents per inch in November 1906 and dropped to 16 cents an inch by August 1907. But during its first full year the rate averaged 19 cents. The Dallas *Dispatch* began with a rate of 28 cents per inch in October 1906, although that dropped; the first-year average was 23 cents. Charles F. Mosher to R. F. Paine, Nov. 11, 1907, series 3.1, box 25, folder 7.

28. J. C. Harper to F. R. Peters, Feb. 12, 1909, subseries 3.1, box 29, folder 5; see also R. F. Paine to H. H. McDonald of the Berkeley *Independent:* "You understand that as editor, under our policies, you are responsible for all advertising that goes into your columns as well as news. You have a right to be consulted about this advertising contracts offered and it is contrary to our policies to publish any free ads." Paine to McDonald, Feb. 11, 1908, subseries 3.1, box 26, folder 7.

29. R. F. Paine to Henry White, Feb. 15, 1906, subseries 3.1, box 20, folder 10.

30. J. C. Harper to N. D. Cochran, Aug. 10, 1910, subseries 3.1, box 32, folder 10.

31. E. W. Scripps to W. W. Thornton, Aug. 24, 1910, subseries 1.2, box 13, folder 1.

32. E. W. Scripps to W. H. Porterfield, Feb. 25, 1905, series 3.1, box 18, folder 4.

33. E. W. Scripps to A. O. Andersson, Oct. 1, 1908, subseries 1.2, box 28, folder 3; E. W. Scripps to J. P. Hamilton, April 25, 1907, subseries 1.2, box 8, folder 15.

34. R. F. Paine to J. C. Harper, July 14, 1906, subseries 3.1, box 21, folder 10; A. R. Hopkins to E. W. Scripps, Oct. 11, 1906, subseries 1.1, box 25, folder 10; J. P. Hamilton to Milton McRae, Aug. 15, 1906, subseries 3.1, box 22, folder 4.

35. J. P. Hamilton to E. H. Bagby et al., March 29, 1905, subseries 3.1, box 18, folder 7. Hamilton was Scripps's secretary at this time and was relaying his words to the western editors.

36. E. W. Scripps to B. H. Canfield, July 30, 1903, subseries 1.2, box 5, folder 1.

37. B. H. Canfield to Coast Editors, Nov. 27, 1908, subseries 3.1, box 28, folder 9; B. H. Canfield to K. J. Murdock, Nov. 11, 1908, subseries 3.1, box 28, folder 7; R. F. Paine to Henry White, Feb. 15, 1906, subseries 3.1, box 20, folder 10.

38. R. F. Paine to Alfred O. Andersson, Nov. 30, 1906, subseries 3.1, box 23, folder 2.

39. Minutes of Conference between E. W. Scripps, E. B. Scripps, and George Putnam, Miramar, Calif., Aug. 17, 1902, subseries 1.2, box 4, folder 19; E. H. Wells to E. W. Scripps, July 1, 1903, subseries 1.1, box 21, folder 14; J. P. Hamilton to E. W. Scripps, March 27, 1906, subseries 1.1, box 25, folder 4; A. O. Andersson and A. J. Richmond to E. W. Scripps, Sept. 3, 1906, and E. S. Fentress and R. W. Hobbs to E. W. Scripps, Sept. 20, 1906, subseries 1.1, box 24, folder 14; LeRoy Sanders to E. W. Scripps, March 5, 1906, subseries 1.1, box 26, folder 3.

40. John Vandercook to E. W. Scripps, July 11, 1905, subseries 1.1, box 24, folder 11.

41. R. F. Paine to All Editors, March 12, 1908, subseries 3.1, box 26, folder 9.

42. E. W. Scripps to H. B. Clark, Feb. 7, 1906, subseries 1.2, box 6, folder 16.

43. F. R. Peters to Charles W. Larsh, Dec. 30, 1908, subseries 3.1, box 28, folder 15.

44. J. C. Harper to F. R. Peters, Oct. 30, 1906, subseries 3.1, box 20, folder 5; Robert F. Paine to A. R. Hopkins and E. L. Rector, Feb. 3, 1907, subseries 3.1, box 23, folder 7. The Pueblo *Sun* was not available for examination, so compliance could not be checked.

45. The boycotts against Scripps newspapers occurred in Cincinnati (1900, 1906), Cleveland (1899), Seattle (1902, 1903), Des Moines (1903), Los Angeles (1903, 1907), San Diego (1906), St. Louis (1906, 1907), Fresno (1907), and Evansville (1908).

46. Milton McRae to H. S. Scott, Sept. 14, 1902, subseries 3.1, box 9, folder 1.

47. Editor, *Press*, to Milton McRae, Oct. 22, 1901, subseries 3.1, box 9, folder 7.

48. Milton McRae to E. W. Scripps, Jan. 19, 1900, subseries 1.1, box 16, folder 1.

49. H. N. Rickey to E. W. Scripps, Jan. 13, 1906, subseries 1.1, box 26, folder 3.

50. W. H. Porterfield to L. T. Atwood, Nov. 27, 1906, subseries 3.1, box 23, folder 2; E. H. Bagby to E. W. Scripps, subseries 1.1, box 20, folder 4.

51. E. W. Scripps to F. J. Zeehandelaar, March 11, 1903, series 2, box 8, letterbook 12, 201.

52. E. F. Chase to E. W. Scripps, Aug. 5, 1903, subseries 1.1, box 20, folder 6.

53. Milton McRae to E. W. Scripps, June 7, 1906, subseries 1.1, box 25, folder 13.

54. J. C. Harper to F. R. Peters, Feb. 17, 1908, subseries 3.1, box 26, folder 7.

55. E. H. Wells to L. T. Atwood, Dec. 22, 1904, subseries 3.1, box 17, folder 7.

56. E. W. Scripps to W. D. Wasson and H. B. Clark, Oct. 9, 1904, and E. W. Scripps to W. D. Wasson, Nov. 18, 1904, subseries 1.2, box 5, folder 3; E. W. Scripps to E. H. Bagby, April 4, 1906, subseries 1.2, box 7, folder 3; E. W. Scripps to R. F. Paine, Sept. 21, 1906, subseries 1.2, box 7, folder 11; R. F. Paine to E. W. Scripps, Sept. 25, 1906, subseries 1.1, box 26, folder 1; Diary of R. F. Paine, Oct. 1906, subseries 3.1, box 22, folder 12; Diary of R. F. Paine, Oct. 1906, subseries 3.2, box 5, folder 12; E. W. Scripps to E. H. Wells, Nov. 15, 1906, subseries 1.2, box 8, folder 4; E. W. Scripps to H. H. Hobbs, May 7, 1907, subseries 1.2, box 8, folder 16; E. W. Scripps to B. F. Gurley, April 10, 1908, subseries 1.2, box 8, folder 15.

57. Flyer, Cincinnati *Post*, Dec. 11, 1908, subseries 3.1, box 28, folder 11.

58. E. W. Scripps to W. D. Wasson, Nov. 18, 1904, subseries 1.2, box 5, folder 3.

59. "Non Advertising Newspaper Scheme," Nov. 23, 1904, subseries 1.2, box 5, folder 3; E. W. Scripps to L. T. Atwood, May 4, 1907, subseries 1.2, box 8, folder 16; see also John Vandercook to E. W. Scripps, March 6, 1906, subseries 1.1, box 26, folder 5; E. W. Scripps to H. B. Clark, May 6, 1906, subseries 1.2, box 7, folder 4; E. W. Scripps to H. B. Clark, Jan. 12, 1907, series 1.2, box 8, folder 8; E. W. Scripps to L. T. Atwood, Feb. 18, 1907, subseries 1.2, box 8, folder 10; and E. W. Scripps to W. B. Colver, Feb. 25, 1907, subseries 1.2, box 8, folder 11.

60. Knight, "Scripps and His Adless Newspaper," 51–64.

61. Advertisers' emphasis on audience demographics tilted news toward the middle

and upper classes. They also sought to censor a wide variety of content they disliked, including unflattering news about themselves.

62. E. W. Scripps to E. F. Chase, Aug. 26, 1910, subseries 1.2, box 13, folder 1.

Chapter 7: An Advocate of the Working Class

1. Cleveland *Press,* May 8, 1889, 2.

2. Cleveland *Press,* May 4, 1889, 1.

3. "Shake!" Cleveland *Press,* May 10, 1889, 1; "Our Typo," Cincinnati *Post,* July 9, 1889, 3; "It's a Great Project," Cincinnati *Post,* May 14, 1889, 1; M. A. McRae to E. W. Scripps, June 11, 1889, subseries 1.1, box 2, folder 6; St. Louis *Chronicle,* July 17, 1888, 1; Cincinnati *Post,* July 19, 1889, 1, July 21, 1889, 1, July 23, 1889, 1, Aug. 6, 1889, 1, Aug. 13, 1889, 3; Detroit *Evening News,* July 21, 1889, 1, July 23, 1889, 1; Cleveland *Press,* July 19, 1889, 1.

4. Cleveland *Press,* May 14, 1889, 3, May 16, 1889, 1, May 18, 1889, 1, May 27, 1889, 1, June 3, 1889, 1, June 4, 1889, 1, June 18, 1889, 3, June 24, 1889, 3, July 4, 1889, 1, July 15, 1889, 2, Sept. 30, 1889, 1; Cincinnati *Post,* May 11, 1889, 2, 4, May 13, 1889, 4, May 14, 1889, 1, May 15, 1889, 4, May 18, 1889, 1, May 20, 1889, 1, May 22, 1889, 4, May 29, 1889, 3, June 3, 1889, 3, June 4, 1889, 3, June 18, 1889, 3, June 26, 1889, 3, July 5, 1889, 4, July 8, 1889, 2, July 9, 1889, 2, 3, July 15, 1889, 2, Sept. 30, 1889, 1; St. Louis *Chronicle,* May 11, 1889, 1, May 14, 1889, 1, May 18, 1889, 3, June 4, 1889, 3, July 8, 1889, 1, Aug. 19, 1889, 3, Oct. 7, 1889, 3; Detroit *Evening News,* May 4, 1889, 1, May 11, 1889, 2, May 13, 1889, 4.

5. Cleveland *Press,* May 4, 1889, 1.

6. Cleveland *Press,* May 14, 1889, 3.

7. Ibid.

8. "A Great Enterprise," Cleveland *Press,* May 4, 1889, 2; George Booth to E. W. Scripps, Sept. 6, 1889, subseries 1.1, box 2, folder 2.

9. M. A. McRae to E. W. Scripps, May 4, 1889, and M. A. McRae to E. W. Scripps, June 22, 1889, subseries 1.1, box 2, folder 6; J. Ridenour to E. W. Scripps, May 4, 1889, subseries 1.1, box 2, folder 9.

10. E. W. Scripps to H. N. Rickey, Aug. 12, 1903, subseries 1.2, box 5, folder 1.

11. E. W. Scripps to J. C. Lee, July 30, 1903, subseries 1.2, box 5, folder 1.

12. Quotation from Minutes of Conference between E. W. Scripps, E. B. Scripps, and George Putnam, Miramar, Calif., Aug. 17, 1902, subseries 1.2, box 4, folder 19 (Spokane *Press*); see also E. H. Wells to E. W. Scripps, July 1, 1903, subseries 1.1, box 21, folder 14 (Tacoma *Times*); J. P. Hamilton to E. W. Scripps, March 30, 1906, subseries 1.1, box 25, folder 3 (Denver *Express*); Jay A. Gove and R. Y. Conant to E. W. Scripps, Oct. 25, 1906, subseries 1.1, box 24, folder 14 (Nashville *Times*).

13. Rutenbeck, "The Rise of Politically Independent Newspapers in the 1870s."

14. This was produced by the Newspaper Enterprise Association and published in the Sacramento *Star,* July 18, 1906, 2. On the journalism of exposure, see Juergens, *News from the White House,* 7, and Hofstadter, *The Age of Reform,* 185.

15. Evansville *Press,* Dec. 1, 1906, 2.

16. Evansville *Press,* Nov. 23, 1906, 1.

17. Los Angeles *Record,* Feb. 20, 1903, 1.

18. E. W. Scripps to W. D. Wasson, Jan. 23, 1904, subseries 1.2, box 5, folder 3.

19. Cleveland *Penny Press,* Jan. 15, 1880, 1.

20. "The Appleton-Rickoff Fraud," Cleveland *Penny Press,* Oct. 9, 1879, 1; see also "A Bare-Faced Fraud," Cleveland *Penny Press,* Oct. 9, 1879, 1.

21. Cleveland *Penny Press,* Aug. 20, 1879, 1.

22. Cleveland *Penny Press,* April 10, 1879, 1.

23. Cleveland *Penny Press,* April 8, 1879, 1, April 10, 1879, 1.

24. E. W. Scripps to H. N. Rickey, Aug. 12, 1903, subseries 1.2, box 5, folder 1.

25. "Help Given the Sufferers," Cincinnati *Post,* Aug. 6, 1887, 2; "A Great Success," Cincinnati *Post,* Aug. 26, 1887, 1; "The Sanitarium Fund," Cincinnati *Post,* Aug. 30, 1887, 1; "Unsafe Theater Buildings," Cincinnati *Post,* Sept. 10, 1887, 2; "That Monopoly Must Go," Cleveland *Press,* Dec. 17, 1883, 1; "Tim's Thanksgiving," Cleveland *Press,* Nov. 29, 1888, 3; "Cleveland Gas Worse Now Than It Ever Was," Cleveland *Press,* Sept. 25, 1900, 1; "Suffering Humanity," St. Louis *Chronicle,* Jan. 15, 1887, 3; "For Free Text Books," St. Louis *Chronicle,* Jan. 15, 1887, 4; "Free Books," St. Louis *Chronicle,* March 4, 1887, 2; "People Aroused for Pure Water," Seattle *Star,* July 5, 1906, 8; "To the Citizens of Seattle," Seattle *Star,* July 6, 1906, 1; "Here Is a Chance to Do Good," Seattle *Star,* Dec. 20, 1906, 1; "Do You Want to Help?" Seattle *Star,* Feb. 13, 1907, 4.

26. E. H. Wells to L. T. Atwood, Dec. 22, 1904, subseries 3.1, box 17, folder 7.

27. Gould, "The Progressive Era," 3.

28. Cleveland *Press,* Aug. 7, 1888, 2.

29. "Nearing 3 Cent Fare at Last," Sacramento *Star,* July 16, 1906, 3; "The People and Street Railways—New Era Opens," *San Diegan-Sun,* Aug. 25, 1906, 1; "Tom Johnson Wins Bitter Fight," Portland *Eastside News,* Nov. 12, 1906, 2; "Three Cent Car Fare Now an Actuality: How the Victory Was Won in Cleveland, O.," *San Diegan-Sun,* Jan. 26, 1907, 5; "A Triumph for Mayor Johnson, the People and One Lone Newspaper Champion," Portland *Daily News,* Jan. 28, 1907, 1; "Low Car Fare Is Wedge to City Ideal for Ideal Citizens," *San Diegan-Sun,* Oct. 30, 1907, 5; "Cleveland—She's a Swift Three-Cent Town Now," Seattle *Star,* May 4, 1908, 1.

30. "Three Cent Fares Will Save the People $1000 a Day," Los Angeles *Record,* March 31, 1903, 1.

31. "Runaway Cars," Cincinnati *Post,* July 15, 1889, 1; "Incline Death," Cincinnati *Post,* Oct. 15, 1889, 1; "Killed by the Cars," Cincinnati *Post,* Oct. 17, 1889, 2; "Another Incline Wreck," Cincinnati *Post,* Oct. 22, 1889, 1; "Victims of the St. Louis Trolley," St. Louis *Chronicle,* July 31, 1895, 5; "Cause of the Street Car Killings," St. Louis *Chronicle,* Aug. 21, 1900, 4.

32. Cleveland *Press,* July 31, 1890, 1.

33. Los Angeles *Record,* March 9, 12, 1903, 1, April 18, 1903, 1, May 12, 15, 1903, 1, May 21, 1903, 4.

34. Los Angeles *Record,* June 17, 1903, 1.

35. Minutes of Conference between E. W. Scripps, E. B. Scripps, and George Putnam, Miramar, Calif., Aug. 17, 1902, subseries 1.2, box 4, folder 19 (emphasis added).

36. Portland *Daily News* (Scripps), 62.6 percent (N = 233.5 column inches); Portland *Oregon Journal,* 13.5 percent (N = 805.25); Portland *Evening Telegram,* 1.9 percent (N = 986); Portland *Oregonian,* 2.7 percent (N = 1,126.5); *San Diegan-Sun* (Scripps), 69.8 percent (N = 185.25); San Diego *Union,* 2.9 percent (N = 466.25); San Diego *Tribune,* 4.7 percent (N = 302.5); Sacramento *Star* (Scripps), 68.8 percent (N = 211.25); Sacramento *Bee,* 10.7 percent (N = 543.75); Sacramento *Union,* 5.2 percent (N = 558.25); Cincinnati *Post* (Scripps), 51.3 percent (N = 611.75); Cincinnati *Times Star,* 3.8 percent (N = 1,180.75). The difference between the Cincinnati *Post* (51.3 percent) and the other three Scripps newspapers (62.6, 6.98, and 68.8 percent) is because only the *Post* provided daily market reports, which were coded as routine business. Still, it presented business in a negative light at least half the time.

37. "Green Lake in the Hands of Coal Trust," Seattle *Star,* Sept. 21, 1904, 1; "Everybody Hitting at the Ice Trusts," Evansville *Press,* July 23, 1906, 4; "Milk Trust Is after Dairies," Evansville *Press,* Dec. 10, 1906, 1; "Did Coal Combine Hold Up the City?" Evansville *Press,* Dec. 27, 1906, 1; "Harvest Trust Is Fully Exposed," *San Diegan-Sun,* July 12, 1905, 7.

38. Evansville *Press,* Oct. 9, 1906, 1; see also "Light on the Standard Oil," Sacramento *Star,* Dec. 4, 1905, 1; and "Again Standard Must Show Missouri," Sacramento *Star,* Dec. 7, 1905, 1.

39. Sacramento *Star,* Nov. 11, 1905, 3.

40. Portland *Daily News,* Sept. 18, 1907, 4; Denver *Express,* July 1, 1907, 4, Sept. 4, 10, 1907, 4; Oklahoma *News,* Sept. 5, 1907, 1.

41. Filene, "An Obituary for 'The Progressive Movement,'" quoted in Buenker, Burnham, and Crunden, *Progressivism,* v.

42. For a discussion of this issue, see Mowry, *The California Progressives,* 23–24; Caine, "The Origins of Progressivism," 27; McCormick, *The Party Period and Public Policy,* 303; and Holli, "Urban Reform in the Progressive Era," 141.

43. Gould, "The Progressive Era," 3.

44. Tacoma *Times,* Jan. 6, 1904, 2 (editorial); see also Holli, "Urban Reform in the Progressive Era," 141.

45. Sacramento *Star,* July 21, 1906, 4.

46. "The City Runs Street Cars, Municipal Ownership in Operation in Liege," Seattle *Star,* Jan. 16, 1901, 1; "Detroit's Example for Other Cities," *San Diegan-Sun,* Jan. 15, 1903, 1; "The Schooling of Glasgow," *San Diegan-Sun,* July 3, 1905, 8 (editorial); "Street Car Accidents Are Few in Glasgow," *San Diegan-Sun,* Aug. 14, 1905, 3; "Muny Ownership Not Corrupting in England," Evansville *Press,* July 16, 1906, 4; "Italy's Railroaders Not Able to Strike," Portland *Eastside News,* Jan. 11, 1907, 4. The NEA series appeared in the Sacramento *Star* on July 19, 20, and 21, 1905.

47. "Public Ownership Inevitable," *San Diegan-Sun,* May 28, 1906, 8.

48. *San Diegan-Sun*, March 23, 1904, 8.

49. "Municipal Ownership," *San Diegan-Sun*, March 2, 1904, 8; "National Irrigation and Public Ownership," *San Diegan-Sun*, April 6, 1904, 8.

50. "As to Building a Water Plant," *San Diegan-Sun*, July 8, 1905, 8.

51. Seattle *Star*, Feb. 13, 1902, 1.

52. Buenker, Burnham, and Crunden, *Progressivism*, 13.

53. Portland *Daily News*, Feb. 18, 1907, 3.

54. Sacramento *Star*, June 6, 1906, 1.

55. "Formaldehyde Is Injurious," Sacramento *Star*, Sept. 21, 1901, 4; "The Poison That Is Used by Some Milk Dealers," Los Angeles *Record*, March 17, 1903, 1.

56. Los Angeles *Record*, Sept. 4, 1903, 1.

57. "The City Milk Supply," Los Angeles *Record*, June 21, 1897, 1; "Milkmen's War," Los Angeles *Record*, March 3, 1896, 3; "Watering Is Shown in City's Tests," Evansville *Press*, Nov. 23, 1906, 1; "Milk and Market Inspectors Must Be Appointed," *San Diegan-Sun*, Jan. 12, 1906, 8; "Renewal of the Crusade against Impure Foods," Sacramento *Star*, Sept. 22, 1905, 2; "Health Board Crusade against Undrawn Poultry Begins with a Flourish," Sacramento *Star*, Dec. 6, 1905, 1; "Inspection of Meat Will Start Wednesday," Evansville *Press*, Oct. 21, 1906, 2.

58. See Sacramento *Star* (all page 1): Jan. 6, 1906 (on Sen. Nelson W. Aldrich of Rhode Island), Jan. 8 (Thomas C. Platt of New York), Jan. 10 (Chauncey De Pew of New York), Jan. 15 (John Kean of New Jersey), Jan. 16 (W. A. Clark of Montana), Jan. 17 (Boies Penrose of Pennsylvania), Jan. 18 (H. H. Rogers of Missouri), Jan. 22 (A. H. Hopkins of Illinois), Jan. 29 (Joseph Foraker of Ohio), Jan. 31 (J. C. Spooner of Wisconsin), Feb. 7 (Steven B. Elkins of West Virginia), Feb. 10 (George Perkins of California), and Feb. 13 (Arthur Gorman of Maryland). For a general discussion of direct democracy issues, see Gould, "The Progressive Era," 2, 4; Cherny, *Populism, Progressivism and the Transformation of Nebraska Politics*, 111; McCormick, *The Party Period and Public Policy*, 277; and Hofstadter, *The Age of Reform*, 259–61.

59. "Recall Is Upheld," Los Angeles *Record*, Aug. 26, 1904, 1; "The Newspaper and the Recall," Los Angeles *Record*, Sept. 12, 1904, 4; "Dav Fails to Keep His Word," Los Angeles *Record*, Sept. 13, 1904, 1.

60. "Initiative-Referendum Idea Sweeping Country," *San Diegan-Sun*, Aug. 16, 1907, 1; "Labor Federation," Sacramento *Star*, April 24, 1906, 2; "Pastor Campaigning for Initiative and Referendum," Evansville *Press*, Oct. 11, 1906, 3; "Direct Primary Bill Should Be a Law," Seattle *Star*, Feb. 2, 1905, 1.

61. On child labor, see "Roosevelt on Child Labor," *San Diegan-Sun*, Dec. 12, 1904, 8; and "Nearly Two Million American Children Are Industrial Slaves," Evansville *Press*, Dec. 1, 1906, 2. On trusts and monopolies, see "Battle of the Trusts," Seattle *Star*, Jan. 22, 1901, 2; and "Beef Trust Men Plead Guilty and Are Punished," Sacramento *Star*, Sept. 21, 1905, 1. On competition, see "Now We Shall Have Telephone Competition," Seattle *Star*, Dec. 27, 1901, 1; and "Citizens Celebrate Freedom from Monopoly," *San Diegan-Sun*, July 13, 1905, 2. On city services, see "Street Sweeping," Los Angeles *Record*,

Jan. 24, 1896, 1; and "City Is Held Up by a Bridge Deal," Los Angeles *Record,* Oct. 3, 1904, 1. On the legal system, see "Money Talks in Court: 'Rich and Poor Not Equal before the Law,'" Seattle *Star,* Sept. 15, 1908, 5.

62. E. W. Scripps to J. C. Harper, July 4, 1903, subseries 1.2, box 5, folder 1; E. W. Scripps to W. D. Wasson, Jan. 23, 1904, subseries 1.2, box 5, folder 3; see also E. W. Scripps, "Profit Sharing Plan," Feb. 19, 1905, subseries 1.2, box 5, folder 4.

63. E. W. Scripps to J. C. Lee, July 30, 1903, subseries 1.2, box 5, folder 1; E. W. Scripps to W. D. Wasson, Jan. 23, 1904, subseries 1.2, box 5, folder 3; E. L. Rector to E. W. Scripps and L. T. Atwood, Aug. 21, 1906, subseries 1.1, box 26, folder 3; W. H. Porterfield to E. W. Scripps, Feb. 3, 1908, subseries 1.1, box 29, folder 1; W. D. Wasson to E. F. Chase, July 1, 1908, subseries 3.1, box 27, folder 9.

64. In 1904 W. D. Wasson, editor of the San Francisco *Daily News,* referred to Scripps's instructions to expand beyond labor union support for the newspaper. W. D. Wasson to E. W. Scripps, Jan. 21, 1904, subseries 3.1, box 15, folder 8; see also R. F. Paine to E. W. Scripps, Feb. 23, 1906, subseries 1.1, box 25, folder 16, and R. F. Paine to H. D. Wheeler, Dec. 4, 1907, subseries 3.1, box 25, folder 11.

65. C. F. Mosher to L. T. Atwood, Nov. 3, 1894, subseries 3.2, box 1, folder 2; H. B. Clark to E. W. Scripps, Feb. 4, 1904, subseries 1.1, box 22, folder 4.

66. Five Scripps newspapers devoted an average of 9.1 percent of their non-advertising content to coverage of labor-related issues, compared to an average of just .97 percent by competitors: Portland *Daily News* (Scripps), 13.1 percent (N = 1,839 column inches); Portland *Oregon Journal,* 1.5 percent (N = 2,711.75); Portland *Evening Telegram,* 1.3 percent (N = 3,881.75); Portland *Oregonian,* 1.2 percent (N = 3,568,75); *San Diegan-Sun* (Scripps), 5.5 percent (N = 1,087); San Diego *Union,* .8 percent (N = 1,895.75); San Diego *Tribune,* 1.1 percent (N = 1,398.25); Sacramento *Star* (Scripps), 7.7 percent (N = 1,047.25); Sacramento *Bee,* 1 percent (N = 2,564); Sacramento *Union,* .8 percent (N = 2,333.75); Cincinnati *Post* (Scripps), 6.02 percent (N = 3,414.5); Cincinnati *Times Star,* .64 percent (N = 5,641.75); Evansville *Press* (Scripps), 13.2 percent (N = 2,336.75); and the Evansville *Journal-News,* .5 percent (N = 3,243.5).

67. Evansville *Press,* Aug. 23, 1906, 2.

68. Los Angeles *Record,* Aug. 31, 1903, 4.

69. On the Knights of Labor, see Cincinnati *Post,* Jan. 7, 1887, 3, and Jan. 31, 1887, 3; Cleveland *Press,* March 11, 1882, 2, and Dec. 17, 1883, 1; and St. Louis *Chronicle,* March 19, 1881, 2. The Scripps newspapers praised nonviolent labor organization. See Cleveland *Press,* April 20, 1881, 1, March 4, 1882, 3, May 11, 1882, 2, July 21, 1888, 1, May 6, 1889, 3, and July 26, 1899, 1.

70. Cincinnati *Post,* Sept. 10, 1887, 2; Cleveland *Press,* Sept. 27, 1900, 4; Seattle *Star,* March 25, 1903, 2. For strikebreaker series, see Portland *Daily News,* Feb. 16, 1907, 1, July 16, 1907, 3, July 23, 1907, 3, July 24, 1907, 3, July 25, 1907, 3.

71. Seattle *Star,* June 6, 1902, 1.

72. Seattle *Times,* June 6, 1902, 1.

73. H. B. Clark to E. W. Scripps, May 9, 1907, subseries 1.1, box 26, folder 8.

74. "Eight Hour Day," St. Louis *Chronicle*, Jan. 14, 1887, 2; "They Strike," Cincinnati *Post*, Feb. 23, 1887, 4; "Ten Hours per Day," Cincinnati *Post*, Sept. 6, 1887, 1; "The Eight-Hour Move," Cincinnati *Post*, Dec. 26, 1889, 1; "May 1, 1890: Eight Hours," Cincinnati *Post*, Dec. 30, 1889, 3; "Job Printing Proprietors Guarantee 8–Hour Day," *San Diegan-Sun*, Sept. 19, 1905, 5; "'Eight Hours' Our Battle Cry," Evansville *Press*, Sept. 3, 1906, 4 (advertisement); "The Eight Hour Day," *San Diegan-Sun*, June 28, 1906, 8.

75. "The Eight Hour Day," *San Diegan-Sun*, June 28, 1906, 8.

76. Portland *Eastside News*, Dec. 27, 1906, 1.

77. Cleveland *Press*, Aug. 16, 1888, 2; "23" for "C.P" [Common People], Portland *Daily News*, Sept. 6, 1907, 2; "The Wolf Has Jumped Up on the Table," Portland *Daily News*, Oct. 3, 1907, p. 2.

78. Portland *Daily News*, Sept. 6, 1907, 3.

79. Los Angeles *Record*, May 15, 1896, 2, May 26, 1896, 3, June 1, 1896, 4; San Francisco *Daily News*, Oct. 1, 1906, 3; Seattle *Star*, Nov. 15, 1901, 4; *San Diegan-Sun*, Jan. 7, 1903, 7; Denver *Express*, Jan. 22, 1907, 4, Feb. 6, 1907, 4; Cincinnati *Post*, July 19, 1883, 2; St. Louis *Chronicle*, July 7, 1900, 4, July 24, 1900, 4.

80. Charles Mosher to W. F. Cronin, May 23, 1908, series 3.1, box 27, folder 4.

81. W. P. Strandborg to E. W. Scripps, May 18, 1903, subseries 1.1, box 21, folder 13.

82. B. H. Canfield to J. P. Hamilton, Sept. 6, 1903, subseries 3.1, box 14, folder 9; Los Angeles *Record*, Aug. 31, 1903, 4.

83. "As Others See Us," Los Angeles *Record*, Sept. 7, 1903, 4; "Sympathetic Action," Los Angeles *Record*, Sept. 14, 1903, 4; "1903–1904," Los Angeles *Record*, Jan. 1, 1904, 4; "Unions Increase Wages," Los Angeles *Record*, Aug. 12, 1903, 4; "Let There Be Fair Play," Los Angeles *Record*, Oct. 27, 1903, 4; "Agitators and Demagogues," Los Angeles *Record*, Aug. 25, 1903, 4; "Dirty Journalism," Los Angeles *Record*, Aug. 29, 1903, 4; "Assaulting the Press," Los Angeles *Record*, Sept. 30, 1903, 4; "Enforce the Law," Los Angeles *Record*, Dec. 18, 1903, 6; "News," Los Angeles *Record*, Dec. 19, 1903, 4.

84. "Labor Conquers All," Los Angeles *Record*, Aug. 31, 1903, 4.

85. St. Louis *Chronicle*, June 29, 1887, 3.

86. "What Gillett Stands For," Sacramento *Star*, Sept. 14, 1906, 2; "Are You Hide Bound?" Sacramento *Star*, Sept. 15, 1906, 2; "Bell Outlines His Campaign," Sacramento *Star*, Sept. 16, 1906, 2; San Francisco *Daily News*, Oct. 16, 1906, 3.

87. R. F. Paine to W. D. Wasson, F. D. Waite, B. H. Canfield, Henry White and Horace Brown, Aug. 31, 1906, subseries 3.1, box 22, folder 5.

88. "Forming a Labor Party," Cleveland *Press*, Nov. 22, 1886, 1; "The Labor Ticket," Cincinnati *Post*, March 16, 1887, 1; "The Reason for a Labor Party," Cincinnati *Post*, Aug. 10, 1887, 2; "Labor Calls a Mass Meeting," Seattle *Star*, Aug. 8, 1901, 1; "Legislation for the Workingman Sought," Seattle *Star*, June 20, 1902, 1; "Labor Party Is in Politics Now," Portland *Eastside News*, Nov. 3, 1906, 3; "Union Labor's Platform," Portland *Eastside News*, Jan. 24, 1907, 1; "Union Labor Party Names Its Ticket," Sacramento *Star*, Oct. 4, 1906, 4; "Unions Here to Enter Politics," Evansville *Press*, July

28, 1906, 1; "Will Elect Laborites if It Is Necessary," Evansville *Press,* Sept. 3, 1906, 2; "Trade Unionists Going into Politics," *San Diegan-Sun,* July 23, 1906, 8; "Union Men Won't Wait in Party Prison for Rights, Says Gompers," *San Diegan-Sun,* Sept. 3, 1906, 5.

89. Seattle *Star,* June 20, 1902, 1; "Gompers to Hurl Labor's Broadside," Evansville *Press,* July 21, 1906, 1; "Union Men Won't Wait in Party Prison for Rights, Says Gompers," Evansville *Press,* Sept. 3, 1906, 2.

90. *San Diegan-Sun,* July 23, 1906, 8.

91. R. F. Paine to W. D. Wasson, Oct. 23, 1905, subseries 3.1, box 19, folder 14.

92. E. W. Scripps to W. D. Wasson, Dec. 12, 1906, subseries 1.2, box 8, folder 5.

93. Los Angeles *Record,* Aug. 21, 1895, 2; Seattle *Star,* Aug. 27, 1901, 4; Seattle *Star,* Aug. 29, 1901, 1; *San Diegan-Sun,* Sept. 7, 1903, 1; Sacramento *Star,* Sept. 4, 1905, 1, 2; *San Diegan-Sun,* Sept. 4, 1905, 1; Sacramento *Star,* Sept. 3, 1906, 1; Evansville *Press,* Sept. 3, 1906, 3.

94. Cincinnati *Post,* Sept. 5, 1887, 2.

95. St. Louis *Chronicle,* Sept. 3, 1900, 1.

96. "Gompers, the Kind of Man Who Leads Two Million Workers," Portland *Eastside News,* Dec. 25, 1906, 4; Evansville *Press,* Dec. 28, 1906, 2; "Local Labor News Chinese Brickmakers Must Go," Los Angeles *Record,* Aug. 17, 1896, 1; "The Jap in the Department Store," San Francisco *Daily News,* Oct. 13, 1906, 4; "Local Labor to Fight Asiatics," Portland *Daily News,* Sept. 14, 1907, 1; "More Power to 'Em," Sept. 16, 1907, 2; "Japs Menacing American Labor," Evansville *Press,* Dec. 20, 1906, 1.

97. *San Diegan-Sun,* Jan. 27, 1903, 7, Jan. 28, 1903, 7, Jan. 29, 1903, 7, Jan. 31, 1903, 7, Feb. 2, 1903, 6.

98. Seattle *Star,* Feb. 23, 1906, 3, Feb. 24, 1906, 3, Feb. 26, 1906, 3; *San Diegan-Sun,* Feb. 22, 1906, 5, March 24, 1906, 3, March 26, 1906, 3; Sacramento *Star,* Feb. 20, 1906, 3, Feb. 21, 1906, 3, Feb. 22, 1906, 3.

99. Cleveland *Press,* Jan. 9, 1880, 1; Los Angeles *Record,* Aug. 21, 1895, 2; *San Diegan-Sun,* March 7, 1903, 2; *San Diegan-Sun,* July 27, 1903, 2; Portland *Daily News,* Jan. 26, 1907, 2; Evansville *Press,* Aug. 2, 1906, 1; H. B. Clark to J. P. Hamilton, Feb. [n.d.], 1903, subseries 3.1, box 12, folder 10 (regarding the Spokane *Press*).

100. E. W. Scripps to J. C. Lee, July 30, 1903, subseries 1.2, box 5, folder 1; E. W. Scripps to E. F. Chase, Oct. 24, 1899, series 2, box 3, letterbook 4, 51.

101. M. A. McRae to Wm. M. Day, Aug. 14, 1899, subseries 3.1, box 5, folder 1.

102. J. C. Harper to B. F. Gurley, Dec. 7, 1908, subseries 3.1, box 28, folder 10.

103. L. T. Atwood to E. S. Wright, June 13, 1899, subseries 3.1, box 4, folder 7; M. A. McRae to E. W. Scripps, April 12, 1900, subseries 1.1, box 16, folder 4.

104. Report of Managing Editor E. S. Wright, Dec. 31, 1894, subseries 3.1, box 2, folder 1; Brommel, *Eugene V. Debs,* 35–37.

105. H. N. Rickey to R. F. Paine, Cleveland *Press* Report for June 1899, subseries 3.1, box 4, folder 10.

106. E. H. Bagby to E. W. Scripps, July 15, 1901, subseries 1.1, box 16, folder 15.

107. Hyacinth Ford to E. W. Scripps, H. B. Clark, W. D. Wasson, and R. F. Paine, June 1, 1907, subseries 1.1, box 26, folder 11.

108. E. H. Wells to H. B. Clark, May 26, 1900, subseries 3.2, box 4, folder 4.

109. E. W. Scripps to W. D. Wasson, Jan. 23, 1904, subseries 1.2, box 5, folder 3.

110. W. D. Wasson to B. H. Canfield, Nov. 19, 1908, subseries 3.1, box 28, folder 8.

111. R. F. Paine to J. C. Harper, July 2, 1906, subseries 3.1, box 21, folder 8; E. H. Wells to E. W. Scripps, Feb. 14, 1901, series 1.1, box 18, folder 1.

112. E. H. Bagby to E. W. Scripps, July 15, 1901, subseries 1.1, box 16, folder 15.

Chapter 8: "Is It Interesting?"

1. Cleveland *Press*, Jan. 10, 1880, 1.

2. Ibid.

3. Ibid.

4. E. W. Scripps to Annie Scripps, Nov. 23, 1878, subseries 1.2, box 1, folder 1.

5. E. W. Scripps to James E. Scripps, Sept. 9, 1880, subseries 1.2, box 1, folder 2.

6. Ibid.

7. Scripps, "Autobiography," series 4, box 11, 370.

8. E. W. Scripps to B. F. Gurley, Sept. 6, 1906, subseries 1.2, box 7, folder 10.

9. Charles Mosher to W. F. Cronin, May 23, 1908, subseries 3.1, box 27, folder 4.

10. B. H. Canfield to John P. Scripps, Nov. 24, 1908, subseries 3.1, box 28, folder 8.

11. Quoted in the *Newspaper Maker*, July 29, 1897, 4.

12. Pittsburgh *Leader*, Jan. 21, 1898, 8.

13. E. W. Scripps to W. D. Wasson, Sept. 25, 1905, subseries 1.2, box 6, folder 3; E. W. Scripps to George Gohen, Jan. 18, 1900, subseries 1.2, box 3, folder 11.

14. Los Angeles *Record*, March 14, 1896, 1.

15. Cleveland *Press*, Feb. 3, 1879, 1, March 1, 1879, 1, March 20, 1879, 1.

16. E. W. Scripps to R. F. Paine, Feb. 20, 1906, subseries 1.2, box 6, folder 7; E. W. Scripps to John Vandercook, Sept. 5, 1905, subseries 1.2, box 6, folder 1; R. F. Paine to Leroy Saunders, Jan. 8, 1906, subseries 3.1, box 20, folder 6; L. T. Atwood to George A. Shives, Jan. 28, 1901, subseries 3.1, box 7, folder 14.

17. Keller, *The Life Insurance Enterprise.*

18. The Seattle *Star*'s article on testimony by Robert McCurdy, president of Mutual Life, covered eighty-nine column lines in mid-October 1905 (forty-five on October 17 and thirty-four on October 18). In contrast, the *Post Intelligencer* gave extensive coverage to the details of vouchers and lobbying by the company and filled 147 lines (195 on October 18 and fifty-two on October 20). The Seattle *Times* covered the same testimony in 175 lines (121 on October 17 and fifty-four on October 18). The *San Diegan-Sun*'s coverage was much more condensed than that of the San Diego *Union*. It covered Senator Platt's testimony in fifty-nine lines as opposed to the *Union*'s 140. Similarly, the *Sun* devoted forty-eight lines to Benjamin Odell's testimony, and the *Union* used 102.

19. Charles Mosher to E. W. Scripps, Feb. 8, 1907, subseries 1.1, box 27, folder 6.

20. E. W. Scripps to George Gohen, Jan. 18, 1900, subseries 1.2, box 3, folder 11; E. W. Scripps to R. F. Paine, Feb. 28, 1906, subseries 6, folder 17.

21. J. C. Harper to B. F. Gurley, March 19, 1908, subseries 3.1, box 26, folder 10.

22. R. F. Paine to H. N. Rickey, Oct. 30, 1905, subseries 3.1, box 19, folder 15.

23. E. W. Scripps to R. F. Paine, Feb. 28, 1906, subseries 1.2, box 6, folder 17.

24. Cleveland *Press*, June 13, 1889, 3.

25. Sacramento *Star*, Dec. 28, 1905, 1.

26. Sacramento *Bee*, Dec. 28, 1905, 1.

27. E. W. Scripps to R. F. Paine, Feb. 28, 1906, subseries 1.2, box 6, folder 17.

28. Portland *Daily News*, May 20, 1907, 2, June 4, 1907, 2; Seattle *Star* Dec. 13, 1906, 4, Jan. 10, 1907, 4, Jan. 11, 1907, 4, Oct. 8, 1907, 4; Los Angeles *Record*, Oct. 3, 1903, 4, Oct. 5, 1903, 2, Oct. 9, 1903, 4, Oct. 19, 1903, 4; *San Diegan-Sun*, Jan. 16, 1907, 8, Feb. 5, 1907, 8; Denver *Express*, Jan. 7, 1906, 2, Jan. 9, 1906, 2, Jan. 15, 1906, 2, Jan. 16, 1906, 19, April 15, 1907, 2; Pueblo *Sun*, Nov. 3, 1906, 2, Nov. 6, 1906, 2, Nov. 12, 1906, 2, Nov. 14, 1906, 2, Nov. 15, 1906, 2, Dec. 3, 1906, 2; *Oklahoma News*, Oct. 4, 1906, 2–3, Oct. 5, 1906, 4, Oct. 13, 1906, 2; Evansville *Press*, Oct. 18, 1906, 2.

29. Evansville *Press*, Oct. 18, 1906, 2.

30. Portland *Daily News*, Feb. 27, 1908, 4, see also Dec. 3, 1907, 8, and *San Diegan-Sun*, Dec. 21, 1907, 8, Dec. 11, 1907, 4, and Feb. 27, 1908, 4 (on the wedding); Portland *Daily News*, April 18, 1908, 4; Seattle *Star*, Oct. 18, 1907, 2, Oct. 21, 1907, 2, Oct. 22, 1907, 2, Oct. 26, 1907, 2, Oct. 28, 1907, 2, Oct. 30, 1907, 2, Nov. 2, 1907, 2.

31. Sept. 5, 1907, 1, Seattle *Star*.

32. R. F. Paine to A. M. Hopkins, Sept. 18, 1906, subseries 3.1, box 21, folder 7; see also *San Diegan-Sun*, Feb. 28, 1907, 8, June 1, 1907, 8 (he throws a yapping dog from a streetcar window), and June 6, 1907, 8 (he attacks a street baseball player whose ball hits him); Seattle *Star*, Oct. 13, 1905, 8, Nov. 8, 1905, 4, Feb. 15, 1906, 5, Jan. 1, 1907, 4, Feb. 27, 1906, 7; Pueblo *Sun*, Sept. 1, 1906, 2, Sept. 3, 1906, 2, Sept. 4, 1906, 2, Sept. 6, 1906, 2, Sept. 17, 1906, 2, Sept. 18, 1906, 2, Oct. 5, 1906, 2, Oct. 12, 1906, 2, Oct. 22, 1906, 2, May 18, 1907, 2; Denver *Express*, Jan. 5, 1907, 4, Jan. 10, 1907, 4, Jan. 15, 1907, 4, April 16, 1907, 4, April 19, 1907, 4; and *Oklahoma News*, Oct. 4, 1906, 4, Oct. 7, 1906, 4, Oct. 11, 1906, 4, Oct. 12, 1906, 4, April 12, 1907, 2.

33. *Oklahoma News*, Oct. 2, 1907, 2, Oct. 3, 1907, 2, Dec. 10, 1907, 2, Dec. 11, 1907, 2, May 12, 1908, 2, May 13, 1908, 2, May 18, 1908, 2; Portland *Daily News*, Jan. 24, 1907, 4, Oct. 8, 1907, 4, May 21, 1908, 4; Seattle *Star*, March 13, 1907, 8; *San Diegan-Sun*, Oct. 15, 1906, 2, Oct. 16, 1906, 2, Oct. 17, 1906, 2, Oct. 18, 1906, 2, Oct. 19, 1906, 2, Oct. 20, 1906, 2, Nov. 7, 1906, 2, Nov. 8, 1906, 2, Nov. 9, 1906, 2, Nov. 10, 1906, 2, Nov. 12, 1906, 2, Nov. 13, 1906, 2; Pueblo *Sun*, April 11, 1907, 2, April 12, 1907, 2, April 13, 1907, 2, April 15, 1907, 2; Denver *Express*, Oct. 13, 1906, 2, Oct. 15, 1906, 2, Oct. 17, 1906, 2.

34. Los Angeles *Record*, July 8, 1903, 6, July 20, 1903, 6, Aug. 1, 1903, 6.

35. "Bump Talks": Portland *Daily News*, Oct. 2, 1907, 2, *San Diegan-Sun*, Oct. 3, 1907,

8, Oct. 15, 1907, 8; "Osgar and Adolf": Seattle *Star*, Jan. 2, 1907, 4, Aug. 9, 1907, 4; Portland *Daily News*, June 4, 1907, 3, July 16, 1907, 2; *San Diegan-Sun*, Dec. 12, 1906, 8, Oct. 30, 1907, 8; Denver *Express*, Jan. 7, 1907, 2, Jan. 14, 1907, 2, April 16, 1907, 2, April 18, 1907, 2; "John Jimpsonweed": Seattle *Star*, Aug. 9, 1907, 4.

36. E. W. Scripps to R. F. Paine, Feb. 26, 1906, subseries 1.2, box 6, folder 17.

37. R. F. Paine to W. D. Wasson, Jan. 27, 1906, subseries 3.1, box 20, folder 8; R. F. Paine to Leroy Saunders, Oct. 19, 1905, subseries 3.1, box 19, folder 14.

38. M. A. McRae to A. O. Andersson and H. J. Richmond, Oct. 3, 1906, subseries 3.1, box 22, folder 9.

39. R. F. Paine to "Dear Sir," [n.d.], and Newspaper Enterprise Association, July 3, 1902, subseries 3.1, box 11, folder 5; R. F. Paine to Milton McRae, May 29, 1902, subseries 3.1, box 11, folder 1; R. F. Paine to E. W. Scripps, Oct. 31, 1903, subseries 1.1, box 5, folder 2; R. F. Paine to M. E. Pew, March 12, 1907, subseries 3.1, box 12, folder 10.

40. Leroy Saunders to R. F. Paine, Oct. 15, 1905, subseries 3.1, box 19, folder 13.

41. Coverage also included forty-nine articles and nine editorials.

42. Seattle *Star*, Oct. 25, 1905, 7, Dec. 27, 1905, 1.

43. R. F. Paine to E. W. Scripps, Sept. 13, 1905, subseries 1.2, box 24, folder 7 (emphasis added).

44. Seattle *Star*, Oct. 3, 1905, 7.

45. *San Diegan-Sun*, Oct. 16, 1905, 1.

46. R. F. Paine to A. M. Hopkins, Dec. 6, 1905, subseries 3.1, box 20, folder 3.

47. Seattle *Star*, Oct. 7, 1905, 8.

48. San Diego *Sun*, Oct. 20, 1905, 1.

49. *San Diegan-Sun*, July 4, 1906, 3; Portland *Daily News*, July 4, 1906, 3; Seattle *Star*, Nov. 28, 1907, 1.

50. E. W. Scripps to George Shives, Nov. 11, 1895, subseries 1.2, box 3, folder 1.

51. Cleveland *Press*, Nov. 2, 1878, 1, April 12, 1879, 1.

52. C. F. Mosher to W. F. Cronin, March 19, 1908, subseries 3.1, box 26, folder 10; C. F. Mosher to W. F. Cronin, April 15, 1908, subseries 3.1, box 26, folder 14; Charles F. Mosher to J. A. Gove and R. G. Conant, May 30, 1907, subseries 3.1, box 24, folder 3; H. B. Clark to E. W. Scripps, Feb. 17, 1903, subseries 1.1, box 20, folder 6; M. A. McRae to E. W. Scripps, March 3, 1905, subseries 1.1, box 24, folder 1.

53. E. W. Scripps to R. F. Paine, Feb. 28, 1906, subseries 1.2, box 6, folder 17.

54. E. W. Scripps to B. F. Gurley, Sept. 5, 1906, subseries 1.2, box 7, folder 10.

55. B. H. Canfield to J. C. Harper, Oct. 8, 1908, subseries 3.1, box 28, folder 11.

56. C. F. Mosher to W. C. Mayborn, June 30, 1908, subseries 3.1, box 27, folder 8.

57. R. F. Paine to A. M. Hopkins, Sept. 1, 1905, subseries 3.1, box 19, folder 7.

58. "Don't Apologize," Seattle *Star*, June 15, 1907, 4; "A Science of Living," Seattle *Star*, Jan. 24, 1907, 4; "Mind and Health," Seattle *Star*, Dec. 1, 1906, 4.

59. "Laugh and the World Laughs with You," Portland *Daily News*, June 7, 1907, 2; "Only a Dog," Los Angeles *Record*, Aug. 25, 1903, 4. From the Portland *Daily News*: "Worry, the Disease of the Age," May 22, 1907, 2; "Three Blind Men at the Theatre,"

May 22, 1907, 2; "Laugh and the World Laughs with You" ("Good Humor Is the Saving Grace of Daily Life"), June 7, 1907, 2; and "The Value of a Smile," June 30, 1908, 2. From the Seattle *Star:* "The Courage of Women," June 13, 1904, 4; "Let's Think When We Talk" and "Worry Makes Disease," both July 17, 1906, 4; "The Transforming Power of Kindness," Sept. 17, 1906, 4; "Wealth or Health?" Nov. 2, 1906, 4; "Happiness," Sept. 27, 1906, 4; "Hobbies—Everybody Should Have at Least One Good One," June 19, 1907, 4; "The Man Who Kicks" [complains], Sept. 30, 1907, 4; and "Real Values," Oct. 8, 1907, 4. From the Los Angeles *Record:* "When a Man Is Ripe," Aug. 4, 1903, 4; "The Man with a Grouch," Aug. 4, 1903, 4; "Can Happiness Be Taught?" Aug. 29, 1903, 4; "The Human Spirit," Sept. 2, 1903, 4; "Some Good Rules for Success in Life," April 29, 1903, 2; and "How to Stay Young," Sept. 17, 1904, 4. From the *San Diegan-Sun:* "Good Manners Are Business Capital," Feb. 13, 1907, 8; "The Benefits of Walking," Oct. 30, 1907, 8; "Does Honesty Pay?" Aug. 21, 1906, 8; and "The Land We Love," Oct. 22, 1906, 8. From the *Oklahoma News:* "Real Values," Oct. 6, 1906, 4; "Sin Is Sexless," Oct. 10, 1906, 4; and "The Value of Time," Oct. 8, 1906, 4. From the Denver *Express:* "A Christmas Tree for Dogs," Jan. 7, 1907, 2; "How to Be Happy though Rich," April 15, 1907, 2; "The Foolish Rich," April 18, 1907, 2; and "Are You Ashamed?" April 19, 1907, 2. From the Pueblo *Sun:* "Happiness," Sept. 26, 1906, 2; "The Irresistible Magnet," Oct. 4, 1906, 2; and "The Tax on Fat," Oct. 10, 1906, 2.

60. Cincinnati *Post,* Feb. 20, 1889, 3, Feb. 27, 1889, 4, June 17, 1889, 3, July 8, 1889, 2, July 19, 1899, 2, Dec. 30, 1889, 3, Oct. 6, 1898, 4, Sept. 1, 1902, 6, Sept. 5, 1902, 4; Cleveland *Press,* Nov. 16, 1881, 2; St. Louis *Chronicle,* April 9, 1881, 1.

61. Seattle *Star,* Aug. 12, 1905, 3.

62. *San Diegan-Sun,* July 6, 1905, 7, July 13, 1905, 3, 7, Sept. 4, 1905, 7; Seattle *Star,* July 15, 1905, 7, July 17, 1905, 2.

63. R. F. Paine to W. D. Wasson, Jan. 27, 1906, subseries 3.1, box 20, folder 8; R. F. Paine to W. D. Wheeler, June 15, 1907, subseries 3.1, box 24, folder 5; R. F. Paine to E. W. Scripps, Sept. 13, 1905, subseries 1.1, box 24, folder 7.

64. W. D. Wasson to B. H. Canfield, Nov. 19, 1908, subseries 3.1, box 28, folder 8.

65. E. W. Scripps to W. D. Wasson, Sept. 25, 1905, subseries 1.2, box 6, folder 3; R. F. Paine to W. D. Wasson, Jan. 27, 1906, subseries 3.1, box 20, folder 8.

66. R. F. Paine to A. M. Hopkins, Sept. 1, 1905, subseries 3.1, box 19, folder 7; R. F. Paine to C. A. Branaman, Dec. 26, 1906, subseries 3.1, box 23, folder 4.

67. "Of Special Interest to Women," Seattle *Star,* May 2, 1908, 5; "What's a 'Model Husband'?" Seattle *Star,* May 31, 1907, 4, June 5, 1907, 4, June 11, 1907, 4, June 15, 1907, 4, Denver *Express,* May 27, 29, 1907, 2, Portland *Daily News,* May 31, 1907, 2; "Shall a Girl Marry Beneath Her?" Seattle *Star,* Aug. 27, 1907, 4; "Symptoms of Insincerity—How Can Girls Tell True from False Men?" Portland *Daily News,* May 4, 1907. Other articles on fashion included: "An Azure Blue," Portland *Daily News,* Feb. 25, 1908, 2; "Crepe de Chene," Portland *Daily News,* March 4, 1908, 4; "New Spring Styles," *San Diegan-Sun,* March 21, 1906, 3; "Fall Hat," *Oklahoma News,* Oct. 4, 1906, 4, "Velvet Hat," *Oklahoma News,* Oct. 9, 1906, 4; "The Peek a Boo Waist Mania Is Dying," Pueblo

Sun, Oct. 8, 1906, 2; "Of Special Woman Interest," Portland *Daily News,* Feb. 28, 1908, 4, March 4, 1908, 4, March 9, 1908, 4; see also "Woman and Home," Pueblo *Sun,* Sept. 1, 1908, 2, Sept. 3, 1908, 2, Sept. 6, 1908, 2, Sept. 8, 1908, 2, Sept. 17, 1908, 2, Sept, 18, 1908, 2, and Oct. 5, 1906, 2.

68. "Twelve Reasons for Marriage," Portland *Daily News,* May 3, 1907, 3. Cynthia Grey's pieces appeared in many other Scripps newspapers as well. From the Los Angeles *Record:* "We 'Homely' Women," Aug. 22, 1904, 3; "The Living Flower Show," Sept. 24, 1904, 3; "What Some Men Fail to See," Sept. 28, 1904, 3; "The Nagging Woman," April 14, 1904, 2; "To Think About," April 21, 1904, 3; "The Man Not to Marry," May 2, 1904, 2; and "The Thanksgiving Turkey," Nov. 23, 1904, 3. From the *San Diegan-Sun:* "The Man Who Buys His Wife's Clothes—and the Wife," July 21, 1905, 7; "How to Dress Well on What We Can Get" (on economizing), Aug. 1, 1905, 8; "It's Your Fault if You Spoil Your Wife," Aug. 8, 1905, 6; and "How Should Man Propose?" June 8, 1907, 8. From the Seattle *Star:* "We Make Our Own Mouths," July 26, 1905, 4; "Home," Nov. 18, 1903, 2; and "The Call of Home," Dec. 13, 1906, 4. From the Pueblo *Sun:* "Woman's Circles and Man's Kicks," Oct. 9, 1906, 2; "The Luxury of a Husband," Nov. 28, 1906, 2; and "Love's Sharp Eyes," Feb. 2, 1907, 2. From the Denver *Express:* "Going Without," Jan. 15, 1907, 2; "Ten Commandments," Jan. 15, 1907, 2; "Hitting the Spots," Jan. 19, 1907, 2; and "Twelve Reasons for Love," April 18, 1907, 2. From the *Oklahoma News:* "A Man and a Frill," Oct. 4, 1906, 2; and from the Toledo *News Bee:* Jan. 4, 1904, 4, and Jan. 5, 1905, 4.

69. "What Is a Kiss?" Los Angeles *Record,* July 28, 1903, 4; "Do the Women Tell Bigger Lies Than the Men Do?" Seattle *Star,* Jan. 4, 1905, 7; "Women Rush in to Defend Their Sex," Seattle *Star,* Jan. 4 , 1905, 7; "Would You Marry Him Again?" Seattle *Star,* Aug. 6, 1908, 1; *San Diegan-Sun,* April 3, 1906, 8, April 4, 1906, 8.

70. E. W. Scripps to W. D. Wasson, Jan. 23, 1904, subseries 1.2, box 5, folder 3; E. W. Scripps to W. H. Porterfield, Aug. 22, 1905, subseries 1.2, box 5, folder 11; R. F. Paine to E. W. Scripps, Feb. 12, 1906, and R. F. Paine to E. W. Scripps, March 19, 1906, subseries 1.1, box 25, folder 16; E. F. Chase to E. W. Scripps, Aug. 8, 1906, subseries 1.1, box 24, folder 17; E. W. Scripps to W. F. Cronin, Oct. 23, 1906, subseries 3.1, box 22, folder 12; R. F. Paine to C. F. Branaman, Dec. 27, 1906, subseries 3.1, box 23, folder 4; R. F. Paine to W. D. Wasson, Jan. 29, 1907, subseries 3.1, box 23, folder 6; R. F. Paine to W. D. Wasson, Feb. 8, 1907, subseries 3.1, box 23, folder 7.

For examples of short stories, see Portland *Daily News:* "Which?" May 6, 1907, 2; "The Turning Point," May 20, 1907, 2; "Kin to the Lilies," June 4, 1907, 2; "Reward of Patience," June 6, 1907, 2; "The Green-Eyed Monster," July 12, 1907, 2; "A Western Lochinvar," July 15, 1907, 2; "What Would You Do?" Sept. 14, 1907, 2; and "A Lucky Accident," Sept. 17, 1907, 2. For the *San Diegan-Sun,* see "The Deception of Victor Dupont," Aug. 5, 1905, 7; "On Midsummer Day," Aug. 7, 1905, 7; "Between the Devil and the Deep," Aug. 12, 1905, 7; and "The Man Who Wouldn't Drink," Aug. 17, 1905, 7. See also *Oklahoma News,* Oct. 12, 1906, 4; Denver *Express,* Jan. 5, 1907, 2, Jan. 7, 1907, 2, Jan. 8, 1907, 2, Jan. 14, 1907, 2, Jan. 16, 1907, 2, Jan. 19, 1907, 2, April 15, 1907, 2, Jan. 16,

1907, 2, Jan. 17, 1907, 2, Jan. 18, 1907, 2; Pueblo *Sun,* Sept. 1, 1906, 2, Sept. 3, 1906, 2, Sept. 4, 1906, 2, Sept. 5, 1906, 2, Sept. 6, 1906, 2, Sept. 17, 1906, 2, Sept. 18, 1906, 2; Cleveland *Press,* Feb. 10, 1880, 4, Nov. 24, 1886, 2, Dec. 3, 1886, 2, July 19, 1888, 4, July 28, 1894, 2; Cincinnati *Post,* Oct. 4, 1892, 2, July 28, 1894, 2, Sept. 8, 1894, 3; and St. Louis *Chronicle,* July 31, 1880, 4, Aug. 2, 1880, 4, Oct. 12, 1880, 4, Dec. 10, 1880, 4, June 10, 1893, 7, June 16, 1893, 7.

71. "NEA Stories for Late 1905," n.d., 1905, subseries 3.1, box 17, folder 11. For serial stories, see the Los Angeles *Record:* George E. Walsh, "The Burglar and the Lady," May 25, 1903, 7, June 3, 1903, 6; "Adventures of Brigadier Gerard," July 29, 1903, 2; "A Legacy of Hate," Dec. 17, 1904, 5; A. Conan Doyle, "The White Company," April 14, 1904, 2; Portland *Daily News:* "The Treasured Trail," Dec. 7, 1907, 2; and *Oklahoma News:* "Strange Tales of a Nihilist," April 10, 1907, 2, April 11, 1907, 2. For poetry, see *Oklahoma News:* "Alice in Wonderland," Oct. 10, 1906, 3; "Following in Father's Foot-steps," Oct. 11, 1906, 3; and Pueblo *Sun:* "Hallowe'en," Oct. 31, 1906, 3; "When Our Teddy Goes to Panama," Nov. 3, 1906, 2; "Memory," Nov. 7, 1906, 2; "The Messenger Boys," Nov. 19, 1906, 2.

72. Nathaniel J. Fowler, Jr., "Reaching the Men through the Women," *Printer's Ink,* July 22, 1891, 51; *Newspaperdom,* March 1892, 23; *Dry Goods Economist,* Jan. 30, 1897, 65; *Newspaper Maker,* May 16, 1895, 7, June 27, 1895, 4, April 9, 1896, 7, Nov. 5, 1896, 3, Nov. 19, 1896, 3.

73. "How to Dress Well on What We Can Get," *San Diegan-Sun,* Aug. 1, 1905, 8, April 3, 1906, 8.

74. "It's Your Fault if You Spoil Your Wife," *San Diegan-Sun,* Aug. 8, 1905, 6; "Our Uncounted Wealth," *San Diegan-Sun,* Aug. 2, 1906, 8; "Cooking Economy," Denver *Express,* Oct. 22, 1907, 2; "Cooking Economy," *San Diegan-Sun,* Nov. 2, 1907, 8, Nov. 4, 1907, 8; "A Thanksgiving Dinner for $2," Denver *Express,* Nov. 16, 1907, 2; "A Thanks-giving Dinner for $3," Denver *Express,* Nov., 19, 1907, 2; "A Thanksgiving Dinner for $4," Denver *Express,* Nov. 20, 1907, 2; "A Thanksgiving Dinner for $5," Denver *Ex-press,* Nov. 21, 1907, 2; Portland *Daily News,* Nov. 23, 1907, 2.

75. "Hundreds of American Women Turn to Jobs Nature Made for Men," Portland *Daily News,* June 2, 1907, 2.

76. "Woman Operator Depicts Hard Life at the Key," Portland *Daily News,* Aug. 22, 1907, 1; "This Dainty Damsel a Wisky Drummer," Los Angeles *Record,* Oct. 3, 1903, 4; "Some Remarkable Working Women," Los Angeles *Record,* Sept. 24, 1904, 3; "Girls in the Army of Toilers," *San Diegan-Sun,* March 12, 19, 1903 (all page 3); Portland *Daily News,* March 4, 1908, 4, March 9, 1908, 4.

77. "Facts about Women Who Work," Spokane *Press,* Jan. 5, 1903, 2; "The Woman Who Works," Spokane *Press,* March 7, 1903, 2; "Workingwomen's Wages," Spokane *Press,* Dec. 6, 1902, 2.

78. "Woman's Wonderful Era in the World's Work," Portland *Daily News,* May 31, 1907, 2.

79. E. F. Chase to John C. Lee and H. Y. Saint, Oct. 19, 1904, subseries 3.1, box 17, folder 2.

80. E. W. Scripps to B. H. Canfield, Jan. 8, 1907, subseries 1.2, box 8, folder 7; R. F. Paine to Edwin A. Nye, Oct. 23, 1905, subseries 1.2, box 6, folder 5.

81. Seattle *Star,* Dec. 25, 1901, 2.

82. E. W. Scripps to B. H. Canfield, May 20, 1903, subseries 1.2, box 5, folder 1.

Chapter 9: The Legacy of E. W. Scripps

1. *Editor and Publisher,* March 20, 1926, 3.

2. Ibid, 8.

3. *Literary Digest,* April 17, 1926, 42.

4. E. W. Scripps, "Non-Advertising Newspaper Scheme," Nov. 2, 1904, subseries 1.2, box 5, folder 3.

5. E. W. Scripps to Robert F. Paine, Feb. 26, 1906, subseries 1.2, box 6, folder 17.

6. E. W. Scripps to W. D. Wasson, Jan. 23, 1904, subseries 1.2, box 5, folder 3.

7. E. W. Scripps to L. T. Atwood, April 14, 1906, subseries 1.2, box 7, folder 3.

8. E. W. Scripps to L. T. Atwood, Aug. 29, 1906, subseries 1.2, box 7, folder 9.

9. E. W. Scripps to R. F. Paine, Jan. 16, 1906, subseries 1.2, box 6, folder 14.

10. E. W. Scripps to L. T. Atwood, Aug. 3, 1907, subseries 1.2, box 9, folder 6.

11. E. W. Scripps to Robert F. Paine, Feb. 26, 1906, subseries 1.2, box 6, folder 17.

12. *Newspaper Maker,* April 12, 1900, p. 6.

Bibliography

Manuscript Collections

George Putnam Papers, University of Oregon, Eugene.

E. W. Scripps Correspondence, Bancroft Library, University of California, Berkeley.

E. W. Scripps Correspondence, Alden Library, Ohio University, Athens. (The two hundred thousand letters in this collection provide a detailed view of the Scripps newspaper business from the 1870s to the 1920s.)

Newspapers

Scripps newspapers: Berkeley *Independent;* Cincinnati *Post;* Cleveland *Press;* Columbus *Citizen; Kentucky Post* (Covington); Denver *Express;* Evansville, Ind., *Press;* Los Angeles *Record;* Oklahoma City *News;* Portland, Ore., *Daily News;* Portland, Ore., *East Side News;* Pueblo *Sun;* St. Louis *Chronicle;* San Diego *San Diegan-Sun;* San Francisco *Daily News;* Seattle *Star;* Spokane *Press;* Tacoma *Times;* Toledo *News-Bee*

Other newspapers: Cincinnati *Times-Star;* Cleveland *Plain Dealer;* Denver *Post;* Denver *Rocky Mountain News;* Evansville, Ind., *Journal News;* Los Angeles *Express;* Los Angeles *Times;* Portland *Journal;* Portland *Oregonian;* Portland *Evening Telegram;* St. Louis *Labor;* St. Louis *Evening Journal;* St. Louis *World;* St. Louis *Post-Dispatch;* St. Louis *Republic;* St. Louis *Star Sayings;* St. Louis *Globe-Democrat;* San Diego *Tribune;* San Diego *Union;* San Francisco *Bulletin;* Seattle *News;* Seattle *Post Intelligencer;* Seattle *Times;* Seattle *Union Record;* Spokane *Chronicle;* Spokane *Spokesman-Review;* Toledo *News;* Toledo *Bee*

Trade Journals

Advertising Experience; Editor and Publisher; Fame; Fourth Estate; The Journalist; Newspaper Maker; Newspaperdom

Books, Articles, and Dissertations

Adams, Edward E. "Secret Combinations and Collusive Agreements: The Scripps Newspaper Empire and the Early Roots of Joint Operating Agreements," *Journalism and Mass Communications Quarterly* 73 (Spring 1996): 199–207.

————. "Market Subordination and Competition: A Historical Analysis of Combinations, Consolidation and Joint Operating Agreements through an Examination of the E. W. Scripps Newspaper Chain, 1877–1993." Ph.D. diss., Ohio University, 1993.

Ambramoske, Donald J. "The Chicago Daily News: A Business History, 1876–1901." Ph.D. diss., University of Chicago, 1963.

American Journalism from the Practical Side: What Leading Publishers Say Concerning the Relations of Advertisers and Publishers and about the Way a Great Paper Should be Made. New York: Holmes Publishing, 1897.

Andriot, John L., comp. *Population Abstract of the United States.* McLean, Va.: Andriot Associates, 1983.

Bain, Joe S. *Barriers to New Competition.* Cambridge: Harvard University Press, 1956.

Baldasty, Gerald J. *The Commercialization of News in the Nineteenth Century.* Madison: University of Wisconsin Press, 1992.

Baldwin, William L. *Market Power, Competition and Antitrust Policy.* Homewood, Ill.: Irwin, 1987.

Bekken, Jon. "'The Most Vindictive and Most Vengeful Power': Labor Confronts the Chicago Labor Trust." Presented at the Association for Education in Journalism and Mass Communication, History Division, Minneapolis, Aug. 1990.

Blondheim, Menahem. *News over the Wires: The Telegraph and the Flow of Public Information about America, 1844–1897.* Cambridge: Harvard University Press, 1994.

Brommel, Bernard J. *Eugene V. Debs: Spokesman for Labor and Socialism.* Chicago: Charles H. Kerr, 1978.

Brundage, David. *The Making of Western Labor Radicalism: Denver's Organized Workers, 1878–1905.* Urbana: University of Illinois Press, 1994.

Buenker, John D., John C. Burnham, and Robert M. Crunden. *Progressivism.* Cambridge: Schenkman Publishing, 1977.

Bunnell, A. O., comp. *New York Press Association, Authorized History for Fifty Years, 1853–1903.* Dansville, N.Y.: F. A. Owen Publishing, 1903.

Busterna, John C. "Concentration and the Industrial Organization Model." In *Press Concentration and Monopoly: New Perspectives on Newspaper Ownership and Operation,* ed. Robert G. Picard, James P. Winter, Maxwell E. McCombs, and Stephen Lacy, 35–54. Norwood: Ablex Publishing, 1988.

————. "Price Discrimination as Evidence of Newspaper Chain Market Power." *Journalism Quarterly* 68 (1991): 501–4.

Caine, Stanley P. "The Origins of Progressivism." In *The Progressive Era,* ed. Lewis L. Gould, 11–34. Syracuse: Syracuse University Press, 1974.

Carlton, Dennis W., and Jeffrey M. Perloff. *Modern Industrial Organization.* 2d ed. New York: HarperCollins, 1994.

Chamberlin, Edward. *The Theory of Monopolistic Competition: A Re-Orientation of the Theory of Value.* 8th ed. Cambridge: Harvard University Press, 1962.

Chandler, Alfred D., Jr. "The Beginnings of 'Big Business' in American Industry." *Business History Review* 33 (Spring 1959): 1–31.

———. *Strategy and Structure: Chapters in the History of the Industrial Enterprise.* Cambridge: M.I.T. Press, 1962.

———. *The Visible Hand: The Managerial Revolution in American Business.* Cambridge: Harvard University Press, 1977.

Cherny, Robert W. *Populism, Progressivism and the Transformation of Nebraska Politics, 1885–1915.* Lincoln: University of Nebraska Press, 1981.

Clarkson, Kenneth W., and Roger L. Miller. *Industrial Organization: Theory, Evidence and Public Policy.* New York: McGraw Hill, 1982.

Cochran, Negley D. *E. W. Scripps.* New York: Harcourt, Brace, 1933.

Cochran, Thomas C., and William Miller. *The Age of Enterprise.* New York: Macmillan, 1942.

Cochran, Thomas D. *Two Hundred Years of American Business.* New York: Basic Books, 1977.

Cundiff, Edward W., and Richard R. Still. *Basic Marketing: Concepts, Decisions and Strategies.* 2d ed. Englewood Cliffs: Prentice-Hall, 1971.

Demsetz, Harold. "Barriers to Entry." *American Economic Review* 72 (March 1982): 47–57.

Dicken-Garcia, Hazel. *Journalistic Standards in the Nineteenth Century.* Madison: University of Wisconsin Press, 1989.

Dimmick, John, and Eric Rothenbuhler. "The Theory of Niche: Quantifying Competition among Media Industries." *Journal of Communication* 34 (1984): 103–16.

Dobson, John. *Politics in the Gilded Age: A New Perspective on Reform.* New York: Praeger Publishers, 1982.

Drucker, Peter F. *Management: Tasks, Responsibilities, Practices.* New York: Harper and Row, 1974.

Dyar, Ralph E. *News for an Empire: The Story of the* Spokesman-Review. Caldwell, Idaho: Caxton, 1952.

Dyer, Carolyn Stewart, and Carol Smith. "Taking Stock and Placing Orders: A Historiographic Essay on the Business History of the Newspaper." *Journalism Monographs* 132 (April 1992): 1–38.

Ekirch, Arthur A., Jr. *Progressivism in America: A Study of the Era from Theodore Roosevelt to Woodrow Wilson.* New York: New Viewpoints, 1974.

Emery, Michael, and Edwin Emery. *The Press and America: An Interpretive History of the Mass Media.* 7th ed. Englewood Cliffs: Prentice-Hall, 1992.

Filene, Peter. "An Obituary for 'The Progressive Movement.'" *American Quarterly* 22 (1970): 20–34.

Flippo, Edwin P., and Gary M. Munsinger. *Management*. 3d ed. Boston: Allyn and Bacon, 1975.

Fowler, Nathaniel C., Jr. *The Handbook of Journalism*. New York: Sully and Kleinteich, 1913.

Frank, Ronald E., William F. Massy, and Yoram Wind. *Market Segmentation*. Englewood Cliffs: Prentice-Hall, 1972.

Gans, Herbert J. *Deciding What's News*. New York: Pantheon Books, 1979.

Gardner, Gilson. *Lusty Scripps: The Life of E. W. Scripps*. New York: Vanguard Press, 1932.

Garraty, John A. *The New Commonwealth, 1877–1890*. New York: Harper and Row, 1968.

Geroski, Paul, Richard J. Gilbert, and Alexis Jacquemin. *Barriers to Entry and Strategic Competition*. New York: Harwood, 1990.

Gould, Lewis L., ed. *The Progressive Era*. Syracuse: Syracuse University Press, 1974.

Harrigan, Kathryn Rudie. "Barriers to Entry and Competitive Strategies." *Strategic Management Journal* 2 (1981): 395–412.

Hart, Jim A. *A History of the* St. Louis Globe-Democrat. Columbia: University of Missouri Press, 1961.

Hays, Samuel P. *The Response to Industrialism, 1885–1914*. Chicago: University of Chicago Press, 1957.

Hofstadter, Richard. *The Age of Reform: From Bryan to FDR*. New York: Alfred A. Knopf, 1955.

Holli, Melvin G. "Urban Reform in the Progressive Era." In *The Progressive Era*, ed. Lewis L. Gould, 133–51. Syracuse: Syracuse University Press, 1974.

Hower, Ralph B. *A History of Macy's of New York, 1858–1915*. Cambridge: Harvard University Press, 1943.

Johnson, Richard M. "Market Segmentation: A Strategic Management Tool." In *Marketing Classics: A Selection of Influential Articles*, ed. Ben M. Enis and Keith, Cox, 89–111. 4th ed. Boston: Allyn and Bacon, 1981.

Jordan, Myron K. "Men Not Money." M.A. thesis, University of Washington, 1983.

Juergens, George. *Joseph Pulitzer and the* New York World. Princeton: Princeton University Press, 1966.

———. *News from the White House: The Presidential-Press Relationship in the Progressive Era*. Chicago: University of Chicago Press, 1981.

Kaplan, Richard. "The Economics of Popular Journalism in the Gilded Age: The Detroit *Evening News* in 1873 and 1888." *Journalism History* 21 (Summer 1995): 65–78.

Karakaya, Fahri, and Michael J. Stahl. *Entry Barriers and Market Entry Decisions: A Guide for Marketing Executives*. New York: Quorum Books, 1989.

Kaufman, Stuart B. *Samuel Gompers and the Origins of the American Federation of Labor, 1848–1896*. Westport: Greenwood Press, 1973.

Keller, Morton. *The Life Insurance Enterprise, 1885–1910: A Study in the Limits of Corporate Power*. Cambridge: Harvard University Press, 1963.

Kirkland, Edward C. *Dream and Thought in the Business Community, 1860–1900*. Ithaca: Cornell University Press, 1956.

Knight, Oliver. "Scripps and His Adless Newspaper, *The Day Book.*" *Journalism Quarterly* 41 (Winter 1964): 51–64.

———, ed. *I Protest: Selected Disquisitions of E. W. Scripps*. Madison: University of Wisconsin Press, 1966.

Kobre, Sidney. *Development of American Journalism*. Dubuque: William C. Brown, 1969.

Koch, James V. *Industrial Organization and Prices*. 2d ed. Englewood Cliffs: Prentice-Hall, 1980.

Kotler, Philip. *Principles of Marketing*. 2d ed. Englewood Cliffs: Prentice-Hall, 1983.

Lacy, Stephen. "The Effect of IntraCity Competition on Daily Newspaper Content." *Journalism Quarterly* 64 (Spring 1987): 281–90.

———. "The Impact of Intercity Competition on Daily Newspaper Content." *Journalism Quarterly* 65 (Summer 1988): 399–406.

———. "A Model of Demand for News: Impact of Competition on Newspaper Content." *Journalism Quarterly* 69 (Winter 1989): 40–48.

Lavine, John M., and Daniel Wackman. *Managing Media Organizations: Effective Leadership of the Media*. New York: Longman, 1988.

Lawson, Linda. *Truth in Publishing: Federal Regulation of the Press's Business Practices, 1880–1920*. Carbondale: Southern Illinois University Press, 1993.

Lee, Alfred McClung. *The Daily Newspaper in America: The Evolution of a Social Instrument*. New York: Macmillan, 1937.

Litman, Barry R., and Janet Bridges. "An Economic Analysis of Daily Newspaper Performance." *Newspaper Research Journal* 5 (Spring 1987): 9–26.

Litterer, Joseph A. "Systematic Management: Design for Organizational Recoupling in American Manufacturing Firms." *Business History Review* 37 (Winter 1963): 375.

———. "Systematic Management: The Search for Order and Integration." *Business History Review* 35 (1961): 461–76.

Mackenzie, Kenneth D. *Organizational Structure*. Arlington Heights: AHM Publishing, 1978.

Mandel, Bernard. *Samuel Gompers: A Biography*. Yellow Springs, Ohio: Antioch Press, 1963.

McCabe, Charles R. *Damned Old Crank: A Self-Portrait of E. W. Scripps, Drawn from his Unpublished Writings*. New York: Harper and Bros., 1951.

McCormick, Richard L. *The Party Period and Public Policy: American Politics from the Age of Jackson to the Progressive Era*. New York: Oxford University Press, 1986.

McRae, Milton A. *Forty Years in Newspaperdom: The Autobiography of a Newspaper Man*. New York: Brentano's, 1924.

Mencken, Henry L. *Newspaper Days, 1899–1906*. New York: Alfred A. Knopf, 1941.

Mott, Frank Luther. *American Journalism*. New York: Macmillan, 1940.

Mowry, George E. *The California Progressives*. Berkeley: University of California Press, 1951.

Nelson, Daniel. *Managers and Workers: Origins of the New Factory System in the United States, 1880–1920*. Madison: University of Wisconsin Press, 1975.

———, ed. *A Mental Revolution: Scientific Management since Taylor*. Columbus: Ohio State University Press, 1992.

Nevins, Allan. The Evening Post: *A Century of Journalism*. New York: Boni and Liveright, 1922.

Nord, David Paul. *Newspapers and New Politics: Midwestern Municipal Reform, 1890–1900*. Ann Arbor: UMI Research Press, 1981.

———. "Working Class Readers: Family, Community and Reading in Late Nineteenth Century America." *Communication Research* 13 (April 1986): 156–81.

O'Connell, Mary Joan. "The Seattle *Union Record,* 1918–1928: A Pioneer Labor Daily." M.A. thesis, University of Washington, 1964.

Owen, Bruce M. *Economics and Freedom of Expression: Media Structure and the First Amendment*. Cambridge: Ballinger Publishing, 1975.

Picard, Robert G. *Media Economics: Concepts and Issues*. Newbury Park: Sage Publications, 1989.

Pollard, James E., ed. "E. W. Scripps' Reflections on Robert F. Paine." *Journalism Quarterly* 45 (1968): 125–29.

Porter, Glen. *The Rise of Big Business, 1860–1920*. 2d ed. Arlington Heights: Harlan Davidson, 1992.

Porter, Michael E. *Competitive Strategy: Techniques for Analyzing Industries and Competitors*. New York: Free Press, 1980.

Ratner, Sidney, James H. Soltow, and Richard Sylla. *The Evolution of the American Economy: Growth, Welfare and Decision Making*. New York: Basic Books, 1979.

Robertson, Ross M., and Gary M. Walton. *History of the American Economy*. 4th ed. New York: Harcourt Brace Jovanovich, 1979.

Rogers, Jason. *Newspaper Building*. New York: Harper and Bros., 1918.

Rosenblatt, S. Bernard, Robert L. Bonnington, and Belverd E. Needles, Jr. *Modern Business: A Systems Approach*. Boston: Houghton Mifflin, 1973.

Rosewater, Victor. *History of Cooperative News Gathering in the United States*. New York: D. Appleton, 1930.

Rosse, James N. "Daily Newspapers, Monopolistic Competition and Economies of Scale." *American Economic Review* 57 (May 1967): 522–33.

Rutenbeck, Jeffrey B. "Newspaper Trends in the 1870s: Proliferation, Popularization and Political Independence." *Journalism and Mass Communications Quarterly* 72 (Summer 1995): 361–75.

Scherer, F. M., and David Ross. *Industrial Market Structure and Economic Performance*. Boston: Houghton Mifflin, 1990.

Schwarzlose, Richard A. *The Nation's Newsbrokers*. 2 vols. Evanston: Northwestern University Press, 1989–90.

Scott, W. Richard. *Organizations: Rational, Natural and Open Systems*. Englewood Cliffs: Prentice-Hall, 1981.

Seitz, Don C. *Joseph Pulitzer: His Life and Letters.* New York: Simon and Schuster, 1924.

Shaw, Archer H. The Plain Dealer: *One Hundred Years in Cleveland.* New York: Alfred A. Knopf, 1942.

Shaw, Donald L. "News Bias and the Telegraph: A Study of Historical Change." *Journalism Quarterly* 44 (Spring 1967): 3–12, 31.

Shimmons, Earl W. "The Labor Dailies." *American Mercury* 15 (1928): 85–93.

Smith, Carol L. "The Development of Monopoly Markets in the Daily Newspaper Industry: An Exploration of the Role of the Early Associated Presses." Ph.D. diss., University of Iowa, 1990.

Smythe, Ted Curtis. "The Reporter, 1880–1900: Working Conditions and Their Influence on News." *Journalism History* 7 (1980): 1–11.

Steffens, J. Lincoln. "The Business of a Newspaper." *Scribner's Magazine* 22 (Oct. 1897): 447–67.

Swanberg, W. A. *Citizen Hearst: A Biography of William Randolph Hearst.* New York: Charles Scribner's Sons, 1961.

Tilley, Nannie. *The R.J. Reynolds Tobacco Company.* Chapel Hill: University of North Carolina Press, 1985.

Tree, Robert L. "Victor Lawson and His Newspapers, 1890–1910." Ph.D. diss., Northwestern University, 1959.

Trimble, Vance. *The Astonishing Mr. Scripps: The Turbulent Life of America's Penny Press Lord.* Ames: Iowa State University Press, 1992.

Turnbull, George S. *History of Oregon Newspapers.* Portland: Binfords and Mort, 1939.

Ware, Norman L. *The Labor Movement in the United States, 1860–1895.* New York: D. Appleton, 1929.

Weaver, David H., and L. E. Mullins. "Content and Format Characteristics of Competing Daily Newspapers." *Journalism Quarterly* 52 (Summer 1975): 257–64.

Weigle, Clifford. "The Young Editor: Keystone of E. W. Scripps' System." *Journalism Quarterly* 41 (1964): 360–66.

Weinstein, Art. *Market Segmentation.* Chicago: Probus, 1987.

Woodard, Joan. *Industrial Organization: Theory and Practice.* New York: Oxford University Press, 1980.

Wren, Daniel A. *The Evolution of Management Thought.* 3d ed. New York: John Wiley and Sons, 1987.

Yates, JoAnne. *Control Through Communication: The Rise of System in American Management.* Baltimore: Johns Hopkins University Press, 1989.

Yip, George S. *Barriers to Entry: A Corporate-Strategy Perspective.* Lexington, Mass.: Lexington Books, 1982.

———. "Gateways to Entry." *Harvard Business Review* 60 (Sept.-Oct. 1982): 86.

Index

GERALD J. BALDASTY is professor of communications and adjunct professor of women's studies at the University of Washington, Seattle. He is the author of *The Commercialization of News in the Nineteenth Century* and senior editor of *Journalism History.* He holds a Ph.D. from the University of Washington and an M.A. from the University of Wisconsin–Madison.

THE HISTORY OF COMMUNICATION

Selling Free Enterprise: The Business Assault on Labor and Liberalism,
    1945–60   *Elizabeth A. Fones-Wolf*
Last Rights: Revisiting *Four Theories of the Press*   *Edited by John C. Nerone*
"We Called Each Other Comrade": Charles H. Kerr & Company, Radical
    Publishers   *Allen Ruff*
WCFL, Chicago's Voice of Labor, 1926–78   *Nathan Godfried*
Taking the Risk Out of Democracy: Corporate Propaganda versus Freedom
    and Liberty   *Alex Carey; edited by Andrew Lohrey*
Media, Market, and Democracy in China: Between the Party Line and the
    Bottom Line   *Yuezhi Zhao*
Print Culture in a Diverse America   *Edited by James P. Danky and
    Wayne A. Wiegand*
The Newspaper Indian: Native American Identity in the Press, 1820–90
    John M. Coward
E. W. Scripps and the Business of Newspapers   *Gerald J. Baldasty*